50 Maps
OF THE WORLD

Publisher's note:

The maps in this book have been designed to tell a story, and show the natural curve of the Earth. They are not drawn to scale, nor do they reflect the longitudinal and latitudinal lines of each country. Please consult an atlas after using this book to plan your journey around the world!

While every effort has been made to obtain permission for copyright material, there may be some cases where we have been unable to trace a copyright holder. The publisher will be happy to correct any omission in future printings.

WIDE EYED EDITIONS

CONTENTS

N

W   E

S

THE NETHERLANDS
20-21

SCANDINAVIA
32-33

UNITED KINGDOM
& IRELAND
8-9

GERMANY
10-11

ESTONIA,
LATVIA &
LITHUANIA
22-23

POLAND
24-25

RUSSIA
14-15

HUNGARY
26-27

SPAIN
16-17

ITALY
12-13

TURKEY
34-35

GREECE
18-19

ISRAEL
50-51

CHINA
42-43

KOREA
60-61

JAPAN
46-47

MOROCCO
70-71

JORDAN
54-55

EGYPT
68-69

IRAN
52-53

NEPAL
48-49

INDIA
36-37

SAUDI ARABIA
& UNITED ARAB
EMIRATES
56-57

THAILAND
40-41

CAMBODIA
64-65

PHILIPPINES
62-63

NIGERIA
74-75

ETHIOPIA
72-73

VIETNAM
38-39

RWANDA
82-83

KENYA
78-79

MALAYSIA
58-59

INDONESIA
44-45

MOZAMBIQUE
80-81

MADAGASCAR
76-77

AUSTRALIA &
NEW ZEALAND
104-105

SOUTH
AFRICA
66-67

WELCOME TO 50 MAPS OF THE WORLD

One of the questions that might pop up for you as you read this book is:

What is a country?

And it's a very good question. After all, the land you're standing on was there long before it became known as a country!

The truth is that a country might exist for a while, and then not exist anymore. This coming and going of countries happens all the time. Some countries become one country over time, like East and West Germany did in 1990, while others separate, like Czechoslovakia did when it became Slovakia and the Czech Republic in 1993. There are about 30 more countries today than there were in 1990. It's worth remembering that when we look at an area of land and call it a country, we might be including people and history that, in years past, might not have been part of the country we know today at all.

So, are you ready to explore? Read on and start your discovery—hopefully you'll plan a great adventure through these places and visit them all one day!

EXPLORING THIS BOOK

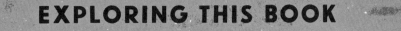

WELCOME BOX

With so much to investigate, it's good to have a plan! For each country, you may want to start by reading the short introduction.

PEOPLE OF NOTE

Meet five people who are part of the history and story of each country.

COUNTRY ICONS

Let your eyes wander over the icons that celebrate a country's people, places, and history —history that we continue to make every day!

KEY FACTS

These provide a quick snapshot of each country, including the capital city, the country's motto, and birds, animals, and flowers that are culturally important, popular, or unique.

MOMENTS TO REMEMBER

Discover some of the significant dates in the country's history.

SPOTLIGHT

These bubbles, featuring a collection of key icons, allow you to discover more about one particular place.

Each of these maps contains information about a different country to give you a look at what you'll find there today, and a glimpse of some **HISTORICAL SITES** that show how it looked in times past. Within each of these countries, we welcome you to explore the many **NATIONAL PARKS**, **ANCIENT HISTORICAL SITES**, **BEAUTIFUL FORESTS**, and **GLIMMERING BODIES OF WATER**, and hope they will inspire you to respect and explore the great outdoors. Just remember: these maps have been designed to tell a story: they aren't drawn to scale.

GET TO KNOW THESE SYMBOLS ON EVERY MAP

CAPITAL CITY

LARGEST CITIES

COUNTRY

BODY OF WATER

BORDERING COUNTRY

BORDER LINE

PEOPLE OF NOTE

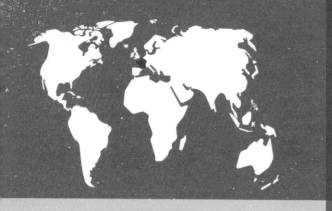

MOMENTS TO REMEMBER

AD 481–511: During his reign, King Clovis I of the Franks takes over much of Gaul that we now call France.

768–814: Charlemagne, known as Charles the Great, rules France and forms an empire across Western Europe.

1431: Joan of Arc is executed for heresy.

1789: The Bastille is stormed during the French Revolution.

1804: Napoleon Bonaparte becomes emperor and later takes control of most of Western Europe.

1900: Impressionist artist Claude Monet paints *The Artist's Garden at Giverny.*

1914–1918: World War I sees fierce fighting in France, killing more than 1.3 million French people.

1914: Marie Curie develops and uses a mobile X-ray machine to treat the wounded at the Battle of Marne.

1940: Germany invades France in World War II.

1944: Paris is liberated from German forces.

1959: Charles de Gaulle becomes president of France.

1969: Concorde, the world's first supersonic passenger jet, takes off from Toulouse in France.

1998: France wins its first soccer World Cup. It wins again in 2018.

2013: Same-sex marriage becomes legal in France.

2019: Notre-Dame cathedral in Paris is almost destroyed in a fire.

WELCOME TO THE LAND OF FASHION AND CROISSANTS!

Are you ready to make decisions? Because there are so many versions of France that you can't possibly experience them all! There's natural France, with its beautiful rivers, gorges, and forests; there's ancient France, with prehistoric paintings and monuments; there's fashion France, with its chic stylings from Paris to the French Riviera; and there's food France, which is absolutely everywhere. And that's just the beginning! No wonder this is the most visited country in the world.

The capital of France is Paris, the "City of Light," which is full of art in its many beautiful galleries—and on the street too! If there's one thing that Paris is famous for, it's sitting in a café, ordering a coffee and watching the world go by. You may want to order a flaky croissant as well . . .

KEY FACTS — LIBERTY, EQUALITY, FRATERNITY

CAPITAL Paris	**MONEY** Euro	**NATION CODE** FR
LARGEST CITIES Paris, Marseille, Lyon, Toulouse	**NAMED FOR** The Franks, a Germanic tribe who took control of Gaul in the 5th century	**OFFICIAL LANGUAGE** French
POPULATION 68,200,000	**FLOWER** Fleur-de-lys (yellow iris)	**BIRD** Gallic rooster

ATLANTIC OCEAN

COCO CHANEL
1883–1971
A fashion designer, she created and ran one of the world's most famous luxury labels.

UK

ROUEN CATHEDRAL
This has been a church since AD 400 and, over hundreds of years, was built into a cathedral.

THE LOUVRE
Don't miss the world's biggest and most-visited art museum.

BELGIUM

ARC DE TRIOMPHE
This war memorial built in the 19th century feels like the gateway to Paris.

EIFFEL TOWER
The universal symbol of Paris! Climb to the top and gaze out over this magnificent city.

JOAN OF ARC
C.1412–1431
This farmgirl turned warrior inspired the French to fight the English invasion during the Hundred Years' War.

SACRÉ-CŒUR
Stroll around Montmartre and head to this basilica at the highest point of the city.

LUXEMBOURG

VICTOR HUGO
1802–1885
This famous author wrote *The Hunchback of Notre Dame* and *Les Misérables*.

LA JUMENT
Lighthouses like La Jument have saved many sailors' lives from the rocky, wild waters off Brittany.

CAMEMBERT
One of the world's most famous cheeses comes from this town!

MONT SAINT-MICHEL
This island's medieval buildings and abbey make it look like a fairy-tale kingdom.

PARIS

PALACE OF VERSAILLES
With gold, statues, gardens, and 2,300 rooms, Versailles is the grandest of palaces!

CHAMPAGNE
Only sparkling wine from this area can be called champagne—the superstar of French wine!

GERMANY

CARNAC STONES
In fields around Carnac, you'll find 3,000 standing stones that are thousands of years old.

CHEFS IN LYON
Lyon has been home to many of France's finest chefs, including the revered Paul Bocuse.

MONT BLANC
At 15,780 feet high, Western Europe's highest mountain is snow-capped all year around.

SWITZERLAND

CHAMBORD
One of France's most famous castles has beautiful gardens and more than 400 rooms.

LASCAUX CAVES
Marvel at these prehistoric cave paintings, made 17,000 years ago.

AZAY-LE-RIDEAU
This island castle in the middle of the Indre River almost looks like a ship!

LYON

PONT DU GARD
This amazing 2,000-year-old, three-level bridge and aqueduct was built by the Romans.

THE FOUNTAIN OF VAUCLUSE
Every year, 166 billion gallons of water pour from this beautiful mineral spring.

ITALY

CHÂTEAU DE CHENONCEAU
This pretty castle spans the Cher River, like a bridge.

TOULOUSE

NICE

MARSEILLE

FRENCH RIVIERA
Dress up and look fabulous on the French Riviera—it's where the rich and famous come to relax.

CHARLES DE GAULLE
1890–1970
Army officer de Gaulle led the French Resistance in World War II and became the nation's first president.

SARAH BERNHARDT
1844–1923
This actor performed on stage all over the world and appeared in some of the earliest films ever made.

SPAIN

CANAL DU MIDI
Jump on a barge and cruise the 300-year-old canal connecting the Atlantic coast to the Mediterranean.

THE CAMARGUE
Explore this wetland national park and look out for the famous flamingos.

OLD PORT OF MARSEILLE
Stop for a drink at one of the Old Port's cafés and soak up 2,500 years of trading history.

VERDON GORGE
Kayak along the Verdon River and marvel at the beautiful scenery.

UNITED KINGDOM and IRELAND

MOMENTS TO REMEMBER

2500 BC: Standing stones are arranged at Stonehenge.

55–54 BC: Roman Emperor Julius Caesar sets out to conquer Britain. The Romans establish Londinium (you guessed it, London!) in AD 43.

866: The Vikings invade Britain.

1066: William the Conqueror defeats King Harold at the Battle of Hastings.

1348: The Black Death, a bubonic plague, reaches England and kills over a third of the population.

1455–1485: A fight for the right to rule England called the War of the Roses takes place between the York family and the Lancaster family.

1666: Most of London is destroyed in the Great Fire.

1845–1852: The Potato Famine in Ireland kills 1 million people.

1914–1918: The United Kingdom fights on the side of the Allies in World War I.

1922: Most of the island of Ireland gains independence from the UK. Six counties in the North remain in the UK.

1928: Women in the UK gain the same voting rights as men.

1997: The first *Harry Potter* novel in J. K. Rowling's series is released.

2020: The UK leaves the European Union, following a referendum in 2016.

2022: Queen Elizabeth II dies, after a 70-year reign spanning 15 British prime ministers and 14 United States presidents. She is succeeded by her son, King Charles III.

CHARLES DARWIN
1809–1882
Naturalist Charles Darwin wrote *On the Origin of Species*, which proposed that all life is descended from common ancestors.

QUEEN ELIZABETH I
1533–1603
Elizabeth I's reign became known as the "Golden Era" because of the peace and prosperity that blossomed under her rule.

CARRICK-A-REDE ROPE BRIDGE
This rickety rope bridge in Antrim spans a 65-foot gap and swings 98 feet above the Atlantic Ocean.

BELFAST

GIANT'S CAUSEWAY
Legend has it that these 40,000 pillars on the Antrim coastline were built by a giant!

THE CLIFFS OF MOHER
Watch Atlantic puffins from these spectacular sea cliffs in Clare.

DUBLIN

THE SPIRE
This 400-foot-high, needle-like monument stands in the heart of Dublin.

IRELAND

ROMAN BATHS, SOMERSET
Explore a complex of heated rooms and pools, built by the Romans over a natural spring.

ATLANTIC OCEAN

THE EDEN PROJECT, CORNWALL
Two giant geodesic biomes re-create a tropical rain forest and a Mediterranean climate, and contain over two million plants!

KEY FACTS

ENGLAND, WALES, NI: GOD AND MY RIGHT

CAPITALS
England: London
Scotland: Edinburgh
Northern Ireland: Belfast
Wales: Cardiff
Ireland: Dublin

LARGEST CITIES
UK: London
Birmingham
Manchester
Glasgow

Ireland: Dublin

MONEY
UK: British Pound
Ireland: Euro

NATION CODES
GBR
IE

OFFICIAL LANGUAGES
English, Welsh, Gaelic, Scots, Irish

FLOWERS
England: Rose
Wales: Daffodil
Northern Ireland & Ireland: Shamrock
Scotland: Thistle

POPULATION
UK 68,100,000
Ireland 5,200,000

BIRDS
UK: Robin
Ireland: Northern lapwing

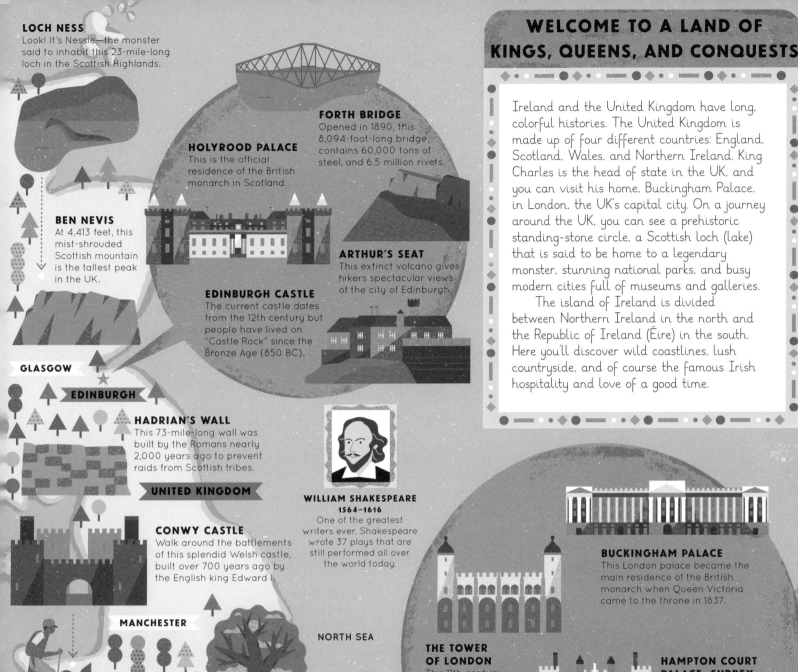

LOCH NESS
Look! It's Nessie—the monster said to inhabit this 23-mile-long loch in the Scottish Highlands.

FORTH BRIDGE
Opened in 1890, this 8,094-foot-long bridge contains 60,000 tons of steel, and 6.5 million rivets.

HOLYROOD PALACE
This is the official residence of the British monarch in Scotland.

BEN NEVIS
At 4,413 feet, this mist-shrouded Scottish mountain is the tallest peak in the UK.

ARTHUR'S SEAT
This extinct volcano gives hikers spectacular views of the city of Edinburgh.

EDINBURGH CASTLE
The current castle dates from the 12th century but people have lived on "Castle Rock" since the Bronze Age (850 BC).

GLASGOW

EDINBURGH

HADRIAN'S WALL
This 73-mile-long wall was built by the Romans nearly 2,000 years ago to prevent raids from Scottish tribes.

UNITED KINGDOM

CONWY CASTLE
Walk around the battlements of this splendid Welsh castle, built over 700 years ago by the English king Edward I.

WILLIAM SHAKESPEARE
1564–1616
One of the greatest writers ever, Shakespeare wrote 37 plays that are still performed all over the world today.

MANCHESTER

NORTH SEA

BIRMINGHAM

[E]RYRI (SNOWDONIA)
[T]his national park is home to Wales's highest [m]ountain, 3,560-foot-high Yr Wyddfa (Snowdon).

SHERWOOD FOREST
The mighty "Major Oak" tree is over 800 years old. Stories say it was the hideout of Robin Hood!

[T]HE COTSWOLDS
[L]ook out for a "Cotswold Lion" in [t]his pretty area of woodland and [h]ills. (Hint: it's actually a sheep!)

CARDIFF

LONDON

STONEHENGE
This Neolithic stone circle is one of the most spectacular prehistoric monuments in Europe.

[J]URASSIC COAST
[T]he rocks and fossils found along this 95-mile [s]tretch of coastline go back 185 million years.

WELCOME TO A LAND OF KINGS, QUEENS, AND CONQUESTS

Ireland and the United Kingdom have long, colorful histories. The United Kingdom is made up of four different countries: England, Scotland, Wales, and Northern Ireland. King Charles is the head of state in the UK, and you can visit his home, Buckingham Palace, in London, the UK's capital city. On a journey around the UK, you can see a prehistoric standing-stone circle, a Scottish loch (lake) that is said to be home to a legendary monster, stunning national parks, and busy modern cities full of museums and galleries.

The island of Ireland is divided between Northern Ireland in the north and the Republic of Ireland (Éire) in the south. Here you'll discover wild coastlines, lush countryside, and of course the famous Irish hospitality and love of a good time.

BUCKINGHAM PALACE
This London palace became the main residence of the British monarch when Queen Victoria came to the throne in 1837.

THE TOWER OF LONDON
This 11th-century fortress has been a prison, a royal palace, an army barracks, an armory, a zoo, and a jewel house!

HAMPTON COURT PALACE, SURREY
King Henry VIII liked to bring guests here so they would be impressed with his wealth and power.

WEMBLEY STADIUM
Known as the "Home of Football," the stadium can hold up to 90,000 passionate soccer fans.

BELGIUM

WHITE CLIFFS OF DOVER
These striking chalk cliffs are over 300 feet tall.

BONO
B.1960
Rock star Bono, from the band U2, is well known for his music and his work on global poverty.

EMMELINE PANKHURST
1858–1928
Pankhurst led Britain's suffragette movement, which fought for women's right to vote.

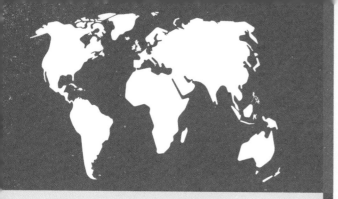

MOMENTS TO REMEMBER

c. 2nd–1st century BC: Early Germanic peoples occupy what will later become Northern Germany.

AD 800: Emperor Charlemagne, Frankish ruler of France and Germany, is crowned Roman emperor by Pope Leo III.

911: The Frankish kingdom disintegrates into separate feudal states—Bavaria, Franconia, Swabia, Lorraine, and Saxony.

1450: Johannes Gutenberg introduces moveable-type printing, contributing to the Renaissance and Scientific Revolution.

1618–1648: The Thirty Years' War devastates Germany and affects most of Central and Western Europe.

1871: The German Empire is founded.

1939: Under Adolf Hitler, Germany invades Poland, starting World War II.

1945: Germany is defeated and is eventually split into two countries, West Germany and communist East Germany.

1961: The Berlin Wall is built, dividing Berlin into East and West.

1989: The Berlin Wall comes down. The following year, East and West Germany are reunited and become one country again.

2014: Germany wins the FIFA World Cup for the fourth time.

WELCOME TO THE LAND OF POETS AND THINKERS

Composers, philosophers, scientists, inventors . . . Germany has had more than its share of great minds, and they have had a huge impact on the world.

Evidence of this wonderful country's history is scattered across the country, from ancient Roman ruins to medieval castles. In Germany's colorful history, there have been times where it's been one empire, then broken apart into feudal states, become an empire again, and once more broken apart. In fact, in its current shape, it's only been one country since 1990!

Germany is a rich land, with beautiful rivers, lakes, and mountains, so there's plenty of opportunity to enjoy the outdoors. And its modern cities and beautiful old towns will keep you entertained for days. The capital, Berlin, is one of the world's great cities, famous for being at the cutting edge of culture, art, and entertainment.

So what are you waiting for? Let's get ready to explore!

HEIDI KLUM
B.1973
Klum has gone from being a supermodel to the host and producer of globally successful TV shows.

STEFFI GRAF
B.1969
One of the greatest tennis players in the world, Graf won 22 Grand Slam singles titles.

ELTZ CASTLE
This medieval castle overlooking the Moselle River has belonged to the same family for 850 years!

GUTENBERG MUSEUM
Johannes Gutenberg pioneered printing in Western Europe. This museum celebrates his influential printing press.

WATERING CAN MUSEUM
This museum in Giessen celebrates the humble watering can.

ENGLISH CHANNEL

FRANCE

GERMANY

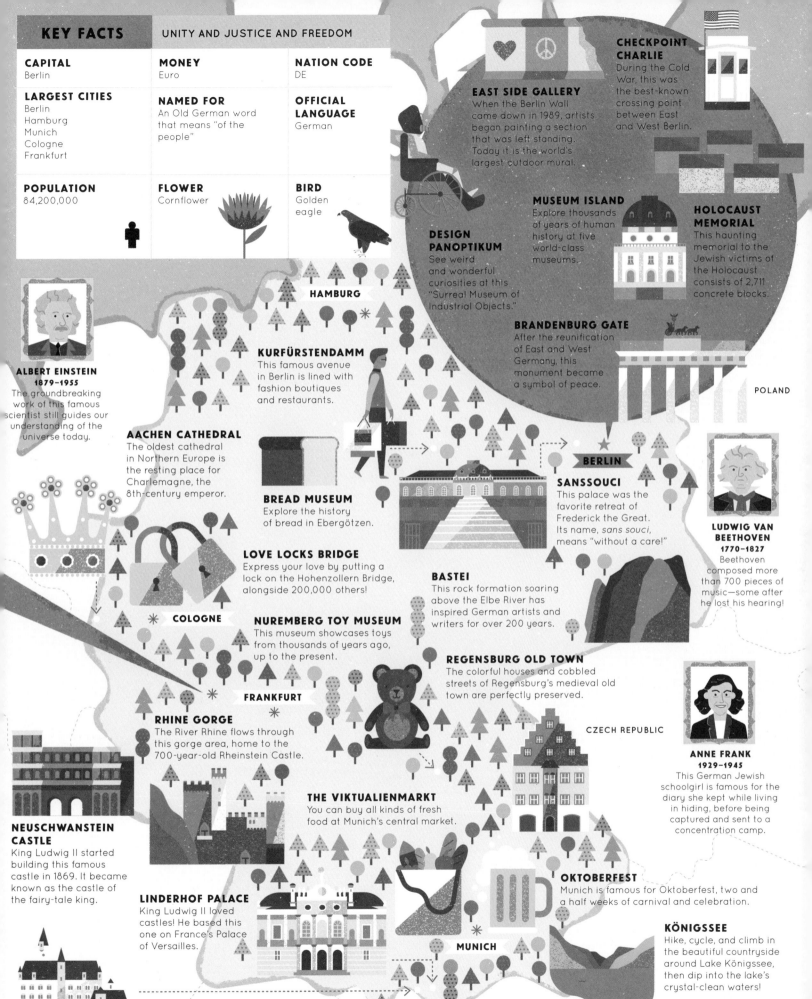

KEY FACTS

UNITY AND JUSTICE AND FREEDOM

CAPITAL Berlin	**MONEY** Euro	**NATION CODE** DE
LARGEST CITIES Berlin Hamburg Munich Cologne Frankfurt	**NAMED FOR** An Old German word that means "of the people"	**OFFICIAL LANGUAGE** German
POPULATION 84,200,000	**FLOWER** Cornflower	**BIRD** Golden eagle

EAST SIDE GALLERY
When the Berlin Wall came down in 1989, artists began painting a section that was left standing. Today it is the world's largest outdoor mural.

CHECKPOINT CHARLIE
During the Cold War, this was the best-known crossing point between East and West Berlin.

DESIGN PANOPTIKUM
See weird and wonderful curiosities at this "Surreal Museum of Industrial Objects."

MUSEUM ISLAND
Explore thousands of years of human history at five world-class museums.

HOLOCAUST MEMORIAL
This haunting memorial to the Jewish victims of the Holocaust consists of 2,711 concrete blocks.

BRANDENBURG GATE
After the reunification of East and West Germany, this monument became a symbol of peace.

POLAND

HAMBURG

KURFÜRSTENDAMM
This famous avenue in Berlin is lined with fashion boutiques and restaurants.

ALBERT EINSTEIN
1879–1955
The groundbreaking work of this famous scientist still guides our understanding of the universe today.

AACHEN CATHEDRAL
The oldest cathedral in Northern Europe is the resting place for Charlemagne, the 8th-century emperor.

BREAD MUSEUM
Explore the history of bread in Ebergötzen.

LOVE LOCKS BRIDGE
Express your love by putting a lock on the Hohenzollern Bridge, alongside 200,000 others!

BERLIN

SANSSOUCI
This palace was the favorite retreat of Frederick the Great. Its name, sans souci, means "without a care!"

LUDWIG VAN BEETHOVEN
1770–1827
Beethoven composed more than 700 pieces of music—some after he lost his hearing!

BASTEI
This rock formation soaring above the Elbe River has inspired German artists and writers for over 200 years.

COLOGNE

NUREMBERG TOY MUSEUM
This museum showcases toys from thousands of years ago, up to the present.

REGENSBURG OLD TOWN
The colorful houses and cobbled streets of Regensburg's medieval old town are perfectly preserved.

CZECH REPUBLIC

FRANKFURT

RHINE GORGE
The River Rhine flows through this gorge area, home to the 700-year-old Rheinstein Castle.

ANNE FRANK
1929–1945
This German Jewish schoolgirl is famous for the diary she kept while living in hiding, before being captured and sent to a concentration camp.

THE VIKTUALIENMARKT
You can buy all kinds of fresh food at Munich's central market.

NEUSCHWANSTEIN CASTLE
King Ludwig II started building this famous castle in 1869. It became known as the castle of the fairy-tale king.

LINDERHOF PALACE
King Ludwig II loved castles! He based this one on France's Palace of Versailles.

OKTOBERFEST
Munich is famous for Oktoberfest, two and a half weeks of carnival and celebration.

KÖNIGSSEE
Hike, cycle, and climb in the beautiful countryside around Lake Königssee, then dip into the lake's crystal-clean waters!

MUNICH

SWITZERLAND

AUSTRIA

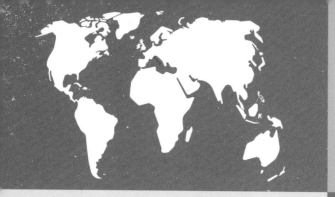

FRANCE

ITALY

WELCOME TO THE LAND OF PIZZA, EMPERORS, AND INGENIOUS INVENTORS

It's hard to imagine what the world we know today would be like without Italy. What if there was no pizza? No pasta? No gelato? Italy also gave us some of the world's greatest artists, explorers, scientists, and inventors. And what would life have been like without the influence of the Romans?

At the height of its power, the Roman Empire was one of the biggest empires the world has ever known. Romans used their engineering skills to build huge aqueducts and created concrete to build structures like the Colosseum and the Pantheon, which still stand today, almost 2,000 years later. In Italy's cities, Roman ruins sit side by side with medieval piazzas and modern buildings.

The countryside in Italy is a highlight—travel from top to bottom and you'll experience rolling hills, soaring alpine peaks, crystal-clear lakes, lush woodlands, and vast vineyards, as well as rocky coastlines dotted with cliffside villages.

MOMENTS TO REMEMBER

c.2000 BC: Indo-Europeans migrate into Italy, and establish the ancient Roman civilization.

280–275 BC: Following the Pyrrhic War, Rome becomes the undisputed master of Italy.

27 BC: The Roman Empire is established by Augustus and two centuries of peace and prosperity follow.

AD 200–300: The Roman Empire suffers under Barbarian invasions and its rule is weakened by conflict.

500–1000: After a series of wars and conquests on the Italian Peninsula, Rome re-emerges as one of the most powerful cities.

1100–1300: Increasing trade in Europe makes city states like Venice and Sicily more powerful. Banks and universities are established.

c.1300–1600: Art, invention, exploration, and science flourish in the Renaissance.

1600s–1800: Succession wars in Europe divide Italy between Austria and Spain. Italy is invaded by France during the age of Napoleon.

1815–1870: "Risorgimento," or Italian unification begins, and the whole of Italy becomes one kingdom.

1915: Italy joins World War I on the side of Britain and France despite being in an alliance with Germany.

1940: Italy fights World War II on the side of Germany and Japan and is defeated, which results in a civil war.

1946–1960: The monarchy is abolished, democracy is reinstated, and Italy experiences an economic boom.

2016: An earthquake in central Italy kills more than 200 people.

SANTA MARIA DEL FIORE BASILICA
When this cathedral was completed in 1436, it was the largest church in the world.

UFFIZI GALLERY
The masterpieces in this gallery are so famous that visitors stand in line for up to five hours to get in!

PONTE VECCHIO
This medieval stone bridge over the River Arno was once lined with butcher shops.

KEY FACTS	ITALY IS A DEMOCRATIC REPUBLIC, FOUNDED ON LABOR	
CAPITAL Rome	**MONEY** Euro	**NATION CODE** ITA
LARGEST CITIES Rome Milan Naples Turin	**NAMED FOR** An ancient name for the people of Southern Italy, Vitalia	**OFFICIAL LANGUAGE** Italian
POPULATION 61,000,000	**FLOWER** Lily	**BIRD** Italian sparrow

LAKE COMO
At the foothills of the Alps, this glacial lake is popular with the rich and famous.

MONTE BIANCO
The highest peak in Western Europe sits on the border with France, where it's known as Mont Blanc.

THE DOLOMITES
This part of the Alps has glacial lakes, limestone peaks, and pretty towns.

AUSTRIA

SFORZA CASTLE
Built on 14th-century fortifications, this castle in Milan has several rooms with frescoes painted by Leonardo da Vinci.

JULIET'S BALCONY
Shakespeare's Juliet supposedly professed her love for Romeo from this stone balcony in Verona.

MILAN

VENICE
Instead of roads and cars, this city has canals and boats—and more than 400 bridges!

TURIN

EGYPTIAN MUSEUM
Turin's Egyptian museum is the oldest in the world, and displays over 40,000 artifacts.

BOLOGNA
Love spaghetti bolognese? You have Bologna to thank. The dish we know today is inspired by the city's meat sauce with fresh tagliatelle.

ELENA CORNARO
1646–1684
One of the first women in the world to receive a university degree, Cornaro went on to complete a PhD.

LEANING TOWER OF PISA
This 185-foot-tall tower sank on one side when it was built in the 12th century.

FLORENCE

MOSAICS IN RAVENNA
Ravenna is famous for the centuries-old mosaics decorating many religious buildings and monuments.

LEONARDO DA VINCI
1452–1519
Inventor, sculpter, painter, scientist, architect, musician, writer, engineer, astronomer, cartographer—there wasn't much da Vinci couldn't do!

CINQUE TERRE
These five villages are built into the rugged coastline and can only be accessed by boat, train, or foot.

PIAZZA DEL CAMPO, SIENA
In the summer, this medieval town square becomes a racetrack for horses in the traditional Palio di Siena.

ROME

PIZZA IN NAPLES
Antica Pizzeria Port'Alba is the first-ever pizza restaurant!

NURAGHI ON SARDINIA
Sardinia is home to Bronze Age ruins known as Nuraghi.

BLUE GROTTO, CAPRI
When sunlight passes through a hole in the rock wall, this underwater cave shines bright blue.

NAPLES

MATERA
The prehistoric caves in this ancient town were the first human settlements in Italy.

MIUCCIA PRADA
B.1949
Miuccia took over the family fashion business in 1978 and turned Prada into one of the world's most respected labels.

COLOSSEUM
Gory gladiator fights entertained the crowds at this ancient Roman amphitheater.

POMPEII
The eruption of Mount Vesuvius in AD 79 covered Pompeii in ash, preserving the city and its people as they were on that tragic day.

PANTHEON
This ancient Roman temple has a massive concrete dome and enormous columns that weigh 60 tons each!

VALENTINO ROSSI
B.1979
Superstar motorcycle racer Valentino Rossi has won nine Grand Prix World Championships.

TREVI FOUNTAIN
Legend says that if you throw a coin into this fountain you will return to Rome.

PALERMO

MOUNT ETNA, SICILY
Europe's tallest and most active volcano towers over the island of Sicily.

GALILEO
1564–1642
Galileo was the first person to prove that the planets in our solar system revolve around the Sun.

WASSILY KANDINSKY
1866–1944
Kandinsky was a painter who pioneered the style known as abstract art.

YURI GAGARIN
1934–1968
This astronaut was the first human to blast into outer space, on April 12, 1961.

MAYA PLISETSKAYA
1925–2015
A world-famous prima ballerina, Plisetskaya danced *Swan Lake* over 800 times!

MOMENTS TO REMEMBER

AD 482: Slavic peoples begin to move south into what is now Russia. They found the Ukrainian city of Kyiv.

862: King Rurik rules over the region from Novgorod. People from this area become known as the "Rus."

1200–1300: Mongol invasions from the southeast drive waves of early European Russians south to Moscow and the city grows.

1480: Moscow's ruler, Ivan III, drives the Mongols out of Russia.

1547: Ivan IV becomes the first tsar (Russian emperor) and sets about extending the kingdom.

1682: Peter the Great becomes co-tsar at only ten years old. He eventually establishes Russia as a world power.

1867: Russia sells Alaska to the United States for $7.2 million.

1917: The tsarist government is overthrown in the Russian Revolution. Months later, Vladimir Lenin's communist Bolsheviks take over and the Union of Soviet Socialist Republics (USSR) is created.

1924–1934: Lenin dies and Joseph Stalin comes to power. To eliminate all opposition Stalin begins the "Great Purge" and millions of people are killed.

1942: Russia, fighting on the side of the Allies during World War II, defeats Germany in the Battle of Stalingrad.

1945–1950: World War II ends, and the USSR controls much of Eastern Europe. Relations with the West deteriorate, and the Cold War begins.

1991: The Soviet Union is dissolved and the country of Russia is established.

2000: Vladimir Putin is elected president.

2022: Russia invades Ukraine, leading to a refugee crisis and thousands of deaths on both sides.

KIZHI ISLAND
An open-air museum on this island in Lake Onega features re-created medieval Russian architecture made entirely of wood.

MURMANSK
Catch the Kirovskaya railway to the northern-most city in the Arctic Circle, which is covered in snow most of the year.

THE KOLA PENINSULA
Up here, beyond the Arctic Circle, the sun doesn't set for 100 days. In winter, there's a spectacular display of the Northern Lights.

RUSKEALA MOUNTAIN PARK
This park contains a 300-foot-deep marble ravine filled with crystal-clear water.

MANPUPUNER ROCK FORMATIONS
These seven stone pillars, up to 130 feet high, were formed by 200 million years of wind and ice.

✳ **ST. PETERSBURG**

MOSCOW ★

✳ **NIZHNY NOVGOROD**

KAPOVA CAVE
Ancient paleolithic rock drawings decorate this limestone cave.

STALINGRAD BATTLEFIELD
When German troops invaded Stalingrad during World War II, Russian troops and residents fought back.

SUZDAL
This city has hundreds of whitewashed buildings with beautiful gold-and-blue domes.

MOUNT ELBRUS
This inactive volcano is Europe's highest peak.

SOCHI
The 2014 Winter Olympics were hosted by this summer resort city.

CATHERINE THE GREAT
1729–1796
One of Russia's longest-reigning rulers, Catherine was a fiercely smart leader who strengthened Russia's position in the world.

RUSSIA

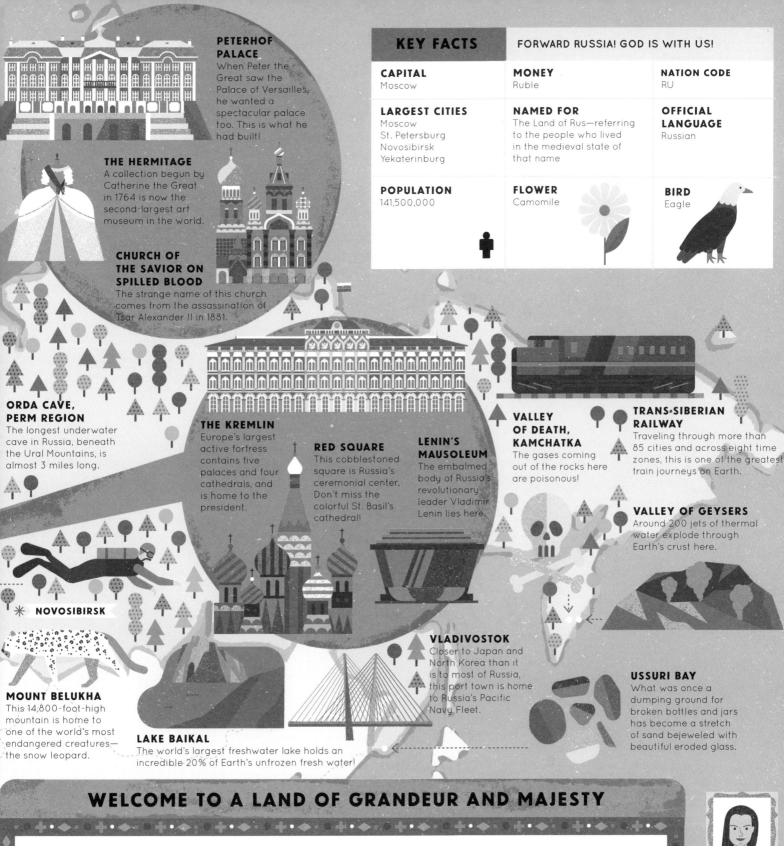

PETERHOF PALACE
When Peter the Great saw the Palace of Versailles, he wanted a spectacular palace too. This is what he had built!

THE HERMITAGE
A collection begun by Catherine the Great in 1764 is now the second-largest art museum in the world.

CHURCH OF THE SAVIOR ON SPILLED BLOOD
The strange name of this church comes from the assassination of Tsar Alexander II in 1881.

KEY FACTS

FORWARD RUSSIA! GOD IS WITH US!

CAPITAL	MONEY	NATION CODE
Moscow	Ruble	RU
LARGEST CITIES	**NAMED FOR**	**OFFICIAL LANGUAGE**
Moscow St. Petersburg Novosibirsk Yekaterinburg	The Land of Rus—referring to the people who lived in the medieval state of that name	Russian
POPULATION	**FLOWER**	**BIRD**
141,500,000	Camomile	Eagle

ORDA CAVE, PERM REGION
The longest underwater cave in Russia, beneath the Ural Mountains, is almost 3 miles long.

THE KREMLIN
Europe's largest active fortress contains five palaces and four cathedrals, and is home to the president.

RED SQUARE
This cobblestoned square is Russia's ceremonial center. Don't miss the colorful St. Basil's cathedral!

LENIN'S MAUSOLEUM
The embalmed body of Russia's revolutionary leader Vladimir Lenin lies here.

VALLEY OF DEATH, KAMCHATKA
The gases coming out of the rocks here are poisonous!

TRANS-SIBERIAN RAILWAY
Traveling through more than 85 cities and across eight time zones, this is one of the greatest train journeys on Earth.

VALLEY OF GEYSERS
Around 200 jets of thermal water explode through Earth's crust here.

✳ NOVOSIBIRSK

MOUNT BELUKHA
This 14,800-foot-high mountain is home to one of the world's most endangered creatures—the snow leopard.

LAKE BAIKAL
The world's largest freshwater lake holds an incredible 20% of Earth's unfrozen fresh water!

VLADIVOSTOK
Closer to Japan and North Korea than it is to most of Russia, this port town is home to Russia's Pacific Navy Fleet.

USSURI BAY
What was once a dumping ground for broken bottles and jars has become a stretch of sand bejeweled with beautiful eroded glass.

WELCOME TO A LAND OF GRANDEUR AND MAJESTY

Welcome to the biggest country on Earth! Russia stretches for more than 6,000 miles from St. Petersburg in the west to Vladivostok in the east. It would take over two weeks of driving nonstop to get all the way from one side to the other! Along the way, you would cross huge deserts, vast mountain ranges, barren plains, enormous pine forests, and giant marshlands. And if at any point on the journey you head north, you'll reach the Arctic Circle, where the winter months are cloaked in total darkness.

Russia is a place of mystery and intrigue, cold and wild. It's also a country rich in history and art, architecture and innovation. You can scale the heights of one of the world's tallest mountains and walk in the footsteps of revolutionaries; watch prima ballerinas perform onstage and explore the expanse of the world's largest freshwater lake. The list of things to do and places to see is as huge as the country itself.

ALEXANDRA KOSTENIUK
B.1984
Kosteniuk was a chess grandmaster at the age of 14 and in 2008 she became the women's world champion.

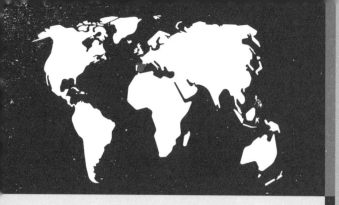

MOMENTS TO REMEMBER

900–600 BC: The Celts arrive in the area.

206 BC: The Romans begin their conquest of Spain.

AD 409–470: Germanic tribes rule Spain.

711: Muslims from North Africa begin their successful conquest of Spain.

1492: The Christians defeat the Muslims in Granada, ending Muslim rule.

1493: Spain begins to colonize the Americas.

1605–1615: Spain's most famous novel, *Don Quixote* by Miguel de Cervantes, is published.

1936: The Spanish Civil War begins between Republicans and Nazi-supported Nationalists.

1939: The Nationalists win the civil war, with Francisco Franco leading the country as dictator for the next 36 years, until his death in 1975.

1978: Spain becomes a democracy with the adoption of its constitution.

1992: The Olympic Games are held in Barcelona.

2023: Spain wins the FIFA Women's World Cup, making it only the second nation, after Germany, to have won both the men's title (in 2010) and the women's.

WELCOME TO THE LAND OF TAPAS

Everything about Spain makes you hungry for more—the food, the beaches, the art, the architecture, the festivals . . . You won't be able to get enough of the place!

Spain has been inhabited for more than 30,000 years. The last 2,500 years of its history has been a story of invaders from all parts of Europe and Africa, which has contributed to its diverse culture.

Pick any one of its wonderful cities and wander through the history-soaked streets. Dig into the national dish, paella, stare at the magnificent architecture, see some art, have an afternoon siesta, then head out for some tapas and dancing. Or maybe one of Spain's beautiful beaches is calling your name! What are you waiting for?

ANTONI GAUDÍ
1852–1926
This architect left his mark on the streets of Barcelona. His Sagrada Família cathedral is an icon of the city.

SAN MIGUEL MARKET
Feeling hungry? Look no further than this market that showcases the best of Spanish food.

ROYAL PALACE OF MADRID
There are more than 3,400 rooms in the home of King Felipe VI, the current monarch of Spain.

CALLE CAVA BAJA
This street is the capital of tapas—Spain's most famous food.

PENÉLOPE CRUZ
B.1974
This actor is known the world over, appearing in both art-house films and international blockbusters.

EDURNE PASABAN
B.1973
This mountaineer was the first woman to climb all 14 of the world's highest peaks.

PABLO PICASSO
1881–1973
When you think of modern art, Picasso is sure to come to mind. He painted colorful, block-like pictures.

SPAIN

KEY FACTS

FURTHER BEYOND

CAPITAL Madrid	**MONEY** Euro	**NATION CODE** ES
LARGEST CITIES Madrid Barcelona Valencia Sevilla	**NAMED FOR** Spania, an ancient name for the Iberian Peninsula	**OFFICIAL LANGUAGE** Spanish
POPULATION 47,200,000	**FLOWER** Red carnation	**BIRD** Iberian imperial eagle

FRANCE

GUGGENHEIM MUSEUM
This striking museum of modern art in the city of Bilbao is a piece of art itself.

DALÍ THEATER-MUSEUM
Salvador Dalí was a 20th-century Spanish artist famous for his Surrealist paintings.

CAMINO DE SANTIAGO
The scallop shell is the symbol of this famous pilgrimage trail.

PICOS DE EUROPA
Spain's first national park is a rocky wonderland—which is probably why chamois and ibex call it home!

ALJAFERÍA PALACE
This Muslim palace-fort was built almost 1,000 years ago.

ZARAGOZA

IBIZA
This Spanish island is famous for its beautiful beaches and dance parties.

BARCELONA

L'OCEANOGRÀFIC
Sharks, whales, and more can be found in the largest oceanarium in Europe!

MADRID

MOSQUE-CATHEDRAL OF CÓRDOBA
Is it a mosque or a cathedral? This magnificent building has been both in its history!

VALENCIA

PORTUGAL

SEVILLE FAIR
April in Seville sees a week of parades and partying!

LA TOMATINA
Ready to get messy? This festival sees crowds of people throwing tomatoes at each other!

LA BOQUERIA
Barcelona's picturesque public market sells food in all shapes and sizes!

LA RAMBLA
This tree-lined boulevard is a tourist hotspot.

SEVILLA

PICASSO MUSEUM
What made Picasso such a revolutionary artist? Come here to find out!

CASA BATLLÓ
Gaudí's "house of bones" is an amazing building of waves and curls.

PLAYA DE BOLONIA
The perfect beach—in a national park, near ancient Roman ruins, and no crowds!

ALHAMBRA
This beautiful fortress dates back to the 9th century. Its name means "the red one."

PARK GÜELL
With its gingerbread houses and mosaics, Gaudí's park is a symbol of Barcelona.

LA SAGRADA FAMÍLIA
Construction of Gaudí's remarkable church started in 1882—and it's still not complete!

RAFAEL NADAL
B.1986
Rafa, as he's commonly known, is one of Spain's greatest tennis players.

CAMINITO DEL REY DE ARDALES
Imagine walking along this narrow path on a rocky cliff face, 300 feet above the ground!

MOROCCO

17

GREECE

BULGARIA

MACEDONIA

MOUNT OLYMPUS
The highest mountain in Greece and, according to legend, home to the ancient Greek gods!

ALBANIA

THESSALONIKI

THESSALONIKI OLYMPIC MUSEUM
Learn about the 3,000-year-old history of this global sporting event.

PANATHENAIC STADIUM
The first modern Olympics was hosted here in 1896.

METEORA
The Holy Monastery of Great Meteoron sits atop this huge rock.

FOKI BEACH
Snorkel in the warm water or do some spear fishing and catch your dinner!

LARISSA

ACROPOLIS MUSEUM
This ancient complex of temples, statues, and other buildings lies in the heart of Athens.

MONASTIRAKI FLEA MARKET
You'll find souvenirs, antiques, and jewelry in this hectic, buzzing market.

THE ORACLE OF DELPHI
In ancient times, people visited Delphi to hear predictions of the future.

THE PELION TRAIN
Chug along on a steam train up the slopes of Pelion, looking out over the bay.

THE PARTHENON
This 2,500-year-old temple is considered the pinnacle of ancient Greek civilization.

EAT A GYROS IN ATHENS
Gyros is the ultimate Greek street food—roasted pork or chicken, wrapped in a pita bread.

PATRAS

MELISSANI LAKE
Take a boat trip to explore this spectacular lake in a collapsed cave.

MYCENAE
This amazing archeological site was one of Greece's most important cities in the Bronze Age.

ATHENS

PYTHAGORAS CAVE
Your favorite mathematician hung out in these caves, teaching, thinking, and looking for right angles.

NAVAGIO BEACH
A hidden beach with a shipwreck would be amazing in itself, but Navagio also has crystal-clear water to swim in.

ANCIENT THEATER OF EPIDAURUS
You can still see performances in this 2,000-year-old amphitheater today.

THE CYCLADES
Greece is famous for its islands—sailing from one to the next is the perfect way to explore.

AKROTIRI RUINS
This town was destroyed by a volcano in the 16th century, but the ruins were preserved by ash.

MUSEUM OF THE OLIVE AND GREEK OLIVE OIL
Olives and olive oil are Greek institutions! Learn all about the little fruit and how oil has been made for thousands of years.

PLATO (C.428–C.348 BC)
The philosopher Plato believed that the perfect human state is made up of courage, wisdom, justice, and self-discipline.

OLIVE TREE OF VOUVES
This special olive tree is one of the oldest in the world. Its branches have been used for Olympic victors' wreaths.

HERAKLION

MOUNT IDA
This is the highest mountain on the Greek island of Crete.

KNOSSOS
Ancient ruins or labyrinth? This Bronze Age site in Crete may well be the oldest city in Europe.

WELCOME TO THE LAND OF THE GODS

This venerable country has had a major influence on the world. Plato, Aristotle, and Socrates are some of the most famous thinkers in human history, and there are many more Greek philosophers too. Of their many achievements, the introduction of democracy is one of Greece's most important gifts to the world.

Greek history is rich with myth and legend. The 12 gods and goddesses of Mount Olympus appear in stories throughout history. You've probably heard of many of these legendary characters, such as Zeus, Apollo, and Poseidon. Many of the temples and great buildings of Greece, such as the Parthenon, were dedicated to these gods.

But Greece isn't all history and ruins! The country has about 6,000 islands, dotted around the Mediterranean Sea. That means beautiful water for swimming, sailing, and beach vacations, and it also means delicious seafood wherever you go!

KEY FACTS
FREEDOM OR DEATH

CAPITAL Athens	**MONEY** Euro	**NATION CODE** GR
LARGEST CITIES Athens Thessaloniki Patras Larissa Heraklion	**NAMED FOR** An ancient tribe in the region	**OFFICIAL LANGUAGE** Greek
POPULATION 10,500,000	**FLOWER** Bear's breeches	**ANIMAL** Dolphin

MOMENTS TO REMEMBER

1600–1100 BC: Mycenaean Greece, the first advanced civilization in the region, thrives.

1194–1184 BC: According to legend, the Trojan War takes place, which ends after the Greeks hide in a giant wooden horse and attack the Trojans.

C.800 BC: Homer composes the *Iliad* and the *Odyssey*, poems about events in and after the legendary Trojan War.

776 BC: The first-ever Olympic Games take place.

508 BC: Cleisthenes establishes democracy in Greece, the first of its kind.

490 BC: The Greeks defeat the Persians at the Battle of Marathon—which is also believed to give rise to the marathon as a sport.

336 BC: Alexander the Great becomes king.

AD 1822: Greece declares independence from the Turkish Ottoman Empire.

1981: Greece joins the European Union.

1999: The worst earthquake in the country for 20 years kills 145 people in Athens.

2004: The Olympic Games are held in Athens.

2018: After ten years of economic crisis, Greece begins to grow again.

2018: A 2,400-year-old Greek shipwreck is discovered intact in the Black Sea.

KALYMNOS
There are more rock-climbing routes than you can imagine on this beautiful Greek island.

NIKOS KAVVADIAS
1910–1975
Nikos was a poet, writer, and sailor who traveled around the world. Today there is a statue of him in Argostoli.

NANA MOUSKOURI
B.1934
Nana is arguably Greece's most popular singer. She has recorded more than 200 albums.

GIORGOS KARAGOUNIS
B.1977
One of Greece's greatest soccer players, Giorgos has played more games for his country than any other player.

HYDNA OF SCIONE
C.500 BC–UNKNOWN
Hydna helped the Greeks defeat Persia in 480 BC by diving under their ships and cutting the ropes tying them to shore.

RIJKSMUSEUM
This enormous museum has over 1 million objects in its collection, including paintings by Rembrandt and Vermeer.

VAN GOGH MUSEUM
Come here to see the world's largest collection of work by Van Gogh—the great Dutch artist.

ANNE FRANK HOUSE
The house where Anne and her family hid from the Nazis in a secret annex is now a museum.

ZAANSE SCHANS
The windmills and houses of this open-air museum take visitors back in time to the 18th and 19th centuries.

ALKMAAR CHEESE MARKET
Dutch cheeses have been traded on the market square in Alkmaar for over 400 years.

IJSSELMEER TOWNS
The old fishing towns around this lake are made up of pretty colored houses.

MARKEN
To avoid being flooded, the wooden houses in Marken were built on stilts.

BINNENHOF
Today this complex of buildings houses the Dutch parliament, but for many years it was the home of the ruling aristocracy.

INTERNATIONAL COURT OF JUSTICE
The ICJ was set up after World War II to help countries settle their disputes peacefully.

MADURODAM
Want to see all of the Netherlands but don't have enough time? Problem solved—Madurodam is a miniature model of the entire country!

DELFT
This city is known for its distinctive blue-and-white pottery.

OUDE HAVEN
There has been a jetty in Rotterdam's old harbor since 1350; these days you'll find restored historical boats here.

HOGE VELUWE NATIONAL PARK
What was once the country's biggest hunting reserve is now the biggest nature reserve.

AMSTERDAM

KEUKENHOF GARDENS
Here, tulips stretch in every direction as far as the eye can see!

OOSTVAARDERSPLASSEN
See Eurasian spoonbills, sea eagles, black storks, and more at this fantastic nature reserve.

THE HAGUE

UTRECHT

ROTTERDAM

KINDERDIJK WINDMILLS
These 19 enormous windmills were built to drain the land.

KASTEEL DE HAAR
The largest castle in the Netherlands looks like it's come straight out of a fairy tale.

KRÖLLER-MÜLLER MUSEUM
Admire art by Van Gogh, Monet, Picasso, and other modern masters, as well as a huge sculpture garden.

EFTELING
The rides at this adventure park are based on fairy tales and folklore.

EINDHOVEN

DELTA WORKS
This is the world's biggest flood protection system made of dykes, dams, sluice gates, and storm-surge barriers.

DWINGELROTS
The ruins of this 12th-century castle are the remains of the only hilltop fortress in the Netherlands.

THERMAE 2000
Bathe in thermal pools with views over the Valkenburg Castle ruins.

KEY FACTS	I WILL UPHOLD	
CAPITAL Amsterdam	**MONEY** Euro	**NATION CODE** NL
LARGEST CITIES Amsterdam Rotterdam The Hague Utrecht Eindhoven	**NAMED FOR** Netherlands means "low country"; half of the Netherlands lies below sea level	**PREFERRED LANGUAGES** Dutch, English, Papiamento, Frisian
POPULATION 17,700,000	**FLOWER** Tulip	**BIRD** Godwit 

ANNA MARIA VAN SCHURMAN
1607–1678
Van Schurman was the first woman to study at a Dutch university. She was a painter and poet, who could speak 14 languages fluently.

VINCENT VAN GOGH
1853–1890
Van Gogh created over 800 paintings but only sold one during his lifetime.

ABEL TASMAN
1603–1659
Tasman was the first European to reach New Zealand and the island previously known as Van Diemen's Land, now called Tasmania.

HUNEBEDDEN, DRENTHE
Thought to be tombstones from the prehistoric age, each massive stone weighs more than 40 tons.

WILLEM-ALEXANDER
B 1967
The current king of the Netherlands is known for his love of sports, particularly soccer and speed skating.

FANNY BLANKERS-KOEN
1918–2004
At the 1948 Olympics, Blankers-Koen won four gold medals for sprinting; she was 30 years old and a mother of two.

GERMANY

WELCOME TO THE LAND OF WINDMILLS!

Is it the Netherlands? Or is it Holland? You may have heard people use either. The official name of the country is the Kingdom of the Netherlands; Holland refers to two of its provinces, Noord Holland and Zuid Holland, but many people use the name when talking about the whole country. You'll also hear people from the Netherlands referred to as "Dutch"—which comes from an Old English word meaning "of the people." It may be a small country, but don't be fooled—the Netherlands' contribution to world history is huge. Famous Dutch kings, queens, explorers, artists, and sportspeople have all shaped the world we know today.

Across the Netherlands you'll find pretty towns with painted wooden houses, giant windmills, Renaissance palaces and medieval castles, tulip gardens, national parks, open-air museums, and galleries with some of the world's greatest works of art. The Netherlands is a place where history can be traced in the streets, from the moving Anne Frank House museum to prehistoric burial sites and the International Court of Justice. The Netherlands is a perfect example of the saying "good things come in small packages."

MOMENTS TO REMEMBER

3400 BC: Farming tribes settle in the region and build stone structures known as "hunebedden," which are thought to be burial sites.

57 BC: Roman general Julius Caesar invades the Netherlands and takes control.

1st century AD: A tribe of people known as the Frisians move into the region.

476: The Romans are overthrown by Germanic tribes.

800–1000: The Vikings begin raiding coastal towns and villages and settle in some areas.

1482–1567: The country comes under the rule of the Habsburg Empire, which is under the control of the king of Spain.

1581: The Dutch declare independence from Spain and become known as the Republic of the Seven United Netherlands.

1814: The Kingdom of the Netherlands is declared. It includes Belgium and has two capital cities: Amsterdam and Brussels.

1830: Belgium breaks away from the Netherlands to form its own country.

1945: After World War II and the horrendous crimes committed against Jewish people by Nazi Germany, an International Court of Justice is established at The Hague.

2002: The Netherlands adopts the Euro as its currency, replacing the Dutch guilder.

2010: Miep Gies, one of the Dutch citizens who hid Anne Frank and her family from the Nazis, dies aged 100.

2010: The Netherlands makes the final of the FIFA World Cup, but is defeated by Spain.

2013: Queen Beatrix abdicates, and her son Willem-Alexander becomes king.

NETHERLANDS

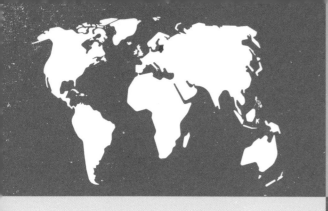

MOMENTS TO REMEMBER

AD 1200s: Two orders of warrior monks, the Teutonic Knights and the Brothers of the Sword, move into the Baltics and establish Riga, in Latvia.

1386: The Lithuanian Grand Duke marries a Polish noblewoman.

1569: The Commonwealth of Poland and Lithuania is formed; it is the biggest state in Europe.

1772: Russia absorbs Lithuania when it moves in and breaks up Poland in a show of force.

1917: The fall of the Russian Empire and the Russian Revolution ignites Baltic independence and, by 1918, Estonia, Latvia, and Lithuania proclaim themselves nation states.

1939–1953: During World War II, the Baltic states come under the influence of the USSR (Union of Soviet Socialist Republics). Lithuania maintains strong resistance.

1970s: Protests, demonstrations, and even riots against Soviet control occur in Estonia, Latvia, and Lithuania.

1990: The Baltic states declare independence from the USSR.

2004: Estonia, Latvia, and Lithuania become part of the European Union.

2011: Lithuania ranks number-one for Internet upload and download speed in the world.

2014: Latvia's capital city, Riga, is declared European Capital of Culture.

2015: An oak tree on a soccer field in Estonia wins European Tree of the Year.

KERLI KÕIV
B.1987
One of the biggest pop stars to come out of Estonia, Kõiv created a signature style known as "Bubble Goth."

JONAS BASANAVIČIUS
1851–1927
This doctor and champion of Lithuania's independence started the first Lithuanian newspaper.

TOWN HALL SQUARE
It's believed that the world's first Christmas tree was erected in this square in 1441.

TOOMPEA HILL
The fortress on Toompea Hill was built in 1229 by the Knights of the Sword.

KADRIORG PARK
This park and palace were built for Catherine I by Russian Tsar Peter the Great. The name in Estonian means "Catherine's Valley."

SAAREMAA
The largest island off Estonia's coast boasts the only intact medieval fortress in the Baltics.

CAPE KOLKA
Thousands of birds can be seen on their annual migration north.

VENTSPILS COWS
In 2002, Ventspils hosted a Cow Parade. It was so popular that some of the life-size cow statues were left in place and you can find them dotted through town.

ESTONIA

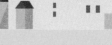

LIEPĀJA

VENTA RAPID
This is Europe's widest waterfall, 800 feet across—but only 6 feet tall!

LATVIA

KLAIPĖDA

CURONIAN SPI[T]
The legend goes that this narrow spit was formed when a giant threw sand in the ocean to protect townships from the wild Baltic Sea.

LITHUANIA

POLAND

KEY FACTS	ESTONIA: NO OFFICIAL MOTTO LATVIA: FOR FATHERLAND AND FREEDOM LITHUANIA: FREEDOM, UNITY, PROSPERITY		
CAPITALS Estonia: Tallinn Latvia: Riga Lithuania: Vilnius	**NATION CODES** Estonia: EE, Latvia: LV Lithuania: LT	**MONEY** Euro	
LARGEST CITIES Estonia: Latvia: Lithuania: Tallinn Riga Vilnius Tartu Liepāja Kaunas Narva Klaipėda	**BECAME A COUNTRY** When the Russian Empire relinquished control after the Russian Revolution in 1917.	**OFFICIAL LANGUAGES** Estonia: Estonian Latvia: Latvian Lithuania: Lithuanian	
POPULATION Estonia: 1,200,000 Latvia: 1,800,000 Lithuania: 2,700,000	**FLOWERS** Estonia: Cornflower Latvia: Daisy Lithuania: Rue	**BIRDS** Estonia: Barn swallow Latvia: White wagtail Lithuania: White stork	

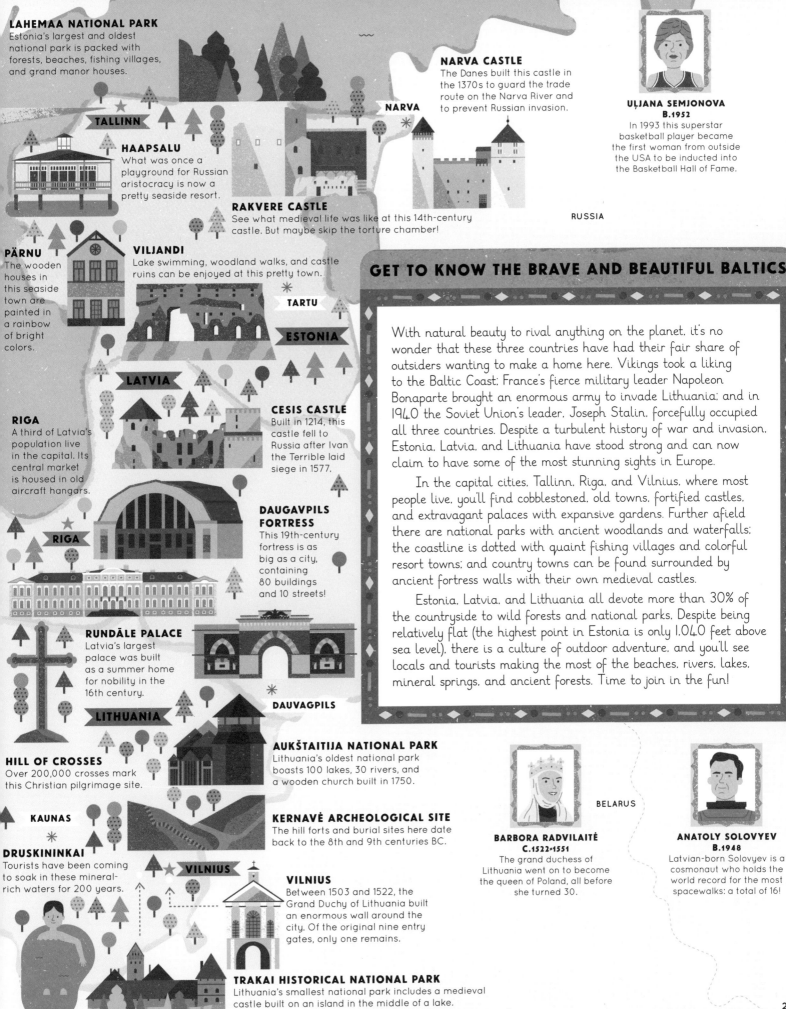

LAHEMAA NATIONAL PARK
Estonia's largest and oldest national park is packed with forests, beaches, fishing villages, and grand manor houses.

TALLINN

HAAPSALU
What was once a playground for Russian aristocracy is now a pretty seaside resort.

PÄRNU
The wooden houses in this seaside town are painted in a rainbow of bright colors.

VILJANDI
Lake swimming, woodland walks, and castle ruins can be enjoyed at this pretty town.

RAKVERE CASTLE
See what medieval life was like at this 14th-century castle. But maybe skip the torture chamber!

TARTU

ESTONIA

LATVIA

NARVA CASTLE
The Danes built this castle in the 1370s to guard the trade route on the Narva River and to prevent Russian invasion.

NARVA

ULJANA SEMJONOVA
B.1952
In 1993 this superstar basketball player became the first woman from outside the USA to be inducted into the Basketball Hall of Fame.

RUSSIA

RIGA
A third of Latvia's population live in the capital. Its central market is housed in old aircraft hangars.

CESIS CASTLE
Built in 1214, this castle fell to Russia after Ivan the Terrible laid siege in 1577.

DAUGAVPILS FORTRESS
This 19th-century fortress is as big as a city, containing 80 buildings and 10 streets!

RIGA

RUNDĀLE PALACE
Latvia's largest palace was built as a summer home for nobility in the 16th century.

DAUVAGPILS

LITHUANIA

HILL OF CROSSES
Over 200,000 crosses mark this Christian pilgrimage site.

KAUNAS

DRUSKININKAI
Tourists have been coming to soak in these mineral-rich waters for 200 years.

AUKŠTAITIJA NATIONAL PARK
Lithuania's oldest national park boasts 100 lakes, 30 rivers, and a wooden church built in 1750.

KERNAVĖ ARCHEOLOGICAL SITE
The hill forts and burial sites here date back to the 8th and 9th centuries BC.

VILNIUS

VILNIUS
Between 1503 and 1522, the Grand Duchy of Lithuania built an enormous wall around the city. Of the original nine entry gates, only one remains.

TRAKAI HISTORICAL NATIONAL PARK
Lithuania's smallest national park includes a medieval castle built on an island in the middle of a lake.

GET TO KNOW THE BRAVE AND BEAUTIFUL BALTICS

With natural beauty to rival anything on the planet, it's no wonder that these three countries have had their fair share of outsiders wanting to make a home here. Vikings took a liking to the Baltic Coast; France's fierce military leader Napoleon Bonaparte brought an enormous army to invade Lithuania; and in 1940 the Soviet Union's leader, Joseph Stalin, forcefully occupied all three countries. Despite a turbulent history of war and invasion, Estonia, Latvia, and Lithuania have stood strong and can now claim to have some of the most stunning sights in Europe.

In the capital cities, Tallinn, Riga, and Vilnius, where most people live, you'll find cobblestoned, old towns, fortified castles, and extravagant palaces with expansive gardens. Further afield there are national parks with ancient woodlands and waterfalls; the coastline is dotted with quaint fishing villages and colorful resort towns; and country towns can be found surrounded by ancient fortress walls with their own medieval castles.

Estonia, Latvia, and Lithuania all devote more than 30% of the countryside to wild forests and national parks. Despite being relatively flat (the highest point in Estonia is only 1,040 feet above sea level), there is a culture of outdoor adventure, and you'll see locals and tourists making the most of the beaches, rivers, lakes, mineral springs, and ancient forests. Time to join in the fun!

BELARUS

BARBORA RADVILAITĖ
C.1522–1551
The grand duchess of Lithuania went on to become the queen of Poland, all before she turned 30.

ANATOLY SOLOVYEV
B.1948
Latvian-born Solovyev is a cosmonaut who holds the world record for the most spacewalks: a total of 16!

BALTIC SEA

What have you heard about Poland? That it was the first country to be invaded by Germany in World War II? Or perhaps you've heard that it was a Polish man who suggested our Earth revolved around the Sun and not the other way around. You may know something about the dark days of the Holocaust or even that Poland was once controlled by the Soviet Union. You'll be surprised to find out that Poland is home to Europe's biggest land mammal, the European bison; the world's biggest castle, Malbork Castle; and that there have been 17 Polish recipients of a Nobel Prize. Poland may be modest about the part it plays on the world stage, but we're here to tell you that there's plenty to shout about.

Poland has some of the world's most important historical sites, from the reminders of Adolf Hitler's atrocities at Auschwitz concentration camp to ancient castles that withstood Mongol invasions. Despite being seriously damaged by World War II bombs, Poland's cities still contain stunning medieval town squares and royal palaces. There are alpine lakes and seaside sand dunes, a salt mine that has chambers carved into chapels, and a village where locals have painted the outside of their houses with colorful flowers. Poland has weathered adversity and is now ready to take a bow.

SŁOWIŃSKI NATIONAL PARK
You might not think of sand dunes when you think of Poland, but here they are, on the Baltic coast.

UPSIDE-DOWN HOUSE IN SZYMBARK
Wander around on the ceiling at this topsy-turvy house, built to symbolize how communism turned Poland upside down.

GDAŃSK

MALBORK CASTLE
This 13th-century fortress is the largest in the world.

BISKUPIN ARCHEOLOGICAL SITE
See how people lived in the Bronze Age at this life-size reconstruction.

TORUN
Torun's medieval old town miraculously survived the bombings in World War II.

POZNAN

CHURCHES OF PEACE
These two churches were built at the end of the Thirty Years' War, in 1648.

STREET MURALS IN ŁÓDŹ
Street artists from all over the world have added their works to the walls.

ŁÓDŹ

NICOLAUS COPERNICUS
1473–1543
Astronomer and mathematician Copernicus was the bright spark who proposed that Earth orbits the Sun, not the other way around.

IRENA SZEWIŃSKA
1946–2018
Szewińska was the only athlete ever to hold world records in 100-, 200-, and 400-meter sprinting.

MARIA SKŁODOWSKA CURIE (MARIE CURIE)
1867–1934
Despite being banned from studying in Poland because she was a woman, Curie went on to win two Nobel Prizes, one in physics and one in chemistry.

GERMANY

KSIĄŻ CASTLE
During World War II, the Germans seized this castle and built a network of tunnels under its foundations.

WROCŁAW

WROCŁAW
Keep a lookout for the city's "krasnale," little statues shaped like gnomes, hiding in doorways and squares.

AUSCHWITZ CONCENTRATION CAMP
During World War II, Hitler had a terrible plan to exterminate Jewish people, and forced them into camps such as this one.

ARBEIT MACHT FREI

SKULL CHAPEL
The interior of this chapel is made up of 3,000 skulls and bones!

ZAKOPANE
Known as the gateway to the Tatra Mountains, Zakopane is full of uniquely decorated wooden buildings.

MORSKIE OKO LAKE
Stay overnight in a wooden hostel on the shores of this emerald-green alpine lake.

POLAND

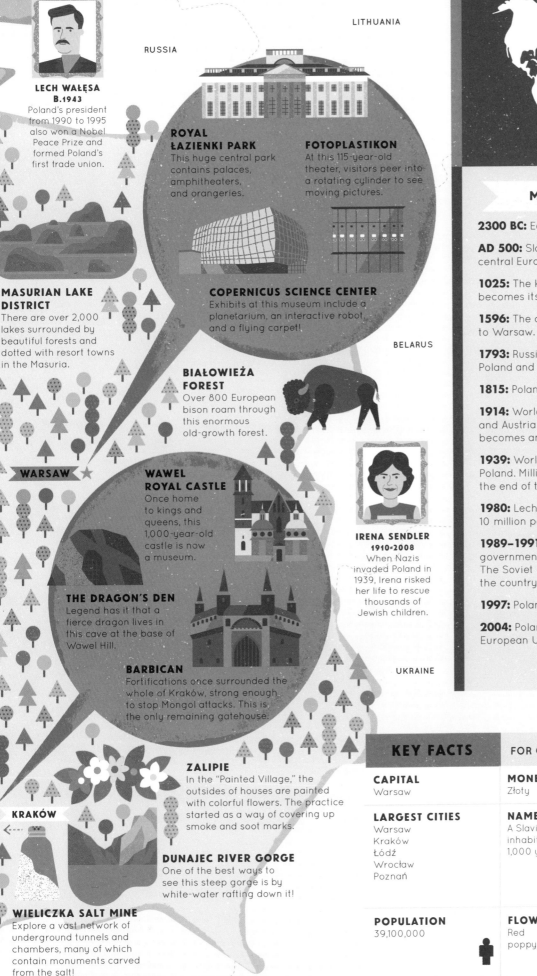

RUSSIA
LITHUANIA
BELARUS
UKRAINE

LECH WAŁĘSA
B.1943
Poland's president from 1990 to 1995 also won a Nobel Peace Prize and formed Poland's first trade union.

ROYAL ŁAZIENKI PARK
This huge central park contains palaces, amphitheaters, and orangeries.

FOTOPLASTIKON
At this 115-year-old theater, visitors peer into a rotating cylinder to see moving pictures.

COPERNICUS SCIENCE CENTER
Exhibits at this museum include a planetarium, an interactive robot, and a flying carpet!

MASURIAN LAKE DISTRICT
There are over 2,000 lakes surrounded by beautiful forests and dotted with resort towns in the Masuria.

BIAŁOWIEŻA FOREST
Over 800 European bison roam through this enormous old-growth forest.

WARSAW

WAWEL ROYAL CASTLE
Once home to kings and queens, this 1,000-year-old castle is now a museum.

IRENA SENDLER
1910–2008
When Nazis invaded Poland in 1939, Irena risked her life to rescue thousands of Jewish children.

THE DRAGON'S DEN
Legend has it that a fierce dragon lives in this cave at the base of Wawel Hill.

BARBICAN
Fortifications once surrounded the whole of Kraków, strong enough to stop Mongol attacks. This is the only remaining gatehouse.

ZALIPIE
In the "Painted Village," the outsides of houses are painted with colorful flowers. The practice started as a way of covering up smoke and soot marks.

KRAKÓW

DUNAJEC RIVER GORGE
One of the best ways to see this steep gorge is by white-water rafting down it!

WIELICZKA SALT MINE
Explore a vast network of underground tunnels and chambers, many of which contain monuments carved from the salt!

MOMENTS TO REMEMBER

2300 BC: Early Bronze Age people settle in Poland.

AD 500: Slavic peoples begin to arrive in Poland from central Europe.

1025: The Kingdom of Poland is established. Boleslaw I becomes its first king.

1596: The capital of Poland is moved from Kraków to Warsaw.

1793: Russia and Prussia (an old German state) invade Poland and divide the country between them.

1815: Poland comes under the sole control of Russia.

1914: World War I begins, and Poland joins Germany and Austria to fight Russia. At the end of the war, Poland becomes an independent nation.

1939: World War II begins when Germany invades Poland. Millions of Jewish people are killed in Poland. At the end of the war, Poland is again under Russian control.

1980: Lech Wałęsa forms the Solidarity trade union and 10 million people join. Russia puts Wałęsa in prison.

1989–1991: Nationwide elections are held, and a new government is formed with Lech Wałęsa as president. The Soviet Union begins withdrawing troops from the country.

1997: Poland adopts a new constitution.

2004: Poland becomes the tenth country to join the European Union (EU).

KEY FACTS
FOR OUR FREEDOM AND YOURS

CAPITAL Warsaw	**MONEY** Złoty	**NATION CODE** PL
LARGEST CITIES Warsaw Kraków Łódź Wrocław Poznań	**NAMED FOR** A Slavic tribe that inhabited the region 1,000 years ago	**OFFICIAL LANGUAGE** Polish
POPULATION 39,100,000	**FLOWER** Red poppy	**BIRD** White-tailed eagle

GET TO KNOW CENTRAL EUROPE'S SPA COUNTRY

This landlocked country in Europe makes up for its lack of seashore with thousands of thermal pools, springs, and lakes, not to mention the medieval castles, expansive grasslands, grand palaces, Roman ruins, and fascinating museums.

The Hungarian translation of "Hungarian" is "Magyar," and they still refer to themselves as the Magyar people. The Magyar tribes made their way from Western Siberia to settle in the region that is now Hungary in the 9th century. By AD 1000, the Kingdom of Hungary was established. This wasn't Hungary's happy ever after, however. From the 14th to the 16th century, the Turkish Ottoman Empire invaded and eventually conquered Hungary. On the heels of the Ottomans came the Austrian Habsburgs, and then, after fighting on the losing side in World War I, the country was occupied by the Soviet Union. Today, it's a democracy with an elected prime minister.

Hungary's past has resulted in a countryside packed with fascinating historic buildings, from immense castles to abandoned palaces. Its countryside is relatively flat and there are many beautiful lakes and rivers, including the River Danube and Lake Balaton, the largest freshwater lake in Central Europe—all of which makes it a popular tourist destination.

JUDIT POLGÁR
B.1976
Chess grandmaster Polgár is regarded as the greatest female player of all time.

SKANZEN OF SZENTENDRE
This open-air museum shows how people from all over Hungary have lived over the centuries.

VISEGRÁD ROYAL PALACE
In the 15th century, King Matthais Corvinus called this 350-room palace home. Today it's a museum.

MICRO WONDER MUSEUM
This collection of art is so tiny it can only be seen through a microscope. Exhibits include a chess set on the head of a pin!

GYŐR

GYERMEKVASÚT
The staff of this scenic railway line is entirely made up of children ages 10–14!

BUDAPEST

CASTLE OF SÜMEG
The fortified walls of this mountaintop castle are dramatically lit at night.

GORSIUM ARCHEOLOGICAL PARK
Before the Magyars arrived, this was a thriving Roman city.

HARRY HOUDINI
1874–1926
Houdini was such an amazing escape artist that he used to challenge the police to keep him locked up.

LÁNGOS
Hungary's favorite street food is this fried bread, often eaten for breakfast topped with sour cream and grated cheese. Yum!

LAKE HÉVÍZ
The world's largest thermal lake has indoor and outdoor baths for visitors to bathe in.

ERNŐ RUBIK
B.1944
Inventor, architect, and professor, Rubik is famous for the well-known puzzle cube he invented.

CITADELLA
This historic fortress was used by the Nazis to observe enemy aircraft and by the communists to quell any uprisings.

BUDA CASTLE
Underneath the castle is a network of caves formed by thermal hot springs.

FISHERMAN'S BASTION
This lookout was built on top of the old defensive walls of Buda Castle and gives the best views of the city.

SHOES ON THE DANUBE
Sixty pairs of shoes cast from iron are lined up along the banks of the Danube as a memorial to the Jewish people killed in World War II.

SEMMELWEIS MEDICAL MUSEUM
This museum of medical oddities contains bizarre old surgical instruments and a shrunken human head.

KEY FACTS

WITH THE HELP OF GOD FOR HOMELAND AND FREEDOM

CAPITAL Budapest	**MONEY** Hungarian forint	**NATION CODE** HU
LARGEST CITIES Budapest Debrecen Miskolc Szeged Pécs	**NAMED FOR** The Latin word "Hungaria," which comes from the name of a local 6th century empire, the Onogur	**OFFICIAL LANGUAGE** Hungarian
		BIRD Turul (mythical)
POPULATION 9,900,000	**FLOWER** Tulip	

BÉLA LUGOSI
1882–1956
Don't believe in vampires? Lugosi's portrayal of Count Dracula in the 1931 film might change your mind.

MÁRIA TELKES
1900–1995
Telkes' nickname is "the Sun Queen," which comes from her groundbreaking work on solar energy technology.

LILLAFÜRED CAVES
These caves were discovered when a dog fell into the Saint István Cave in 1910.

BÜKK NATIONAL PARK
Natural springs and forested mountains make this place a favorite hiking spot.

KÉKES
The highest mountain in Hungary, at over 3,300 feet, is a popular for snow sports.

★ MISKOLC

CASTLE OF EGER
In 1552, the Ottoman Empire attempted to invade the town of Eger, but was foiled by the impenetrable walls of this castle.

HORTOBÁGY NATIONAL PARK
The vast grasslands of Hungary's oldest national park make it an excellent spot for stargazing.

DEBRECEN

THE HOLY RIGHT HAND OF ST. STEPHEN
The thousand-year-old mummified hand of Saint Stephen is displayed in an ornate cabinet. Every year, it leads a parade in his name.

SZÉCHENYI THERMAL BATH
Come and soak in one of the grandest spa baths in Europe, backed by its own palace.

TIMEWHEEL
It takes a whole year for the sand to pass through the center of this huge "hourglass" in the center of Budapest.

KIRÁLY THERMAL BATH
The city's oldest thermal bath was built by the Ottoman Turks in the 16th century.

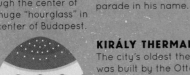

LUKÁCS THERMAL BATH
Back in the 12th century, monks bathed here. Nowadays there's a spa hotel.

VAJDAHUNYAD CASTLE
This castle was built in 1896 to mark the 1,000-year anniversary of the Magyar conquest of the Carpathian Basin.

SERBIA

ROMANIA

MOMENTS TO REMEMBER

AD 896: Hungarian tribes known as the Magyars conquer the Carpathian Basin (Southern Hungary) and force the Romans out.

1241: The Tartars from Mongolia invade and devastate the region.

1361: Buda becomes the capital of the Kingdom of Hungary.

1526: The Turks invade Hungary and divide the country into three parts: the north goes to the Austrian Habsburgs; the south stays with Hungary; Turkey rules the center.

1867: The Habsburgs create a dual monarchy to be divided between Vienna and Pest-Buda.

1873: The cities of Pest, Buda, and Óbuda are joined to become one major city in Europe.

1914: Hungary fights in World War I on the losing side, and as a result, the Hungarian monarchy collapses.

1939–1945 World War II begins, and the Nazis invade Hungary; when the war ends, the Soviet Union makes Hungary part of the Soviet bloc.

1990: The Soviet Union leaves Hungary, and democracy is established. József Antall becomes the first democratically elected prime minister of Hungary.

2004: Hungary becomes part of the European Union (EU).

2015: Hungary faces a migrant crisis when those fleeing war in Afghanistan, Syria, and Northern Africa arrive into Europe.

HUNGARY

ICELAND

JÓHANNA SIGURÐARDÓTTIR
B.1942
This politician was the world's first openly LGBTQ+ head of government.

LÁTRABJARG
These spectacular cliffs are home to millions of seabirds, including puffins.

DRANGSNES HOT POTS
Iceland's natural geothermal springs are perfect for bathing outside on a chilly Icelandic day.

THE ICELANDIC ELF SCHOOL
Do you believe in elves, trolls, and fairies? This school does and will teach you all about them!

THE SETTLEMENT EXHIBITION
This open excavation, the remains of Viking Age structures, is the earliest evidence of human settlement here.

MUSEUM OF ICELANDIC SORCERY & WITCHCRAFT
Explore Iceland's long history of magic and mythology here.

INTO THE GLACIER
Wrap up warm, and journey deep inside a glacier! It's the largest ice tunnel in the world.

HVÍTSERKUR
Legend says this sea stack is the remains of a troll. Its name means "white shirt" —it's covered in seabird poop!

HALLGRÍMSKIRKJA
This striking Lutheran church can be seen from all over Reykjavík.

THE NATIONAL MUSEUM OF ICELAND
Explore artifacts and exhibitions that tell the country's history.

MOUNT ESJA
Hike up Reykjavík's neighboring mountain for perfect views of the city's colorful rooftops.

AURORA REYKJAVÍK
The aurora borealis lights up the sky in swirls of green and blue. Discover what causes them at this Northern Lights Center.

WHALES OF ICELAND
Before you head out on a whale-watching trip, learn all about these majestic mammals in the world's largest whale museum.

STROKKUR
Look out! Strokkur is a geyser that erupts every few minutes, shooting a blast of water up to 130 feet into the air.

THE BLUE LAGOON
The milky blue water of this geothermal seawater spa is said to be good for your skin.

REYKJAVÍK

KÓPAVOGUR

REYKJANESBÆR

HAFNARFJÖRÐUR

VIKING WORLD MUSEUM
Iceland's epic Viking history is on full display here. Don't miss the replica Viking ship.

KEY FACTS	IT WILL ALL WORK OUT OKAY	
CAPITAL Reykjavík	**MONEY** Icelandic króna	**NATION CODE** IS
LARGEST CITIES Reykjavík Kópavogur Hafnarfjörður Akureyri Garðabær	**NAMED FOR** Um . . . ice!	**OFFICIAL LANGUAGE** Icelandic
POPULATION 360,000	**FLOWER** Mountain avens	**BIRD** Gyrfalcon

BJÖRK
B.1965
This avant-garde pop singer is probably the most well-known Icelander in the world.

LEIF ERIKSON
C.970–1020
Leif Erikson was the first known European to have landed in North America—a few hundred years before Columbus.

ERIK THORVALDSSON
C.950–1003
Erik the Red—Leif's father—founded the first European settlement in Greenland. As you might guess, he was named after his hair color!

MOMENTS TO REMEMBER

AD 874: Ingólfur Arnarson, a Norse settler from Norway, sails to Iceland and founds Reykjavík.

930: An annual parliament—the Althing—is established, to make laws and solve disputes.

986: Erik the Red sets sail from Iceland and settles in Greenland.

1000: Iceland adopts Christianity.

1262: Iceland comes under Norwegian rule.

1402: The Black Death hits Iceland, killing huge numbers.

1662: Denmark controls Iceland.

1783: The volcanic fissure Laki erupts, poisoning air and land, and destroying livestock. A quarter of the population dies.

1918: The independent nation of Iceland is formed, though the Danish king remains head of state.

1926: The population reaches 100,000.

1944: Iceland becomes a fully independent nation.

1980: Vigdís Finnbogadóttir becomes the first woman president of Iceland.

2006: Iceland recommences commercial whaling, to protests from around the world.

2010: The Eyjafjallajökull volcano erupts, creating an ash cloud that disrupts flights in Europe for months.

AKUREYRI

DETTIFOSS
You're going to get wet here! The waterfall drops about 150 feet, creating a mighty spray.

GOÐAFOSS WATERFALL
One of the country's most beautiful waterfalls is steeped in Icelandic lore.

CHRISTMAS HOUSE
It's close to the North Pole, there's snow . . . seems like Christmas! This magical store is jam-packed full of Christmas stuff!

TRAVEL BY ICELANDIC HORSE
Explore some Icelandic countryside on the back of a famously friendly Icelandic horse.

BREIÐAMERKURJÖKULL
This glacier ends in a lagoon known as Jökulsárlón, where it breaks apart and forms icebergs.

SVARTIFOSS
The dark lava columns surrounding this waterfall look a bit like organ pipes.

LAKI
Take a flight over these volcanic craters, formed by a eruption in 1783. The lava didn't stop flowing for eight months!

INGÓLFUR ARNARSON
AD 849–910
Iceland's original settler—Arnarson arrived here in AD 874 and gave Reykjavík its name.

PREPARE FOR THE LAND OF FIRE AND ICE!

Straddling the Eurasian and North American tectonic plates, Iceland is a geological firecracker. It has one of the world's most active volcanoes, and its landscape tells the story of lava flows. There are 130 volcanoes on the island; combine that with sweeping glaciers, crashing waterfalls, and, of course, the spectacular Northern Lights, and you have one of the most incredible-looking places on the planet.

With dramatic landscapes, there's a lot of opportunity to be adventurous here—snowmobiling, skiing, hiking, caving . . . If you're feeling particularly brave, you could even scuba dive the chilly waters. You can always warm up after in one of the many geothermal spas. Alongside nature, there's also the country's Viking history to explore, and don't forget to spend some time in the buzzing capital Reykjavík—a small city with strange and wonderful museums.

KEY FACTS — ONE FOR ALL, ALL FOR ONE

CAPITAL Bern	**MONEY** Swiss franc	**NATION CODE** CH
LARGEST CITIES Zurich Geneva Basel Lausanne Bern	**NAMED FOR** One of the country's original provinces, Schwyz	**OFFICIAL LANGUAGES** French, Swiss, German, Italian, and Romansh
POPULATION 8,800,000	**FLOWER** Edelweiss	**BIRD** No official bird

MOMENTS TO REMEMBER

500 BC: A Celtic tribe, the Helvetians, settle in the region.

58 BC: The Roman Empire takes control.

AD 600: The Franks invade and bring Christianity to the Indigenous people.

1291: The Old Swiss Confederacy is established, beginning the formation of the nation.

1499: Switzerland gains independence from the German Swabian League.

1798: The French under Napoleon invade Switzerland.

1802: The Swiss revolt against the French and take back the land.

1815: Switzerland becomes a neutral country after the Congress of Vienna.

1848: Switzerland becomes a unified state with a constitution.

1863: The International Committee for Relief to the Wounded is formed in Geneva, later becoming the Red Cross.

1914: Switzerland stays neutral in World War I.

1939: The Swiss remain neutral in World War II.

1971: Switzerland becomes one of the last countries in Europe to grant women the vote.

2010: The Gotthard Base Tunnel, the longest in the world, running through the Swiss Alps, is completed.

CERN
The Large Hadron Collider at CERN is the biggest particle accelerator in the world, built to smash together particles and grow our understanding of physics.

CARL GUSTAV JUNG
1875–1961
Carl Jung was a psychologist who worked with Sigmund Freud. He had a deep impact on modern psychology.

GOTTFRIED KELLER
1819–1890
One of Switzerland's most treasured writers, Keller's most famous book is *Green Henry*.

LE CORBUSIER
1887–1965
This famous architect revolutionized urban planning, with simple, large apartment buildings.

ROGER FEDERER
B.1981
One of the greatest men's tennis players of all time, Federer won 20 Grand Slam titles.

FRANCE

BASEL

HAMMETSCHWAND ELEVATOR
You could climb to the top of Mount Bürgenstock . . . or you could take Europe's tallest outdoor elevator.

GRUYÈRE CHEESE FACTORY & MUSEUM
Take an audio tour as you taste your way around this cheese museum —a cow does the talking!

OLYMPIC MUSEUM
Test your sporting prowess with a series of physical challenges at this museum in Lausanne. The city is the Olympic headquarters.

BERN

LAUSANNE CATHEDRAL
Every night for more than 600 years, a lookout has called out the time each hour from the 800-year-old bell tower.

LAUSANNE

CHILLON CASTLE
Hidden on an island on Lake Geneva, this 1,000-year-old castle looks like it's straight out a fairy tale.

GENEVA

BARRYLAND
St. Bernards used to be used for mountain rescues. Celebrate (and pat!) these heroic dogs at this museum dedicated to them.

MARMITE DE L'ESCALADE
Feast on a chocolate cauldron during this festival, which celebrates a foiled attack on the city in 1602.

THE FLOWER CLOCK
Switzerland is the home of watch-making. Don't miss this clock made of flowers in bloom —if you have time!

MATTERHORN GLACIER PARADISE
Europe's highest mountain station gives you views of 14 glaciers!

SWITZERLAND

GERMANY

LAKE LUCERNE
Cruise around this beautiful lake on a paddlewheel steamer, taking in the views.

KYBURG CASTLE
You can touch many of the artifacts on display at this 11th century fortress, one of the oldest surviving castles in Switzerland.

FIFA MUSEUM
If you're a soccer fan, this is the place for you. Try a game of soccer pinball in the giant pinball arena.

LINDT & SPRÜNGLI CHOCOLATE FACTORY
Even if you don't know this chocolate, you'll want to visit to enjoy making it and tasting it!

ZURICH

STOOSBAHN FUNICULAR
This funicular (a kind of cable car) is the steepest in the world.

BOTANIC GARDEN
Flower-filled meadows, a beautiful pond, and 9,000 different types of plants make these gardens a breath of fresh mountain air.

AUSTRIA

TITLIS CLIFF WALK
Cross this 3-foot-wide suspension bridge and look down to a glacier 1,600 feet below.

MARTINA HINGIS
B.1980
Hingis spent 209 weeks as world number-one women's tennis player, and won five Grand Slam titles.

REICHENBACH FALLS
These falls are the setting for the supposed demise of fictional detective Sherlock Holmes.

GOTTHARD BASE TUNNEL
The world's longest train tunnel cuts 37 miles through the mountains of the Alps.

ITALY

VERZASCA RIVER
If you're feeling adventurous, you can bungee-jump into this river from a dam!

CASTLES OF BELLINZONA
The medieval castles of Castelgrande, Castello Montebello, and Castello Sasso Corbaro once protected the city of Bellinzona.

THE EIGER
Get your crampons ready—you'll need those spiky shoe accessories, and a whole lot of rope, to climb this 13,000-foot iconic mountain!

IT'S THE LAND OF CHOCOLATE, CHEESE, AND MOUNTAINS!

One thing is for sure, when you visit Switzerland, you'll see mountains! And with those mountains comes trekking, hiking, skiing of all kinds, climbing, and paragliding. Luckily there's famous Swiss chocolate to give you the energy to keep adventuring. The country is surrounded by the Swiss Alps and the Jura Alps. The highest peak is Dufourspitze in the Swiss Alps, at 15,203 feet.

With Italy, France, and Germany close neighbors, there are several official languages spoken here: Swiss German, French, Italian, and Romansch. The nation code for the country, CH, comes from Switzerland's Latin name, *Confoederatio Helvetica*.

Switzerland is one of the richest countries in the world and is well known for its banks, which are famously secretive and secure. The country's neutral status means that it doesn't get involved in wars. It's been this way since 1815, which has made Switzerland a very peaceful place!

SCANDINAVIA

WELCOME TO THE LANDS OF THE MIDNIGHT SUN

Reindeer and royalty. Vikings and fairy tales. In these lands that experience bitter winters with no sunlight to speak of and summers when the sun never sets, it's not surprising that Scandinavian culture is sprinkled with mystery and majesty. Experience the wonder of the aurora borealis from the Arctic Circle and enjoy spectacular glacial fjords, fascinating open-air museums, and one of the world's oldest amusement parks.

Norway, Sweden, and Denmark make up what we know today as Scandinavia. The history of these countries has been intertwined for centuries, and it wasn't until the 20th century that each country became independent. The Kingdom of Denmark still encompasses the countries of Greenland and the remote Faroe Islands.

In the cities and towns, you'll see evidence of a proud maritime history and a reverence for royalty. Striking palaces and castles, reconstructed shipwrecks, and hotels made entirely of ice—time to put your long johns on and get involved!

GEIRANGERFJORD
Ice Age glaciers created this stunning fjord, complete with towering cliffs, snow-capped peaks, and plunging waterfalls.

NIDAROS CATHEDRAL TRONDHEIM
Deep below this Gothic cathedral lies the tomb of Norway's patron saint, the Viking King Olav II.

TRONDHEIM

MYKINES ISLAND
This island is home to thousands of puffins—the world's cutest bird!

LAKE SØRVÁGSVATN
The largest lake in the Faroe Islands looks like it is balanced precariously on the edge of a cliff.

MÚLAFOSSUR WATERFALL
This waterfall on the island of Vágar plunges over 500 feet into the sea.

TROLLTUNGA
One look at this extraordinary rock formation shows you why it became known as the Troll's Tongue.

HANSEATIC WHARF, BRYGGEN
Fishing boats have been docking at this colorful wharf for more than 600 years.

LINDHOLM HØJE MUSEUM
This Viking burial ground has nearly 700 graves, each marked with a stone.

VIKING SHIP MUSEUM, OSLO
The real-life Viking ships on display here are believed to be the best-preserved in the world.

NORWAY

BERGEN

OSLO

SWEDEN

SKAGEN
Denmark's northernmost town has a beach where the waters of the Baltic and North Sea meet and swirl.

GOTHENBURG

DENMARK **AARHUS** **MALMÖ**

COPENHAGEN

ODENSE

LEGO HOUSE, BILLUND
The exhibits here include a life-size T. rex and some of the first Lego sets ever made.

SINGING TREES IN AALBORG
Since 1987, famous musicians visiting the town of Aalborg have planted a tree here and donated a song.

EGESKOV CASTLE
Straight out of a fairy tale, this 500-year-old castle comes complete with drawbridge and moat.

KEY FACTS

NORWAY: ALL FOR NORWAY
SWEDEN: FOR SWEDEN—WITH THE TIMES
DENMARK: GOD'S HELP, THE LOVE OF THE PEOPLE, DENMARK'S STRENGTH

CAPITALS
Norway: Oslo
Sweden: Stockholm
Denmark: Copenhagen

MONEY
Norway: Norwegian krone
Sweden: Swedish krona
Denmark: Danish krone

OFFICIAL LANGUAGES
Norway: Norwegian, Sámi
Sweden: Swedish, Finnish, Sámi; Denmark: Danish

LARGEST CITIES
Norway: Oslo, Bergen, Stavanger
Sweden: Stockholm, Gothenburg, Malmö
Denmark: Copenhagen, Aarhus, Odense

NATION CODES
N: NO, S: SE, D: DK

FLOWERS
Norway: Purple heather
Sweden: Twinflower
Denmark: Marguerite daisy

BIRDS
Norway: White-throated dipper
Sweden: Eurasian blackbird
Denmark: Mute swan

POPULATION
Norway: 5,500,000
Sweden: 10,500,000
Denmark: 5,900,000

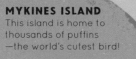

AURORA BOREALIS, TROMSØ

This city is one of the best places to see the Northern Lights.

ABISKO NATIONAL PARK, LAPLAND

For thousands of years, the Sámi people have hunted and herded reindeer in this area. Keep an eye out for their ancient huts.

FINLAND

GRETA THUNBERG
B.2003
Thunberg took her frustration at world leaders' inability to act on the climate crisis and created her own movement for change.

GTUNA

is medieval town is the dest in Sweden, founded by k the Victorious in AD 970.

ICE HOTEL, JUKKASJÄRVI

Check out the rooms at the Ice Hotel. Your bed is made of ice, but they give you cozy animal pelts to sleep on. Phew!

HARALD HARDRADA
1015–1066 AD
The last great Viking ruler, Harald Sigurdsson was given the nickname "Hardrada," meaning "hard ruler."

VASA MUSEUM, STOCKHOLM

The 230-foot-long *Vasa* warship sank on its maiden journey in 1628. Over 300 years later, it was salvaged, restored, and put on display here.

BJÖRN BORG
B.1956
Swedish tennis legend Borg racked up a total of 62 singles titles in his day, 11 of which were Grand Slams.

SKANSEN

The oldest open-air museum in the world shows how Swedes lived and worked hundreds of years ago.

STOCKHOLM

ALES STENAR

Legend has it that these enormous standing stones, arranged in the shape of a long boat, mark the resting place of an ancient king.

CHRISTIANSBORG PALACE

Located on its own island, the palace is used by the royal family for special events and also hosts the Danish parliament and the supreme court.

TIVOLI GARDENS

Thought to be the inspiration behind Disneyland, this is one of the world's oldest amusement parks.

THE ROUND TOWER

Built in the 17th century, this stone tower is the oldest functioning observatory in Europe.

MØNS KLINT

Fossils from 70 million years ago have been discovered at the base of these chalky cliffs, which stretch for almost 4 miles and rise nearly 425 feet out of the sea.

MOMENTS TO REMEMBER

2500 BC: People from Northern Scandinavia begin exploring south on wooden skis. They learn farming techniques and the population grows.

1st century AD: Norwegians trade fur and skins with the expanding Roman Empire.

8th century: Vikings announce themselves as fierce warriors by invading Lindisfarne island, off the coast of England.

1397: Sixteen-year-old Eric of Pomerania becomes the king of Norway, Denmark, and Sweden.

1586: Danish astronomer Tycho Brahe establishes an observatory on Ven island. It catalogs over 1,000 stars.

1668: The Bank of Sweden is established and produces Europe's first paper currency.

1832: The Göta canal is completed. Now ships can travel across Scandinavia from the Baltic to the North Sea.

1905: Norwegians vote overwhelmingly to be independent of Sweden.

1939: Sweden, Norway, and Denmark decide to remain neutral during World War II.

1957: Danish architect Jørn Utzon wins a competition to design the Sydney Opera House in Australia.

2012: A pastel artwork called *The Scream* by Norwegian artist Edvard Munch sells for US $120 million at auction.

2014: Norwegian Major General Kristin Lund becomes the first woman to be the commander of a UN peacekeeping force.

HANS CHRISTIAN ANDERSEN
1805–1875
This famous Danish storyteller is the man behind classics such as *The Little Mermaid*, *Thumbelina*, and *The Ugly Duckling*.

VITUS BERING
1681–1741
Cartographer Bering was the first person to sail through the Bering Strait, proving that the Asian and American continents are separate.

THE GRAND BAZAAR
Explore over 4,000 stalls, all under one roof, at one of the world's biggest and oldest markets.

TOPKAPI PALACE
The center of the Ottoman court from 1478 to 1856 is now a museum showing off jewelry, weaponry, and more.

HAGIA SOPHIA
A church, a mosque, a museum, and now a mosque again, this grand structure was built using the finest marble and the labor of over 10,000 men.

PERGAMON
The nearby thermal springs made this ancient city a favorite destination of kings and queens. It later became a center for health and wellness.

ISTANBUL

BURSA

ANKARA
Here you can visit the hilltop mausoleum of Atatürk, the country's first president.

EPHESUS
At this ancient Greek and Roman site, the standout ruin is the Temple of Artemis.

ASPENDOS
Marvel at the best-preserved Roma amphitheater in the world. It could seat up to 20,000 people.

PAMUKKALE
Soak your feet in warm, mineral-rich spring water at these spectacular brilliant-white terraces on the mountainside.

IZMIR

BODRUM CASTLE
Standing for over 600 years, this castle has also been used as a military base, a monastery, and a mosque.

ANTALYA
The eternal flame of Chimera, fuele by natural gas seeping out of the hillside, ha been burning since ancient times!

DALYAN MUD BATH
This huge mud bath attracts people who believe the mineral-rich mud will cure their skin ailments.

LYCIAN ROCK TOMBS, FETHIYE
The Lycians built these tombs high on the cliffs to help angels reach the dead.

ÖLÜDENIZ
Laze on a sandy beach and swim in the turquoise waters of a protected lagoon.

PATARA
This 11-mile stretch of sand is Türkiye's longest uninterrupted beach.

BUTTERFLY VALLEY
Around 100 different species of butterfly flutter by the pretty waterfall and lavender trees in this valley.

MOMENTS TO REMEMBER

6500 BC: The city of Çatalhöyük is established; it is one of the earliest human settlements.

1900–1260 BC: The Hittite Empire becomes the dominant power in the region.

130 BC: Anatolia (ancient Turkey) falls to the Roman Empire.

AD 330: Emperor Constantine the Great establishes the new capital city of the Roman Empire at Byzantium; he renames it Constantinople (now Istanbul).

1071: The Seljuk Turks defeat the Byzantine army and gain control of Anatolia.

1453: The powerful Ottoman Empire conquers Constantinople, which ends the Byzantine Empire.

1520: Suleyman the Magnificent expands the Ottoman Empire to include all of Turkey and much of the Middle East, Greece, and Hungary.

1914–1918: During World War I, the Ottoman Empire sides with Germany and is defeated by the Allies.

1923: Mustafa Kemal Atatürk founds the Republic of Turkey and becomes the first president. The capital is moved to Ankara.

1974: Turkey invades Cyprus after a military coup.

2019: Turkey invades northern Syria in an attempt to overthrow the Syrian Democratic Forces.

2022: Turkey changes its official name to Türkiye.

2023: A deadly earthquake strikes southern and central Türkiye and parts of northern Syria, killing almost 60,000 people and leaving 1.5 million people homeless.

CONSTANTINE THE GREAT
C. AD 272–337
Roman emperor Constantine built his palace in Byzantium and renamed the city Constantinople, after himself!

MUSTAFA KEMAL ATATÜRK
1881–1938
Atatürk was the leader of the Turkish National Movement and became the founder of the modern Republic of Turkey.

ORHAN PAMUK
B.1952
Bestselling author Pamuk won the Nobel Prize for Literature in 2006. His work has been translated into 63 languages.

TÜRKIYE

SAFRANBOLU
Have a soak in a 17th-century hammam (bathhouse) in this historic Ottoman city.

ANKARA

GÖREME OPEN-AIR MUSEUM
Carved into the rockface are dozens of churches from the 10th to 12th centuries. The largest, known as the Nunnery, is seven stories high.

KAYMAKLI UNDERGROUND VILLAGE
In 3000 BC, the Hittites carved out underground homes, connected by tunnels.

RED AND ROSE VALLEYS
At sunset, the pink-colored rock peaks of these valleys are at their most beautiful.

CAPPADOCIA

ÇATALHÖYÜK
The houses in this Stone Age settlement had no doors or windows; people used a hole in the roof to get in and out.

ADANA

CAVES OF HEAVEN AND HELL
These caves and sinkholes were carved by an underground river. You can still hear it running below.

SUMELA MONASTERY
Built in the 4th century, this huge monastery is carved into the side of a sheer cliff face.

ANI
Once home to over 200,000 people, this Armenian medieval city is now a ruined ghost town.

ARMENIA

MOUNT NEMRUT
At the top of this mountain, huge stone heads of ancient gods surround what is thought to be a burial site from the 1st century BC.

SYRIA

CYPRUS

SABIHA GÖKÇEN
1913–2001
Gökçen was the first woman in the world to fly as a fighter pilot in combat when she was 23 years old.

ALI QUSHJI
1403–1474
Astronomer, mathematician, and physicist, Qushji was one of the first people to prove that Earth revolves on an axis.

CONQUERING EMPIRES AND CAVE-DWELLING CULTURES

Türkiye occupies an important geographical location between Europe and Asia, and has centuries of cultural connections with powerful empires such as the ancient Greeks, Persians, Romans, Byzantines, and Ottomans. The wave upon wave of conquering armies and power-hungry emperors has left Türkiye's countryside with an abundance of ancient ruins, as well as impressive palaces, castles, rock-cut tombs, mosques, churches, monasteries, and even underground cities.

Spanning a large area and lying across two continents means this country has a rich and varied culture. Its national cuisine has influences from Asia and Mediterranean Europe, and its markets are some of the busiest and biggest in the world.

Türkiye's main cities are modern metropolises studded with jewels of the past. Istanbul, the country's biggest city, contains the awe-inspiring Hagia Sophia, while in the capital city, Ankara, you can see the mausoleum of the independence hero, Kemal Atatürk. Away from the cities, Türkiye's majesty continues in wild beaches, giant sinkholes formed by underground rivers, and valleys filled with butterflies. Türkiye's beauty brings out the best of all worlds.

KANGRA VALLEY TEA PLANTATIONS
India is the tea capital of the world. See it growing in the lush hills of Kangra.

THE GREAT HIMALAYAN NATIONAL PARK
Look out for snow leopards and the Himalayan tahr at this beautiful national park.

KEY MONASTERY
Hear the mystical chants of monks in this remote Buddhist monastery.

SPITI VALLEY
Travel on a high mountain road like the Kunzum Pass —but don't look down!

THE VALLEY OF FLOWERS
300 species of flower make this a very colorful place to trek in the Himalayas.

CHINA

PARANTHE GALI WALI
This street is famous for its paratha—a flatbread eaten with vegetarian sauces, chutneys, and pickles.

JIM CORBETT NATIONAL PARK
India's oldest national park is home to tigers, elephants, and sambar deer.

LOTUS TEMPLE
This temple really does look like a lotus flower, with its 27 white petals.

AKSHARDHAM
There are 148 elephant statues in this grand Hindu temple.

PAKISTAN

JAISALMER FORT
Looking just like a golden sandcastle, this 850-year-old fort is still a thriving town.

NEPAL

NEW DELHI

AGRA FORT
This 16th-century complex was home to India's Mughal rulers.

KUMBHALGARH WALL
India has its own great wall! It is 24 miles long and protects the Kumbhalgarh Fort.

LIVING ROOT BRIDGES OF CHERRAPUNJI
At one of the wettest places in the world, who needs to build bridges when you can train the roots of the rubber fig tree!

BANGLADESH

AHMEDABAD

RANTHAMBORE NATIONAL PARK
Travel to Rajasthan's largest national park to see tigers, leopards, and crocodiles.

VARANASI
With 3,000 years of history and the sacred Ganges River running through it, Varanasi is considered India's spiritual capital.

ORCHHA
The quiet town of Orchha is full of ancient temples and palaces.

MYANMAR

KONARK SUN TEMPLE
This World Heritage Site was built in the 13th century as a tribute to the Hindu sun god, Surya.

TAJ MAHAL
India's most famous building was built in the 17th century by Shah Jahan as a mausoleum for his wife, Mumtaz Mahal.

MUMBAI

ELLORA CAVES
Marvel at these 1,500-year-old temples and monasteries that were cut from the rock by hand.

HYDERABAD

ELEPHANTA ISLAND
Explore the island's cave temples, decorated with statues and carvings.

PALOLEM BEACH
This is one of the prettiest beaches in India's beach capital, Goa.

NAGARJUNSAGAR-SRISAILAM TIGER RESERVE
See ancient ruins of forts, temples, and caves—and India's national animal, the Bengal tiger.

LATA MANGESHKAR
1929–2022
Lata had one of the most famous singing voices in India. She appeared on the soundtrack for hundreds of Bollywood movies.

BANGALORE

HAMPI RUINS
Hampi was a great city destroyed in the 16th century, but even in ruins, it looks incredible.

GOMATESHVARA
This is the world's tallest statue carved from a single stone.

SRI LANKA

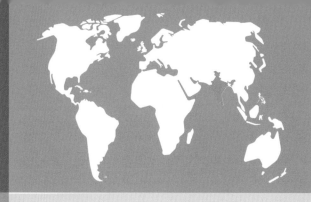

INDIA

3000 BC: The Indus Valley civilization begins. It is the foundation of what becomes India.

1500–1000 BC: The sacred texts called the Vedas are composed. They go on to inform many of India's religious and philosophical traditions.

273 BC: Ashoka the Great becomes emperor of the ancient Indian empire of Maurya.

AD 1526: The Muslim Mughul Empire begins under Babur.

1608: The East India Company, founded in England, begins trading out of India. It grows powerful and eventually takes control of India.

1858: The British crown takes direct control of India.

1920: Mahatma Gandhi launches his campaign against British rule.

1947: India achieves independence from Britain.

1966: Indira Gandhi becomes India's first female prime minister.

1983: India wins its first Cricket World Cup.

2023: India becomes the fourth country ever to land a spacecraft on the Moon.

KEY FACTS

TRUTH ALONE TRIUMPHS

CAPITAL New Delhi	**MONEY** Rupee	**NATION CODE** IN
LARGEST CITIES Mumbai New Delhi Bengaluru	**NAMED FOR** The Indus River	**OFFICIAL LANGUAGES** Hindi and English (plus 20 others recognized in the constitution)
POPULATION 1,425,700,000	**FLOWER** Sacred lotus	**BIRD** Indian peafowl

WELCOME TO THE LAND OF DIVERSITY

Everything about India seems huge, from the towering Himalayan range that stretches across its northern border to its population of more than 1.4 billion people—the highest of any country in the world.

Thousands of years of history surround you as you journey across the landscape, passing ancient temples, palaces, forts, and city ruins. India is one of the most spiritual countries in the world, with religions and major schools of thought having been founded here.

In the many large cities, it's easy to lose yourself in the sights, sounds, and smells. Follow your nose to the delicious food India is famous for, then find a movie theater and watch a Bollywood film—usually a big musical movie with a lot of energetic dancing!

INDIRA GANDHI
1917–1984
Politician Indira Gandhi was the first—and is still the only—woman to become prime minister of India.

SACHIN TENDULKAR
B.1973
Tendulkar is considered one of the greatest batsmen to have played cricket—he's often called the "god of cricket" in India.

MOTHER TERESA
1910–1997
This Catholic nun's name has become synonymous with helping those in need. She was eventually made a saint by the Catholic Church.

MAHATMA GANDHI
1869–1948
Gandhi led India to independence from British rule and his philosophy of nonviolent protest inspired activists all around the world.

SAPA HILL TRIBES
Hike the mountainous lands of the Sapa Hill tribes and learn about the culture of the minority peoples who live here.

HẠ LONG BAY
There are 1,600 limestone karsts poking up from the sea in Hạ Long Bay.

HANOI

HO CHI MINH'S MAUSOLEUM
Uncle Ho, as he is affectionately known, didn't want a mausoleum, but he got one! His embalmed body rests here.

HANOI'S OLD QUARTER
This part of Hanoi has streets dedicated to particular goods, such as shoe street and silver street.

HOÀN KIẾM LAKE
This lake is also known as "Sword Lake," after a legend about a golden turtle and a magic sword.

HAI PHONG

HANOI CYCLO
Why not take a ride on a cyclo? It's a three-wheeled bicycle taxi.

TEMPLE OF LITERATURE
This temple was a center for learning for almost 1,000 years.

THANG LONG WATER PUPPET THEATER
This 1,000-year-old tradition sees wooden puppets performing on water, retelling ancient tales.

PERFUME PAGODA
Canoe along a stream through rice fields to Huong Tich cave and find the Perfume Pagoda.

EAT PHO
Pho is the national dish. Dig into a bowl of steaming beef or chicken, broth, and soft, wide noodles.

MY KHE BEACH
People sell fresh fruit, seafood, and other snacks while you sunbathe or swim. Bliss!

DA NANG

THE MARBLE MOUNTAINS
Five marble and limestone hills rise from the surrounding countryside, each with pagodas, tunnels, and caves.

IMPERIAL CITY HUẾ
Emperor Gia Long built this royal complex in the 18th century.

THIÊN MỤ PAGODA
A symbol of Huế, this pagoda was built in 1601 on the banks of the Perfume River.

HỘI AN
Wander the riverside streets of picturesque old Hội An and watch boats sail by on the river.

ROYAL THEATER OF HUẾ
You can listen to traditional music and song at this restored theater.

DA LAT MARKET
Da Lat is cooler than most of Vietnam, so put on a coat and explore the central market—strawberries are a local specialty!

PO NAGAR TEMPLE
This temple was built more than 1,300 years ago during the Cham civilization.

CỦ CHI TUNNELS
During the Vietnam War, the Northern Vietnamese soldiers used underground tunnels to move around. Try and squeeze through them yourself!

PHÚ QUỐC ISLAND
This island paradise is home to the best fish sauce. Anchovies are dried in the sun and then left to ferment—yum!

HO CHI MINH CITY

CAN THO

THE DUNES OF MŨI NÉ
Rent a sand board and surf down some mountains of sand!

NGUYỄN QUANG HẢI
B.1997
A household name in Vietnam, this soccer player is considered one of the best in Asia.

MEKONG DELTA
The waterways of the Mekong Delta are so busy it can seem like a city on the water!

BẾN THÀNH MARKET
This bustling market is packed with clothes, food, and souvenirs.

CÁI RĂNG FLOATING MARKET
Hundreds of boats crowd the riverbanks, selling produce from all around the Mekong.

TRƯNG TRẮC AND TRƯNG NHỊ
C.AD 12–43
These sisters are considered national heroes, having rebelled against the Chinese from the backs of their trusty elephants.

HỒ CHÍ MINH
1890–1969
Hồ Chí Minh is the father of modern Vietnam: he led North Vietnam against the French and against South Vietnam and the USA to form one country.

KEY FACTS	INDEPENDENCE—FREEDOM—HAPPINESS	
CAPITAL Hanoi	**MONEY** Đồng	**NATION CODE** VN
LARGEST CITIES Ho Chi Minh City Hai Phong Can Tho Bien Hoa Da Nang	**NAMED FOR** There is some debate about what the name means but we think it means "Viet people of the South."	**OFFICIAL LANGUAGE** Vietnamese
POPULATION 104,800,000	**FLOWER** Red lotus	**ANIMAL** Water buffalo

WELCOME TO THE LAND OF THE ASCENDING DRAGON

Could a country be any brighter, louder, and more colorful than Vietnam? It's difficult to imagine!

It is perhaps one of the most beautiful places in the world. That would explain why, throughout its history, people have been fighting over who gets to call it home. For much of its history, it has been a region ruled by China. And many of the country's most famous people are soldiers or warriors who defied Chinese rule.

Today it's a peaceful place, despite the high energy of its cities. Learning to walk across a busy road will be one of your very first challenges as the traffic swirls around you—cars, bicycles, motorcycles, and cyclos (three-wheeled bike taxis). Before you know it, you'll be on the other side, looking at a street cart selling the most delicious fresh fruit you can imagine—with a tiny bag of salt and chilli to dip each piece into.

MOMENTS TO REMEMBER

2879 BC: Kinh Dương Vương forms the state that will eventually become the northern part of Vietnam.

AD 1516: Portuguese explorers arrive.

1809: Poet Nguyễn Du writes one of the country's most treasured stories, *The Tale of Kiều*.

1858: French colonial rule begins.

1926: The last emperor of Vietnam, Bảo Đại, takes the throne.

1954: After the French are forced out of the north, Vietnam is split into two countries: North Vietnam and South Vietnam.

1964: The USA officially declares war on North Vietnam.

1973: The USA withdraws from Vietnam.

1976: Vietnam is unified after North Vietnam defeats South Vietnam. Hundreds of thousands flee abroad.

1977: Vietnam is admitted to the United Nations.

2016: Vietnam wins its first Olympic gold medal, for pistol shooting.

NGÔ QUYỀN
AD 897–944
Ngô Quyền led Vietnam to victory against China, ending 1,000 years of Chinese rule over the land.

VÕ NGUYÊN GIÁP
1911–2013
Giáp defeated the French in 1954, bringing the country one step closer to independence.

VIETNAM

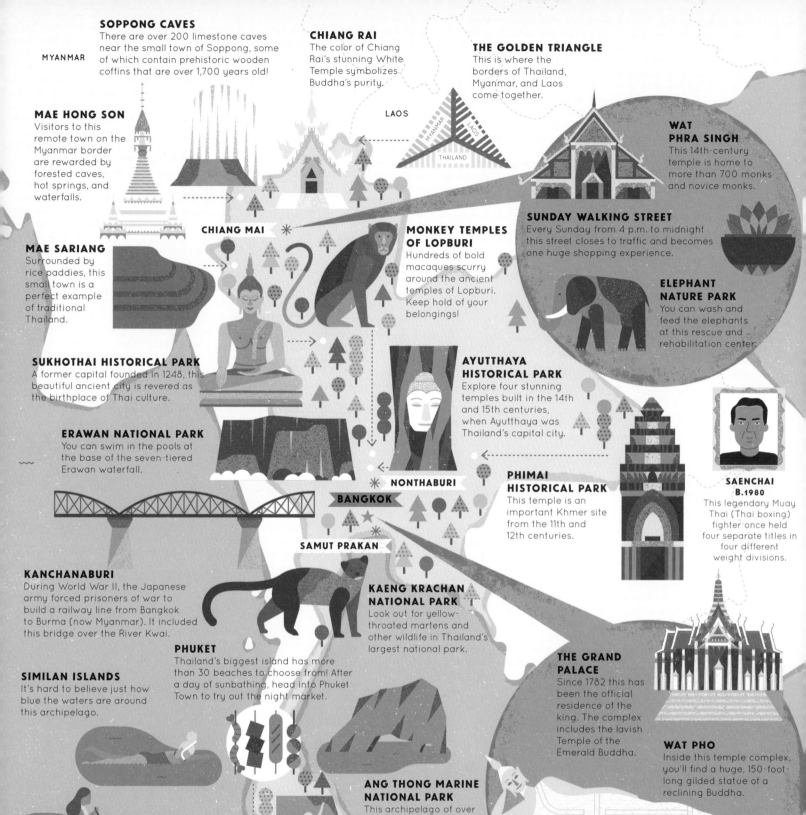

SOPPONG CAVES
There are over 200 limestone caves near the small town of Soppong, some of which contain prehistoric wooden coffins that are over 1,700 years old!

MYANMAR

CHIANG RAI
The color of Chiang Rai's stunning White Temple symbolizes Buddha's purity.

THE GOLDEN TRIANGLE
This is where the borders of Thailand, Myanmar, and Laos come together.

LAOS

MYANMAR
LAOS
THAILAND

WAT PHRA SINGH
This 14th-century temple is home to more than 700 monks and novice monks.

MAE HONG SON
Visitors to this remote town on the Myanmar border are rewarded by forested caves, hot springs, and waterfalls.

CHIANG MAI

MONKEY TEMPLES OF LOPBURI
Hundreds of bold macaques scurry around the ancient temples of Lopburi. Keep hold of your belongings!

SUNDAY WALKING STREET
Every Sunday from 4 p.m. to midnight this street closes to traffic and becomes one huge shopping experience.

ELEPHANT NATURE PARK
You can wash and feed the elephants at this rescue and rehabilitation center.

MAE SARIANG
Surrounded by rice paddies, this small town is a perfect example of traditional Thailand.

SUKHOTHAI HISTORICAL PARK
A former capital founded in 1248, this beautiful ancient city is revered as the birthplace of Thai culture.

AYUTTHAYA HISTORICAL PARK
Explore four stunning temples built in the 14th and 15th centuries, when Ayutthaya was Thailand's capital city.

ERAWAN NATIONAL PARK
You can swim in the pools at the base of the seven-tiered Erawan waterfall.

NONTHABURI

BANGKOK

PHIMAI HISTORICAL PARK
This temple is an important Khmer site from the 11th and 12th centuries.

SAENCHAI
B.1980
This legendary Muay Thai (Thai boxing) fighter once held four separate titles in four different weight divisions.

SAMUT PRAKAN

KANCHANABURI
During World War II, the Japanese army forced prisoners of war to build a railway line from Bangkok to Burma (now Myanmar). It included this bridge over the River Kwai.

KAENG KRACHAN NATIONAL PARK
Look out for yellow-throated martens and other wildlife in Thailand's largest national park.

THE GRAND PALACE
Since 1782 this has been the official residence of the king. The complex includes the lavish Temple of the Emerald Buddha.

PHUKET
Thailand's biggest island has more than 30 beaches to choose from! After a day of sunbathing, head into Phuket Town to try out the night market.

SIMILAN ISLANDS
It's hard to believe just how blue the waters are around this archipelago.

WAT PHO
Inside this temple complex, you'll find a huge, 150-foot-long gilded statue of a reclining Buddha.

ANG THONG MARINE NATIONAL PARK
This archipelago of over 40 islands includes coral reefs, rock arches, and inland lagoons.

PHI PHI ISLANDS
Hop on a kayak to explore these islands' stunning white-sand beaches.

FLOATING MARKETS
Bangkok's canals host floating markets full of boats selling everything from fresh fruit to souvenirs.

KING CHULALONGKORN/RAMA V
1853–1910
This monarch's greatest achievement was to prevent Thailand from being colonized by Western forces.

RAILAY BEACH
This beautiful beach is the best place in the country to rock climb limestone karsts.

KOH TARUTAO
What was once an isolated island prison is now a destination for intrepid travelers seeking pristine beaches without lots of tourists.

MALAYSIA

What do you know about Thailand? Perhaps you've heard about its beautiful white-sand beaches and the delicious, spicy, fragrant food that it is famous for. But did you also know that there are close to 40,000 temples in Thailand, or that it's the only Southeast Asian country that has never been colonized?

Bangkok is the capital of Thailand and the largest city in the country. The streets of this lively metropolis are lined with modern skyscrapers and food carts, luxury cars and tuk-tuks, tourists and temples, monks and business people.

To the south of Bangkok, you'll find Thailand's famous beaches and to the north you'll uncover its forests and jungles, and the country's foodie paradise, Chiang Mai. From top to bottom, this is a country with wondrous wilderness, fascinating historical monuments, unique wildlife, and intriguing cities and towns.

MOMENTS TO REMEMBER

AD 900s: Tai people begin to migrate from Southern China into areas of present-day Thailand.

1200s: Powerful regional empires, such as the Khmer and Dvaravati, decline and Tai city-states unify and identify as Thai.

1350s: The kingdom of Ayutthaya becomes the dominant power and is the first to trade with Europeans.

1569–1767: The Ayutthaya kingdom is overpowered by Burmese forces. The succession line of kings is broken.

1767–1782: A former military general, Taksin, claims power and moves the capital to Thonburi. In 1782, he is deposed by the military.

1782: Chao Phraya Chakri assumes the throne as King Yot Fa (Rama I). The capital is moved to Bangkok.

1850–1910: King Mongkut (Rama IV) and King Chulalongkorn (Rama V) modernize the country, building railways to unite the land and protecting it from colonization.

1932: Military officers and bureaucrats, calling themselves the Khana Ratsadon (People's Party) overthrow the king and introduce a constitutional monarchy.

1939: The country, known as Siam up until now, becomes known as Prathet Thai.

1957: Thailand comes under a military dictatorship. It lasts until 1973, when democracy returns.

1997: The Asian Economic Crisis occurs.

2011: Yingluck Shinawatra becomes the first female prime minister of Thailand.

2016: King Bhumibol Adulyadej dies after 70 years on the throne. His son, King Vajiralongkorn, succeeds him.

KEY FACTS	NATION, RELIGION, KING	
CAPITAL Bangkok	**MONEY** Baht	**NATION CODE** TH
LARGEST CITIES Bangkok Samut Prakan Nonthaburi Udon Thani	**NAMED FOR** The name Thailand translates to "land of the free"	**OFFICIAL LANGUAGE** Thai
POPULATION 69,800,000	**FLOWER** Golden shower tree	**BIRD** Siamese fireback

RATCHANOK INTANON
B.1995
Intanon was the first Thai woman to become a world champion in badminton.

YINGLUCK SHINAWATRA
B.1967
Thailand's first female prime minister was just 43 when she became leader.

KING BHUMIBOL ADULYADEJ
1927–2016
At the time of his death, this monarch was the longest-reigning head of state in the world and the longest-reigning monarch in Thai history.

THAILAND

KEY FACTS — SERVE THE PEOPLE

CAPITAL	MONEY	NATION CODE
Beijing	Renminbi (Yuan)	CN

POPULATION	NAMED FOR	OFFICIAL LANGUAGE
1,425,600,000	In Chinese it means "middle kingdom"	Standard Chinese (Mandarin)

LARGEST CITIES	FLOWER	ANIMAL
Shanghai Beijing Chongqing Tianjin Guangzhou	Plum blossom	Giant panda

MOMENTS TO REMEMBER

7500 BC: People begin cultivating rice in the region.

551 BC: Confucius, the famous philosopher and thinker, is born.

221 BC: Qin Shi Huang becomes the first emperor of a unified China.

AD 105: Paper is invented by Cai Lun.

142: Gunpowder, a Chinese invention, is mentioned in texts for the first time.

206–220: The compass is invented in China, revolutionizing travel.

1041–1048: Bi Sheng invents moveable type printing.

1421: Beijing becomes the capital of China.

1912: China becomes a republic.

1949: The communist revolution sees Mao become the leader of Communist China.

1966–1976: China undergoes the Cultural Revolution—a time of great change throughout its society.

1989: Many demonstrators are killed while protesting in Beijing's Tiananmen Square.

2008: Beijing hosts the Olympic Games.

2013: China lands the Jade Rabbit rover on the Moon.

2022: Xi Jinping begins a third term as president. Before this, presidents were only allowed to serve two terms.

MAO ZEDONG
1893–1976
Chairman Mao was the founder of the People's Republic of China.

FAYE WONG
B.1969
Wong is a hugely popular and groundbreaking Chinese pop star.

YAO MING
B.1980
Basketballer Yao Ming is China's most famous sportsperson. He played in the US NBA as well as in China.

HEAVENLY LAKE OF TIANSHAN
Melted snow from the mountains makes the water here crystal clear.

XINJIANG INTERNATIONAL GRAND BAZAAR
This busy Islamic market is one of the largest bazaars in the world.

POTALA PALACE
This 1,000-room palace was home to Tibet's Dalai Lamas for 400 years until communist rule in 1959.

TIGER LEAPING GORGE
The rocky cliffs of this World Heritage Site run for 9 miles along the Jinsha River.

MOGAO GROTTOES
The "Caves of the Thousand Buddhas" are a treasure-trove of Buddhist art.

WELCOME TO THE LAND OF THE DIVINE

One of the most populous countries on Earth, China has had an amazing influence on the world throughout history. It's the home of printing, gunpowder, and the compass. Rice—one of the world's most important food sources—was first cultivated in China around 10,000 years ago.

Throughout its history China has controlled large areas of East Asia, and almost every country in the region has Chinese traditions as part of their own, from religion to food. The Chinese traded with other parts of the world, spreading their technology and culture, but also adopting from the people they interacted with.

Chinese cities are enormous—Shanghai alone has around 24 million people! A visit to China will keep you entertained for weeks, if not years. With thousands of years of history, each part of China is completely unique. As well as speaking Mandarin, each region usually has its own language. The cuisine in each region is also distinct, with noodles in the north, rice in the south, and spicy dishes in the west.

CHINA

MONGOLIA

EAST TAIHANG GLASSWALK
Gulp! This glass bridge on the side of mountain is designed to look like it's cracking as you walk on it!

DRAGON ESCALATOR
The world's longest outdoor escalator runs down a hillside inside a yellow dragon!

HARBIN ICE AND SNOW WORLD
Ice sculptors from all over the world compete here every year.

GREAT WALL OF CHINA
China's famous collection of defensive walls is more than 13,000 miles long. (You can't see it from space though!)

TERRACOTTA ARMY
In 201 BC, around 8,000 warrior statues were buried with emperor Qin Shi Huang to protect him in the afterlife.

TEMPLE OF HEAVEN
Six hundred years ago, leaders prayed for good harvests at this temple complex.

PEKING DUCK
Peking duck is a multi-course experience, from crispy-skin pancakes to soup—all of it delicious!

BEIJING

LESHAN GIANT BUDDHA
This statue of Buddha, carved into a cliff, stands 230 feet tall!

CHENGDU PANDA BASE
Learn about these amazing bears on a visit to a panda research center.

TIANANMEN SQUARE
It's estimated this huge city square can hold 10 million people!

WATERMELON MUSEUM
Watermelons are one of China's most popular fruits —so it's no surprise to find a museum dedicated to them!

THE FORBIDDEN CITY
There are almost 1,000 buildings within the walls of this imperial palace!

CHONGQING

SHANGHAI

HANGZHOU

XIAO LONG BAO
Shanghai is home to the wonderful soup dumpling—a small parcel of meat that magically contains a delicious soup inside.

GIANT WILD GOOSE PAGODA
This temple was built in AD 652 to house Buddhist relics.

GUANGZHOU

TAIWAN

HONG KONG

WEST LAKE
The West Lake is famed for pagodas, bridges, and gardens. Jump on a bike and ride around the whole lake.

STONE FOREST YUNNAN
Marvel at a huge forest of giant limestone stalagmites, dotted with waterfalls and caves.

THE PEAK TRAM
The Peak Tram that rolls up the side of Victoria Peak in Hong Kong is so steep you'll feel like you're going to fall backward!

YUM CHA
Hong Kong is famed for its yum cha—small plates of single bites, from wontons to chicken feet.

KAYAK THE LI RIVER
The Li River winds through incredible limestone rock formations—paddle a kayak for a peaceful tour of this beautiful area.

KEY FACTS   UNITY IN DIVERSITY

CAPITAL	MONEY	NATION CODE
Jakarta	Indonesian rupiah	ID
LARGEST CITIES	**NAMED FOR**	**OFFICIAL LANGUAGE**
Jakarta Surabaya Medan Bandung	The Latin and Greek words *Indus* and *nesos*—meaning "Indian" and "island"	Indonesian (a standardized variant of Malay)
POPULATION	**FLOWER**	**BIRD**
279,500,000	Sambac jasmine	Javan hawk-eagle

SUKARNO
1901–1970
The first president of Indonesia, Sukarno is credited with being the champion of independence.

JAVA MAN
ONE MILLION YEARS AGO
The fossilized remains of Java Man were discovered in 1891–92; they are one of only a few examples of an early upright-standing human.

ORANGUTANS, KALIMANTAN
See these intelligent apes in the wild in Kutai and Tanjung Puting National Parks.

KAKABAN ISLAND
You can dive with thousands of stingless jellyfish in the lake in the center of this island.

MEDAN

MALAYSIA

LAKE KAOLIN, BELITUNG
Looking almost like the surface of the Moon, the white banks of this blue lake are made up of mineral deposits.

LABUAN CERMIN LAKE
The water in this lake is so clear that boats look like they're floating in midair!

LAKE TOBA
This massive lake lies in the caldera of an ancient volcano.

DIENG PLATEAU
The volcanic landscape of this plateau includes bubbling mud pools and steaming sulfur lakes.

BOROBUDUR TEMPLE
This stunning 9th-century Buddhist temple is the largest in the world.

GILI ISLANDS
Made up of three small islands ringed by coral reefs, the Gilis are famous for snorkeling with sea turtles.

TANA TORA
The Indigenou Torajan peopl are known for their elaborate funeral rituals. These include bodies being placed in loca caves and the mummified.

KRAKATOA
When this volcano erupted in 1883, it could be heard over 2,800 miles away!

UJUNG KULON NATIONAL PARK
It's thought that there are fewer than 70 Javan rhinos left on the planet and this is the only place you can see them.

JAKARTA

WAE REBO
This mountain village is famous for its large, cone-shaped, wooden houses.

BANDUNG

SURABAYA

MOUNT BROMO
If you brave the plumes of smoke from this active volcano and walk to the top, you'll be rewarded with awesome views.

ISTIQLAL MOSQUE
There are more people of Islamic faith in Indonesia than anywhere else on Earth, so it's not surprising that Jakarta has Southeast Asia's biggest mosque.

TAMAN MINI
Ornate pavilions showcase Indonesia's varied cultures with examples of Indigenous art, architecture, and costume.

NATIONAL MONUMENT
This 450-foot-high monument, topped with a bronze flame, is Indonesia's symbol of independence.

SEMINYAK
Surfing, sunbathing, and shopping are the main attractions at this beach town on the island of Bali.

PINK BEACH, LOMBOK
Yes, the sand on this beach on the island of Lombok really is pink!

KOMODO NATIONAL PARK
Don't get too close! Komodo dragons, the world's largest lizards, have a venomous bite.

ULUWATU TEMPLE
Sitting atop a steep cliff with a sheer 230-foot drop to the sea below, this Balinese Hindu temple is dedicated to the spirits of the sea.

SACRED MONKEY FOREST SANCTUARY
The long-tailed monkeys at this Ubud sanctuary like to help themselves to visitors' belongings!

There aren't many countries that count close to 300 different ethnic groups with over 700 languages as their inhabitants. In fact, it wasn't until foreign traders reached the region that it became known as the Indonesian archipelago instead of a group of distinct and separate islands.

Over 17,000 islands make up Indonesia. Across the area, you'll find volcanoes and tropical beaches, rice paddies and rain forests, mangroves and temples. Did you know that Indonesia is home to the world's largest flower too? Its name is *Rafflesia arnoldii*, but locals know it as the corpse flower because of its terrible smell!

Indonesia's capital city, Jakarta, is enormous and hectic. There are towering skyscrapers, an old town lined with Dutch colonial buildings, huge national monuments, and giant shopping malls. It's bright, loud, busy, bustling—and never boring!

MOMENTS TO REMEMBER

100,000 to 1.6 million years ago: *Homo erectus* (a direct ancestor of modern humans) walks the land on the island of Java.

2000 BC: People from Taiwan begin to arrive and settle in the archipelago.

AD 600s: A kingdom known as the Srivijaya is in power in areas of the Indonesian archipelago.

1200s: Islam arrives in Sumatra and gradually becomes the dominant religion.

1512: Portuguese traders are the first Europeans to arrive in Indonesia.

1619: Traders from the Dutch East India Company take over Java and other Indonesian islands.

1945: During World War II, the Dutch lose control and nationalist leader Sukarno declares Indonesian independence.

1967: In the aftermath of a failed coup, Sukarno hands over power to military leader General Suharto.

1999: East Timor votes for independence from Indonesia.

2004: More than 220,000 people die after a massive earthquake and tsunami hits the islands.

2010: Indonesia becomes the third-fastest-growing economy in the world, after China and India.

AGNES MONICA
B.1986
Aka AGNEZ MO, one of Indonesia's favorite pop stars and actors, has won more awards than any other Indonesian singer.

RAJA AMPAT
This archipelago of over 1,500 islands is home to coral reefs with thousands of colorful fish.

PUNCAK JAYA
The highest peak in all of Indonesia, this mountain range has snow and glaciers, despite being so close to the equator.

KELIMUTU
At the summit of this volcano, you can look down into three beautifully colored crater lakes.

RADEN ADJENG KARTINI
1879–1904
Human rights activist Kartini pioneered educational rights for girls and women in Indonesia.

SRI MULYANI INDRAWATI
B.1962
Economist Indrawati has been a director of the World Bank as well as Indonesian Finance Minister.

INDONESIA

CAPITAL Tokyo	**MONEY** Yen	**NATION CODE** JP
LARGEST CITIES Tokyo Yokohama Osaka Nagoya Sapporo	**NAMED FOR** Its name in Japanese, which means "the sun's origin"	**OFFICIAL LANGUAGE** Japanese
POPULATION 123,700,000	**FLOWERS** Chrysanthemum and cherry blossom	**BIRD** Japanese green pheasant

SAPPORO SNOW FESTIVAL
Each year Sapporo's Odori Park is turned into a winter wonderland with enormous snow sculptures made by people from across the world.

SAPPORO

CHŪBU-SANGAKU NATIONAL PARK
Nicknamed "the Japan Alps," this park contains high peaks, deep gorges, snow fields, and alpine wildflowers.

STUDIO GHIBLI
This animation studio has produced some wonderfully unique films over the years. *Spirited Away, Princess Mononoke,* and *My Neighbor Totoro* are just a few.

KENROKU-EN GARDEN (ISHIKAWA)
This 200-year-old garden is considered one of Japan's most beautiful.

KINKAKU-JI TEMPLE
The top two floors of this Zen temple are completely covered in gold leaf, making it glimmer in the sunlight.

GION
This Kyoto district is famous for its geishas, who sing, dance, and serve guests wearing traditional kimonos, hair, and make-up.

THE ATSUTA JINGU SHRINE
Legend has it that an ancient samurai sword is housed in this 2,000-year-old Shinto shrine.

JIGOKUDANI MONKEY PARK
What would you do if you came across a natural hot spring in the freezing snow? Follow the lead of the macaques and take a bath!

ARASHIYAMA BAMBOO GROVE
The soft light and gentle swaying of thousands of bamboo trunks makes this grove feel like another world.

KOREA

HIROSHIMA PEACE MEMORIAL PARK
This park was created to remember the awful destruction of the cities Hiroshima and Nagasaki in August 1945, when the USA dropped atomic bombs on them.

NAGOYA

TOKYO ★

YOKOHAMA

OSAKA

GREAT BUDDHA OF KAMAKURA
When the giant statue was built in 1252, it was entirely covered in gold leaf. You can still see some on the ears.

HENN NA HOTEL, NAGASAKI
Don't expect a human to help you at this hotel—it's run by robots, including a dinosaur!

NAOSHIMA
This incredible art island is full of curiosities big and small. Look out for enormous sculptures scattered around the area.

OSAKA CASTLE
When Toyotomi Hideyoshi succeeded in unifying Japan in the 16th century, he built this five-story castle as a display of power.

ITSUKUSHIMA SHRINE, HIROSHIMA
This "island of worship" has been a place of pilgrimage since ancient times, and the "floating" torii gate rising from the ocean is a sight to see!

FUKUOKA CASTLE
Visitors come in droves to see the cherry blossoms from high up in the crumbling turret ruins.

THE HAKONE OPEN-AIR MUSEUM (KANAGAWA)
If you think art museums are boring, then this open-air sculpture park might change your mind—look out for the giant head lying on its side.

HIMEJI CASTLE
The Japanese call this 400-year-old castle the White Heron castle because it is white and looks so elegant.

OKINAWA
Snorkel with sea turtles in Japan's southernmost prefecture.

MOUNT FUJI
Snow-capped "Fuji-san" is an active volcano and Japan's highest peak. Join the 300,000 people who climb it every year.

WELCOME TO THE LAND OF THE RISING SUN

You may think of Japan as an island off the eastern edge of Asia, but it's actually an archipelago of nearly 7,000 islands! The four major islands are Hokkaido, Honshu, Shikoku, and Kyushu. The city of Tokyo, Japan's busiest city and its capital, is on the largest island of Honshu. Because Japan sits near three of Earth's tectonic plates, it experiences around 1,500 earthquakes every year.

Japanese culture celebrates hard work and humility, and respecting your elders is very important. Did you know that Japanese people are some of the longest-living in the world? It could be down to their diet, which is rich in fish, rice, and vegetables. You might have tried the country's delicious signature dish, sushi.

From one end of the country to the other, you will come across snow-capped mountain peaks and beautifully manicured gardens, high-tech skyscrapers and bendy, bamboo forests, monkeys bathing in hot springs, and hotels run by robots! There is nowhere else on the planet quite like Japan.

MOMENTS TO REMEMBER

2500 BC: People on the Japanese archipelago are using stone tools and earthenware.

AD c.250–552: The Yamato court expands and rules; they will become known for their large burial mounds.

607: The Horyuji Temple is built, which contains the oldest surviving wooden structure in the world.

794: Kyoto becomes the capital.

1590: Toyotomi Hideyoshi unifies Japan after 100 years of instability and fighting among feudal lords.

1639: Japan rejects Western colonialism and religion, closing itself off from the rest of the world for 200 years.

1854: Japan and the USA sign the Treaty of Peace and Amity, which ends Japan's isolation.

1868: Tokyo becomes the capital.

1941–1945: Japan enters World War II. Hiroshima and Nagasaki are the targets of the first atomic bombs.

1956: Japan becomes a member of the United Nations.

2005: The Kyoto Protocol is drawn up and signed by nations determined to reduce climate change.

2011: More than 20,000 people die as a tsunami causes widespread destruction across the country.

2021: Tokyo hosts the 2020 Olympic Games . . . in 2021! The event is postponed by a year due to the COVID-19 pandemic.

TOKYO SKYTREE
This tower's observation deck has a glass walkway—look down and see tiny people far below!

TSUKIJI FISH MARKET
It might sound like a stinky place to visit, but this is one of the busiest fish markets on Earth in a country that invented eating raw fish!

UENO PARK AND ZOO
This huge park is popular during cherry blossom season, and is home to museums, temples, and a zoo.

HAYAO MIYAZAKI
B.1941
Miyazaki, who co-founded the famous Studio Ghibli and directed *My Neighbor Totoro*, is known as one of the world's greatest makers of animated films.

NAOMI OSAKA
B.1997
Osaka is the first Asian player to reach world number-one in women's singles tennis,

CHIAKI MUKAI
B.1952
The first Japanese woman in space and the first Japanese citizen to go on two spaceflights, Mukai happens to be a heart surgeon too!

TAIHŌ KŌKI
1940–2013
Perhaps the greatest sumo wrestler of all time, Taihō won 45 consecutive matches and achieved the highest rank at just 21 years old.

TOYOTOMI HIDEYOSHI
1537–1598
Hideyoshi became one of Japan's preeminent warriors, samurai, and politicians, and is credited with unifying the nation of Japan.

JAPAN

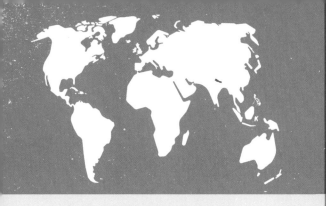

SUSHILA KARKI
B.1952
Karki is the first (and only) woman in Nepal to become the Chief Justice of the Supreme Court.

SANDUK RUIT
B.1954
Ruit is a pioneering eye surgeon responsible for restoring sight to over 120,000 people across Africa and Asia.

JHAMAK GHIMIRE
B.1980
Ghimire was born with cerebral palsy and taught herself to write with her left foot. She has gone on to be an award-winning author and poet.

CHINA

MOMENTS TO REMEMBER

AD 450–750: The ancient kingdom of Licchavi is established in Nepal after losing power in India.

1200–1800: The Malla dynasty comes to power and rules over the Kathmandu Valley, dividing it into city-states under a Malla king.

1769: Gurkha ruler Prithvi Narayan Shah conquers Kathmandu and lays the foundations for a unified kingdom.

1814–1816: War breaks out between the Kingdom of Gorkha (Nepal) and the East India Company because both want to expand their region of control.

1914–1918: Nepalese citizens fight for Britain in World War I.

1923: A treaty with Britain ensures Nepal's sovereignty.

1953: Tenzing Norgay from Nepal and Edmund Hillary from New Zealand become the first climbers to reach the summit of Mount Everest.

1994–1999: A communist government is formed, then dissolved before Maoists (Chinese communists) take over; this results in many Nepalese leaving for India.

2005: Maoists and opposition leaders agree on a plan to bring back a democratic process in Nepal.

2008: Nepal becomes a republic, and a Maoist leader becomes prime minister.

2015: A massive earthquake hits Nepal, killing more than 8,000 people and destroying historic buildings.

2020: Nepal and China jointly agree an official new height for Mount Everest: 8,848.86 meters (29,032 feet). The mountain is slightly higher than previously thought!

TILICHO LAKE
One of the highest lakes in the world sits at 3 miles above sea level.

ANNAPURNA MASSIF
Annapurna is known as the most dangerous mountain to climb because of its frequent avalanches.

ANNAPURNA SANCTUARY
A trek up this 13,000-foot-high plateau rewards hikers with a 360-degree view of towering Himalayan mountains.

KALI GANDAKI RIVER
This river through the Gandaki Gorge is popular with white-water rafters.

POKHARA

PHEWA LAKE
On a windless day, this lake reflects the majestic mountains of the Annapurna Range in perfect detail.

LUMBINI
Thousands of Buddhist pilgrims come here to pay respect to the birthplace of the Buddha.

DEVI'S FALLS
During the monsoon season water roars into this narrow canyon and then disappears into underground caves.

INDIA

SHANTI STUPA
This enormous white stupa was built by Japanese monks as a monument to world peace.

NEPAL

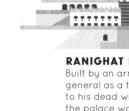

RANIGHAT PALACE
Built by an army general as a tribute to his dead wife, the palace was left abandoned and crumbling by the river until recent restoration.

WELCOME TO THE TOP OF THE WORLD

Most people know about Nepal because of the steady stream of adventurers and mountaineers arriving with a dream to climb the world's highest mountain, Mount Everest, or Sagarmatha as it's known in Nepal. Only a few will make it to the peak, but most will go home with a newfound love of the country that hosts no less than eight of the ten highest mountain peaks on Earth!

While it's famous for its mountains, Nepal has a diverse landscape that stretches down to hot and humid lowland plains. Most Nepalis live in the capital city, Kathmandu, and most of the population are Hindu, which means they believe in reincarnation—where the soul lives on through many lives and in different forms.

From bustling Kathmandu to small southern villages, you'll see stunning temples, busy marketplaces, ancient palaces, and national parks that are home to rhinoceroses, elephants, and Bengal tigers.

TENZING NORGAY
1914–1986
With Sir Edmund Hillary, this mountaineer was the first to reach the summit of Mount Everest.

GAUTAMA BUDDHA
C.563–483 BC
Credited as being the spiritual leader whose teachings were responsible for founding Buddhism.

MONKEY TEMPLE
Climb the 365 steps to Swayambhunath temple and you'll be mobbed by hundreds of monkeys!

HANUMAN DHOKA
The royal palace takes its name from Hanuman, the Hindu monkey god.

PASHUPATINATH TEMPLE
The largest temple complex in Nepal, this is one of the four most sacred Hindu sites in Asia.

ASAN MARKET
You can buy anything from colorful fabrics to interesting spices at this vibrant market.

BOUDHANATH STUPA
This huge stupa, built in the 14th century, is an important pilgrimage site for Buddhists.

GORKHA DURBAR
This 16th-century palace, fort, and temple sits precariously on the edge of a cliff overlooking the Trisuli Valley.

MANAKAMANA TEMPLE & CABLE CAR
The cable car trip up the mountain to this two-tiered Hindu temple is 2 miles long!

LANGTANG NATIONAL PARK
In the high meadows of this national park, you can see red pandas and Himalayan black bears. You might even be lucky enough to see a snow leopard.

NAGARKOT
This small village has the best views of the Himalayas. Eight out of thirteen ranges can be seen from here.

KATHMANDU

LALITPUR

BHARATPUR

BHAKTAPUR
One of the most striking sights in this ancient town is "pottery square," which is covered in clay pots drying in the sun.

MOUNT EVEREST
Mighty Mount Everest, the tallest mountain on Earth, was formed over 60 million years ago when the Indian and Asian tectonic plates crashed together.

CHITWAN NATIONAL PARK
Nepal's oldest national park is home to rhinos, tigers, leopards, monkeys, and sloth bears.

GOLDEN TEMPLE (KWA BAHAL)
This temple gets its name from its intricate gold-covered exterior.

DURBAR SQUARE
There are over 130 courtyards and 55 temples, as well as an ancient palace, in this busy and beautiful square.

PATAN MUSEUM
Housed in a former royal palace, the museum displays sacred and traditional artworks of Nepal.

KEY FACTS
MOTHER AND MOTHERLAND ARE GREATER THAN HEAVEN

CAPITAL	MONEY	NATION CODE
Kathmandu	Nepalese rupee	NP

LARGEST CITIES	NAMED FOR	OFFICIAL LANGUAGE
Kathmandu Pokhara Lalitpur Birgunj Biratnagar Bharatpur	Thought to be named after an ancient dynasty called "Nepa"	Nepali

FLOWER
Rhododendron

BIRD
Danphe

POPULATION
30,900,000

49

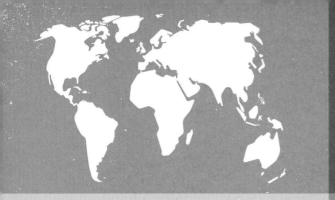

WELCOME TO THE LAND OF MILK AND HONEY

Israel is a young country, but an ancient land—people have been living here for thousands of years. But even more remarkable, Israel is at the center of much of human culture's roots. It's the spiritual home of two of the world's biggest religions, Christianity and Judaism, and is also an important part of Islamic culture. Wherever you travel in Israel, you'll find towns, rivers, mountains, and seas that will be familiar from the Christian Bible, the Jewish Tanakh, and the Islamic Koran.

Alongside the incredible cultural history centered around Israel, there's the amazing desert landscape, the super-salty Dead Sea, and cities rich in diversity—people from all over the world call Israel home. It's also home to some delicious Middle Eastern food—make sure you find a falafel to munch on as you explore the sights of this wonderful country.

MOMENTS TO REMEMBER

1917: Britain decides to create a national home for Jewish people in already-inhabited Palestine.

1939: The British government attempts to limit the number of Jewish people migrating to Palestine to 10,000 per year.

1940s: The persecution of Jewish people by the Nazis in World War II creates a mass migration of Jews to Palestine.

1947: The United Nations steps in and recommends that Palestine be divided into separate Jewish and Arab states.

1948–1949: Israel declares independence. Almost immediately, war breaks out between Palestinians and Israelis.

1949–1960: Close to 1.3 million Jewish refugees settle in Israel.

1967: Israel attacks Egypt over access to the Suez Canal—it becomes known as the Six Day War and leaves Israel with control over more of Palestine.

1982: Israel invades Lebanon in an attempt to expel leaders of the Palestinian Liberation Organization (PLO).

1993: The Israeli Prime Minister and the PLO leader sign an agreement to plan for Palestinian self-government.

2003: The United States, European Union, Russia, and the United Nations all step in to try and resolve Israeli-Palestinian conflict.

2023: Palestinian militants attack Israel, leading to war.

KEY FACTS

NO NATIONAL MOTTO

CAPITAL Jerusalem	**MONEY** New shekel	**NATION CODE** IL
LARGEST CITIES Jerusalem Tel Aviv Haifa Rishon LeZion	**NAMED FOR** An ancient tribe in the region	**OFFICIAL LANGUAGE** Hebrew
POPULATION 9,300,000	**FLOWER** *Anemone coronaria*	**BIRD** Hoopoe

URI GELLER
B.1946
Illusionist and magician Geller is most famous for a trick where he would seemingly bend spoons with his mind.

ADA YONATH
B.1939
Yonath won the Nobel Prize for Chemistry in 2009, becoming the first woman in the Middle East to win a Nobel Prize for science.

ISRAEL

GAL GADOT
B.1985
Gadot's role as Wonder Woman made her an international movie star.

ROSH HANIKRA GROTTOES
The beautiful grottoes in this chalky cliff face are mesmerizing.

HAIFA ✳

THE WESTERN WALL
One of the holiest places for Jews and Christians, the Western Wall is about 2,000 years old.

THE MOUNT OF OLIVES
Once covered in olive groves, this hill remains an important religious site for Christians and Jews alike.

DOME OF THE ROCK
This temple is one of the oldest Islamic monuments still standing —it's about 1,300 years old.

CARMEL MARKET
This buzzing market is a great place for food, jewelry, art . . . almost anything you can think of!

BASILICA OF THE ANNUNCIATION
It's thought that this site is where Mary was told by an angel that she would give birth to the son of God.

KING DAVID'S TOMB
It may not actually be the resting place of King David, but this 1,000-year-old tomb still makes you imagine a boy, a slingshot, and a giant named Goliath!

TEL AVIV ✳

WEST BANK

RISHON LEZION ✳

MEDITERRANEAN SEA

SYRIA

JORDAN

FLOAT IN THE DEAD SEA
It's almost ten times saltier than the ocean, which makes floating in it very easy!

THE POOL OF ARCHES
Row a boat through this 1,000-year-old underground reservoir and admire its incredible arches and pillars.

JERUSALEM ★

GAZA AND WEST BANK
A small strip of land on the coast called Gaza, and parts of the area called the West Bank around Jerusalem, are governed by the Palestinian people.

GAZA

THE GARDEN TOMB
This tomb, cut from rock, is said by some to be the tomb where Jesus Christ was buried.

MINI ISRAEL MUSEUM
If you don't have time to see all of Israel, you can see models of all the most important sites here in miniature scale!

ROCKEFELLER MUSEUM
See a statue made 9,000 years ago at this archeological museum, which has artifacts dating back to prehistoric times.

GETHSEMANE
This is believed to be the garden where Jesus was arrested after being betrayed by Judas.

AVDAT
Explore the remains of this 2,300-year-old Nabatean city destroyed by an earthquake in the 7th century.

MASADA NATIONAL PARK
This national park preserves an iconic Israeli fortress and thousands of years of human history.

THE ISRAEL MUSEUM
This is the country's most important museum and gallery. You'll find ancient objects, art, and lots of fun things to do.

RAMON NATURE RESERVE
Israel's largest national park is famous for the Makhtesh—a crater-like feature formed by erosion. Keep your eyes peeled for ibex and gazelles.

EGYPT

FIND A FALAFEL
Falafel is the street food of choice in Israel, made with chickpeas and served in a fresh pita bread.

UNDERWATER OBSERVATORY PARK
There's more than 800 species of marine life in Israel's largest aquarium.

TIMNA PARK
Zip around this stunning desert park on a go-anywhere mountain bike.

YOTAM OTTOLENGHI
B.1968
Accomplished chef Ottolenghi became internationally famous with his cookbooks featuring Israeli and Middle Eastern cuisine.

DOLPHIN REEF
Dive into the Red Sea and swim with bottle-nosed dolphins and colorful tropical fish.

SIGALIT LANDAU
B.1969
Artist Landau is best known for her *Salt Works* sculptures, where she immersed metal objects in the Dead Sea until they became calcified.

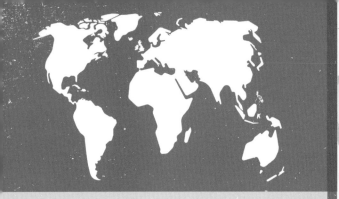

IRAN

MOMENTS TO REMEMBER

3000–2000 BC: Inscriptions uncovered near Jiroft, in Southeastern Iran, are thought to be the world's earliest known writing.

1340–1250 BC: The Elamite civilization builds the Chogha Zanbil ziggurat (stepped tower) to honor the Elamite god, Inshushinak.

522–486 BC: Darius the Great creates the world's first superpower by dividing Persia (Iran) into provinces, creating a system of money, and choosing one common language.

AD 632: The Prophet Muhammad dies and Arab forces attack Persia. By AD 651, the last Persian king is dead.

1051: Turkish Seljuks conquer Persia and create an empire reaching to Syria, Palestine, and Constantinople.

1218: Genghis Khan and his Mongol army invade and conquer most of Persia.

1786: Agha Mohammad Khan moves the capital of Persia to Tehran before he is murdered by his servants.

1797–1834: Persia fights wars with Russia and loses Azerbaijan and Armenia.

1935: Persia asks other countries to refer to it as "Iran."

1962: Iranian leader Mohammad Reza implements the "White Revolution," improving education and women's rights and minimizing the power of the clerics.

1979: The Iranian Revolution results in a theocratic state, ruled by clerics.

1980–1988: The Iran–Iraq War takes place. More than 900,000 people are killed on both sides.

2022: Wide-scale protests are triggered by Mahsa Amini's death in custody for supposedly breaking hijab head-covering rules.

OMAR KHAYYAM
1048–1131
Astronomer, poet, and mathematician, Khayyam developed an accurate solar calendar and helped create the basic principles of algebra.

CYRUS THE GREAT
C.600–530 BC
Responsible for creating a vast empire, Cyrus the Great was known for his political and military intelligence.

TABRIZ

LAKE URMIA
When the algae in this saltwater lake blooms, the water turns red.

DAMAVAND
The highest mountain in Iran is considered a "potentially active volcano."

URAMAN VILLAGE
The mountainous Kurdistan province is known for its stepped houses.

KARAJ

TEHRAN

SULTAN AMIR AHMAD BATHHOUSE, KASHAN
This ancient bathhouse was a place not just for washing but for relaxing with friends.

CHOGHA ZANBIL ZIGGURAT
No one knows what these giant structures were used for. Maybe as shrines dedicated to gods? This one was built in 1250 BC.

ABYANEH
The "Red Village," known for its red mud-brick houses, is thought to be over 1,500 years old.

IRAQ

ISFAHAN

ISFAHAN
Naqsh-e Jahan Square was built by Shah Abbas in 1598, and is lined with impressive buildings.

SHUSHTAR HISTORICAL HYDRAULIC SYSTEM
This centuries-old system of tunnels and canals was built to divert water from the Karun River to mills in Shushtar.

SHIRA

NAQSH-E ROSTAM TOMBS
Four tombs of Achaemenian kings are cut high into the cliff face.

MARGOON WATERFALL
At these falls, the water cascades not from the top, but from dozens of holes in the rock wall.

PERSEPOLIS
These are ruins of the ancient capital of the Achaemenian dynasty that flourished from 559–330 BC.

SHRINE OF IMAM REZA
Over 20 million Muslims make the pilgrimage to this mosque every year. It's just as well it's one of the world's largest!

KARIM KHAN CITADEL
This fortress was once part of the royal court of Karim Khan, founder of the Zand dynasty.

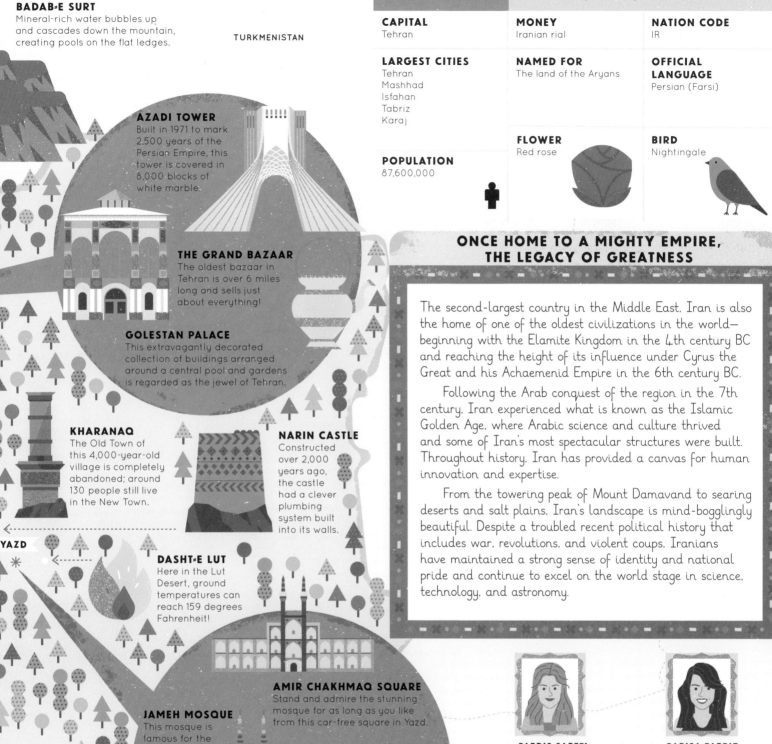

BADAB-E SURT
Mineral-rich water bubbles up and cascades down the mountain, creating pools on the flat ledges.

TURKMENISTAN

AZADI TOWER
Built in 1971 to mark 2,500 years of the Persian Empire, this tower is covered in 8,000 blocks of white marble.

THE GRAND BAZAAR
The oldest bazaar in Tehran is over 6 miles long and sells just about everything!

GOLESTAN PALACE
This extravagantly decorated collection of buildings arranged around a central pool and gardens is regarded as the jewel of Tehran.

KHARANAQ
The Old Town of this 4,000-year-old village is completely abandoned; around 130 people still live in the New Town.

NARIN CASTLE
Constructed over 2,000 years ago, the castle had a clever plumbing system built into its walls.

YAZD

DASHT-E LUT
Here in the Lut Desert, ground temperatures can reach 159 degrees Fahrenheit!

NAMAKDAN SALT CAVE, QESHM ISLAND
The longest salt cave in the world is over 4 miles long and has salty white stalactites and stalagmites!

JAMEH MOSQUE
This mosque is famous for the intricate mosaic tiling on its 15th-century dome and 160-foot-high minarets (towers).

AMIR CHAKHMAQ SQUARE
Stand and admire the stunning mosque for as long as you like from this car-free square in Yazd.

ZOROASTRIAN TOWERS OF SILENCE
Zoroastrians traditionally placed the bodies of the deceased on the top of these towers to be eaten by birds.

PAKISTAN

KEY FACTS

INDEPENDENCE, FREEDOM, (THE) ISLAMIC REPUBLIC

CAPITAL Tehran	**MONEY** Iranian rial	**NATION CODE** IR
LARGEST CITIES Tehran Mashhad Isfahan Tabriz Karaj	**NAMED FOR** The land of the Aryans	**OFFICIAL LANGUAGE** Persian (Farsi)
POPULATION 87,600,000	**FLOWER** Red rose	**BIRD** Nightingale

ONCE HOME TO A MIGHTY EMPIRE, THE LEGACY OF GREATNESS

The second-largest country in the Middle East, Iran is also the home of one of the oldest civilizations in the world—beginning with the Elamite Kingdom in the 4th century BC and reaching the height of its influence under Cyrus the Great and his Achaemenid Empire in the 6th century BC.

Following the Arab conquest of the region in the 7th century, Iran experienced what is known as the Islamic Golden Age, where Arabic science and culture thrived and some of Iran's most spectacular structures were built. Throughout history, Iran has provided a canvas for human innovation and expertise.

From the towering peak of Mount Damavand to searing deserts and salt plains, Iran's landscape is mind-bogglingly beautiful. Despite a troubled recent political history that includes war, revolutions, and violent coups, Iranians have maintained a strong sense of identity and national pride and continue to excel on the world stage in science, technology, and astronomy.

PARDIS SABETI
B.1975
Dr. Sabeti is a geneticist who developed an algorithm that explains how genes affect disease. She's also the lead singer of a rock band!

PARISA TABRIZ
B.1983
Tabriz calls herself the "Security Princess" because she's a computer security whiz. She's also a director of engineering at Google.

PIERRE OMIDYAR
B.1967
Omidyar studied computer science and worked at Apple before creating another company you might have heard of: eBay.

JORDAN RIVER
This is the lowest river in the world, starting on the slopes of Mount Hermon and ending at the Dead Sea.

GADARA (UMM QAIS)
These ancient Greco-Roman ruins were once a popular resort town for wealthy Romans.

DAR AS-SARAYA MUSEUM, IRBID
Jordan's second-largest city is home to this fascinating museum, with artifacts from the Bronze and Iron Ages, and Neolithic statues that are 9,000 years old.

SYRIA

ROMAN THEATER
This 6,000-seat Roman amphitheater dates from the 2nd century, when Amman was called Philadelphia.

JERASH
Here lie the ruins of a once huge and powerful Roman city. You can still see the Forum, surrounded by 160 giant columns.

CAVE OF THE SEVEN SLEEPERS
According to legend, seven Christian boys hid in this cave to escape persecution. They fell asleep and emerged 300 years later!

AJLOUN CASTLE
This 12th-century hilltop castle was built to defend against Crusaders.

IRBID

QUSAYR 'AMRA, ZARQA
Admire beautiful 8th-century wall paintings at this imposing desert castle.

AMMAN CITADEL
High on Amman's tallest hill, the citadel site includes a Bronze Age wall, a Roman temple, and the 8th century Umayyad Palace.

AL-MAGHTAS
This natural spring is thought to be the place where Jesus was baptized.

AMMAN ZARQA

RUSSEIFA

MOUNT NEBO
From the summit, you can see the Dead Sea, Bethlehem, and Jerusalem. Christians believe it was here that Moses first laid eyes on the "Promised Land."

MADABA

MADABA MAP
In the church of Saint George, an incredible mosaic map covers part of the floor. It dates from the 6th century and is the oldest surviving map of the Holy Land.

DEAD SEA PANORAMA
This lookout above the Dead Sea is the best place to get a view of the world's lowest body of water.

MOSES'S SPRING,
Some people believe this natural spring at Wadi Musa is the place where Moses struck water from the rock for his followers.

WADI MUJIB NATURE RESERVE
Hike along the Wadi Mujib River, as it runs through a canyon of towering cliffs, and swim in the pools.

DANA BIOSPHERE RESERVE
Jordan's biggest nature reserve is a haven for wildlife. Look out for ibex, gazelles, sand cats, and wolves.

ISRAEL

AMMAN BEACH
The Dead Sea has such a high concentration of salt that nothing can live in it. The salt makes it easy to float in.

MA'IN SPRINGS
Choose from over 60 hot springs with varying temperatures, or cool down in one of the waterfalls.

KING'S HIGHWAY
This ancient roadway was an important trade route, connecting Africa with Mesopotamia.

SHOBAK CASTLE
The grounds of these 12th-century castle ruins include catacombs and a secret passage leading to a natural spring.

LITTLE PETRA
Rock-carved houses, temples, and dining rooms are densely packed in this ancient Nabatean village.

QUEEN RANIA OF JORDAN B.1970
Born in Kuwait, the wife of King Abdullah II is known for her work in supporting education, health, and disadvantaged communities.

AHMAD ABUGHAUSH B.1996
This tae kwon do athlete won Jordan's first-ever Olympic gold medal in 2016.

RED SEA
Shipwrecks, sharks, coral, and colorful fish make the Red Sea perfect for scuba diving.

AL-KHAZNEH, PETRA
Yes, there really is a temple carved into the mountain! This stunning building is thought to be the tomb of Nabatean King Aretas IV.

WADI RUM
This red sand desert, dotted with gnarly rock formations, has featured in dozens of movies, including *Star Wars*.

MOSES C.14TH CENTURY
Was Moses a real or legendary figure? Biblical scholars say that he was a prophet who could speak with a divine being.

WHERE BIBLE STORIES MEET ANCIENT CIVILIZATIONS

Jordan is part of an area of land located between Asia, Africa, and Europe, and it is an important place to three of the world's largest religions—Christianity, Islam, and Judaism. Jordan has been home to many different civilizations: the Nabateans, the Babylonians, the Greeks and Romans, and even the Ottomans used Jordan as a base for their empires. As a result of all this human activity over the millennia, there are more ancient sites here than in almost any country on Earth.

Jordan's most visited site is the 1,500-year-old city of Petra, also known as the Rose City because of the color of the rock the buildings are carved from. Other major archeological sites include the Roman city of Jerash, the Ayyubid Ajloun Castle, and the Umayyad ruins of Qusayr 'Amra. There are also religious sites, such as Mount Nebo, where Moses is said to have sighted the promised land, and the natural spring where Jesus was reported to be baptized. All this and we haven't even started on Jordan's natural wonders, such as the Dead Sea and the desert, Wadi Rum.

Jordanians are known for being particularly hospitable and will always greet you by saying "ahlan wa sahlan" ("I welcome you") before feeding you copious amounts of food. They are also big sports fans, with soccer and basketball followed by millions.

KEY FACTS — GOD, COUNTRY, KING

CAPITAL
Amman

MONEY
Jordanian dinar

NATION CODE
JO

LARGEST CITIES
Amman
Zarqa
Irbid
Russeifa
Madaba

NAMED FOR
The Jordan River, which is thought to be derived from the Semitic word *Yarad*, meaning "the descender"

OFFICIAL LANGUAGE
Arabic

POPULATION
11,100,000

FLOWER
Black iris

BIRD
Sinai rosefinch

SAUDI ARABIA

MOMENTS TO REMEMBER

10,000–4000 BC: Humans settle in the area known as the Fertile Crescent; they build houses, domesticate animals, and grow crops.

1200 BC: Three distinct kingdoms emerge in Jordan; they are Edom, Moab, and Ammon. They had little contact with one another.

300 BC–AD 400: The Greeks, the Nabateans (nomadic Arabs), and the Romans are all attracted to the region because of its position between Africa and Asia.

600s: The Sunni dynasty of the Umayyads brings Islam to the region, and it becomes the dominant religion.

1100s–1200s: Conflict between Christians and Muslims, known as the Crusades, sweeps across the Middle East, including Jordan.

1516: Ottoman Turks invade and defeat the Mamluks in Jordan, as well as taking the holy city of Jerusalem and Damascus in Syria.

1914–1918: Arab nationalists revolt against Ottoman rule, and by 1918 Arabs control Saudi Arabia, parts of Southern Syria, and Jordan.

1946: Jordan becomes an independent nation under King Abdullah.

1951: King Abdullah I is assassinated by a Palestinian extremist. His son Talal reigns for just one year due to illness. Talal's 17-year-old son, Hussein, becomes king in 1952.

1994: Jordan and Israel sign a peace treaty and agree to work together on security, water, and the economy. The first road between the two countries is built.

2002: Jordan and Israel agree to pipe water from the Red Sea to the Dead Sea, which is shrinking.

JORDAN

DIMA AND LAMA HATTAB
B. 1980
These twin sisters were the first women in the Middle East to take part in the Marathon des Sables—a 156-mile ultramarathon.

KING ABDULLAH I
1882–1951
One of the key players in overthrowing Ottoman rule, he became the first king of independent Jordan.

AMEERA AL-TAWEEL
B.1983
Saudi princess Al-Taweel works to end poverty and empower women in Saudi Arabia and around the world.

MANAL AL-SHARIF
B.1979
When Saudi women were finally granted the right to drive in 2017, it was largely because of the efforts of this woman.

IRAQ

JORDAN

AL ULA
More than 800 mud-brick and stone houses make up this maze-like village. Built over 2,000 years ago, it's now abandoned.

ZAABAL CASTLE
There's more to this centuries-old fort than meets the eye—the courtyard catches rainwater that drains into a well system that waters Sakakah city.

WORLD SIGHTS PARK
No time to fly to France to see the Eiffel Tower? No worries, just see the smaller version here.

OLD AD DIRIYAH
These ruins are what's left of the Saudi dynasty's first capital city, established in 1744.

AL MASMAK FORTRESS
It was from this fort that Abdul Aziz Al Saud made his plan to conquer and unite the provinces that make up the modern Kingdom of Saudi Arabia.

SARAH ATTAR
B.1992
Attar was one of two female athletes allowed to compete in the Olympics for Saudi Arabia for the first time in 2012. She ran the 800 meters.

MADAIN SALEH
Over 130 intricately carved rock-tombs lie in the ruins of this ancient desert city, including the giant Qasr al-Farid.

SAUDI ARABIA

UMLUJ
You might not expect to see a tropical beach with clear blue water so close to the desert, but that's exactly what you'll find at Umluj.

JEBEL FIHRAYN (EDGE OF THE WORLD)
The top of this dizzying escarpment gives amazing views over the desert.

JEDDAH TOWER
If completed, the Jeddah Tower will be the world's tallest building—at 3,280 feet.

AL WAHBAH CRATER
You can climb down inside this enormous volcanic crater.

RIYADH

DESERT DYNASTIES, SOARING SKYSCRAPERS, AND FAST CARS

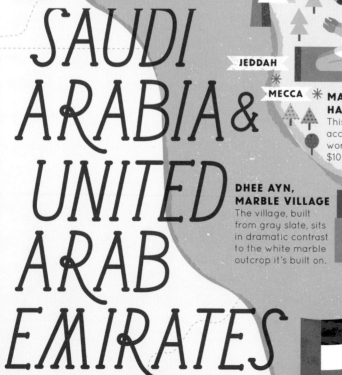

JEDDAH

MECCA

MASJID AL HARAM, MECCA
This mighty mosque can accommodate 4 million worshippers and cost $100 billion to build.

DHEE AYN, MARBLE VILLAGE
The village, built from gray slate, sits in dramatic contrast to the white marble outcrop it's built on.

SAUDI ARABIA & UNITED ARAB EMIRATES

Prior to the 7th century the land that is now Saudi Arabia and the United Arab Emirates (UAE) was largely made up of the crisscrossing paths worn by nomadic tribes. That's hard to imagine now, when you see the sky-piercing megastructures that make up cities such as Dubai and Abu Dhabi. The discovery of huge oil reserves has a lot to do with the kind of luxury on display these days.

Hotels, shopping malls, expensive resorts, and Formula One race tracks are some of the first things people think of when you mention these countries, but below the sparkling surface of the big cities, there are fascinating historical sights, including ancient Nabatean burial tombs carved from rock, abandoned mud-brick towns, grand forts, and exquisite mosques.

You can find spectacular Islamic places of worship in both Saudi Arabia and the UAE. The biggest mosques can fit millions of worshippers. The natural wonders of the region are slowly beginning to attract their fair share of worshippers too. There are beautiful beaches, as well as sheer cliffs rising from the desert floor to be explored.

PALM JUMEIRAH
This palm-leaf shaped artificial island is packed with fancy hotels, luxury stores, and restaurants.

BURJ AL ARAB
The sail-like shape of this luxury hotel, built on its very own island, is one of Dubai's most iconic sights.

BURJ KHALIFA
The world's tallest building, Burj Khalifa is 2,700 feet tall and has 163 floors!

DHAYAH FORT
This is the only remaining hilltop fort in the UAE, with great views over the palm groves below.

AL JAZIRAT AL HAMRA
Locals believe this abandoned 14th-century town is haunted.

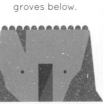

AL BADIYAH MOSQUE
This mud-brick mosque is one of the oldest in the UAE, believed to have been built in 1446.

BLUE SOUQ
Shop for crafts, clothes, or carpets inside Sharjah's biggest and busiest souq.

UNITED ARAB EMIRATES

SHARJAH

DUBAI

FERRARI WORLD
Ride on roller coasters, drive simulators, and sit in some famous Ferraris at this fast-car theme park.

ABU DHABI

EMIRATES PALACE
This super-luxurious hotel boasts 114 domes, more than 100 elevators, and over 1,000 chandeliers.

FUJAIRAH FORT
One of the oldest and biggest forts in the UAE, it was occupied by Wahhabists—a strict sect of Islam.

FORMULA ONE RACETRACK
Abu Dhabi's Grand Prix racetrack is the Yas Marina Circuit. Drivers race for 55 laps around the island of Yas.

SHEIKH ZAYED GRAND MOSQUE
Abu Dhabi's huge grand mosque holds the world's largest hand-woven carpet.

KEY FACTS

SAUDI ARABIA: THERE IS NO GOD OTHER THAN GOD AND MUHAMMAD IS THE MESSENGER OF GOD
UAE: GOD, NATION, PRESIDENT

CAPITALS
Saudi Arabia: Riyadh
UAE: Abu Dhabi

MONEY
Saudi Arabia: Saudi riyal
UAE: UAE dirham

NATION CODES
Saudi Arabia: SA
UAE: AE

LARGEST CITIES
Saudi Arabia:
Riyadh
Jeddah
Mecca
UAE:
Dubai
Abu Dhabi
Sharjah

FLOWERS
Saudi Arabia: Royal jasmine
UAE: *Tribulus omanense*

OFFICIAL LANGUAGE
Arabic

BIRDS
Saudi Arabia:
Falcon
UAE:
Falcon

POPULATION
Saudi Arabia:
35,900,000
UAE: 10,000,000

MOMENTS TO REMEMBER

SAUDI ARABIA

15th century AD: The Bedouin chieftain Mani al Muraidi establishes the town of Diriyah, which is now part of Riyadh.

1744: Muraidi's great-great-great-grandson, Sheikh Muhammad bin Saud, allies with Wahhabists to expand the Al Saud domain.

1818–1824: The first Saudi state is invaded and Diriyah is destroyed by Egyptian and Ottoman forces. The Saud family establishes a second state, with the capital at Riyadh.

1932: The Kingdom of Saudi Arabia is proclaimed and Abd Al-Aziz is the first king.

1938–1945: Oil is discovered in the Dammam Dome and the Saudis agree to allow the US access to oil if the US will protect the Saudi royal family.

2018: Women are issued licences and allowed to drive for the first time in Saudi Arabia.

UNITED ARAB EMIRATES

AD 1760: The Baniyas tribe discovers fresh water on the island of Abu Dhabi and establishes settlements there.

1958–1962: Oil is discovered in Abu Dhabi and production begins; the first export occurs in 1962.

1971: The United Arab Emirates (UAE) is founded, with Sheikh Zayed bin Sultan Al Nahyan as the first leader.

1985: The UAE establishes its national airline, Emirates.

1999: Construction on the world's tallest hotel, Burj Al Arab, is completed.

2009: Dubai becomes the first city in the region to have a mass public transportation system.

2010: Burj Khalifa tower opens in Dubai, the world's tallest building.

AHLAM
B.1969
This popular Emirati singer has made 14 albums and appeared as a judge of *Arab Idol* and *The Voice Ahla Sawt*.

HAMDAN BIN MOHAMMED AL MAKTOUM
B.1982
The Crown Prince of Dubai, Hamdan, is an expert horse rider, winning gold medals in the World Equestrian Games.

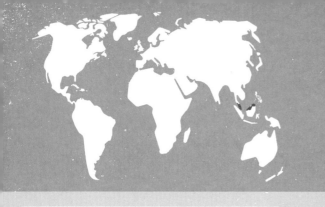

MOMENTS TO REMEMBER

1.8 million BC: A hand tool found in the Lenggong Valley, Perak, dates human habitation back to this time.

10,000–2500 BC: Austronesian peoples begin settling in the region and establish the first trade villages.

AD 200–700: Buddhist-Hindu kingdoms are formed around important trade routes in Kedah and Sarawak.

1400s: The Malay chief Parameswara founds Malacca and converts to Islam. His empire expands and this era becomes known as Malacca's Golden Age.

1511: The Portuguese attack and conquer Malacca in order to secure its important position in the rich spice trade.

1641: Dutch colonists attack Malacca, and after a desperate siege finally overpower the Portuguese.

1786–1826: The British occupy Penang and sign a treaty with the Dutch that divides the Malay area into colonial zones. Singapore, Malacca, and Penang come under British control.

1840s: The discovery of tin at Perak attracts waves of Chinese miners to the area.

1953–1963: The first general elections on the Malay peninsula are easily won by an Indian and Chinese Alliance. Malaya, Singapore, Sabah, and Sarawak form an independent Malaysia.

1990s: Malaysia begins some big building projects, including the Petronas Twin Towers (the tallest buildings in the world at the time).

2004: A devastating tsunami hits Southeast Asia. In Malaysia, the islands of Penang and Langkawi are the worst affected.

2017: As part of the 60th National Day celebrations, the government launches the Negaraku initiative, designed to instill in people a love of their country.

LEE CHONG WEI
B.1982
With 69 badminton titles under his belt, Lee Chong Wei is one of the world's greatest players.

SHEIKH MUSZAPHAR SHUKOR
B.1972
As if being an orthopedic surgeon wasn't enough, Dr. Shukor is also Malaysia's first astronaut. He visited the International Space Station in 2007.

THAILAND

BATU FERRINGHI
At Penang's top beach destination, choose from chilled-out sunbathing or adrenalin-pumping parasailing.

GEORGE TOWN
Penang's capital city has a fascinating mix of cultures, food, and religious buildings.

PENANG HILL
Jump on a funicular up Penang Hill for spectacular views over the island.

LANGKAWI SKY BRIDGE
Stretching 400 feet long and 2,100 feet above sea level, this cable bridge gives pedestrians a bird's eye view of the jungle below.

PERHENTIAN ISLANDS
These remote islands are some of Malaysia's most beautiful, and a top scuba diving top.

CAMERON HIGHLANDS
Colonialists established a hill station here because of the cool weather. Today the lush hillsides are covered in tea plantations.

TAMAN NEGARA
At 130 million years of age, this spectacular rain forest is believed to be the oldest on the planet.

GEORGE TOWN

IPOH

CHILING WATERFALL
After a sweaty hour-long walk through the rain forest, cool down in this pretty waterfall and swimming hole.

PETALING JAYA

KUALA LUMPUR

MALACCA

BATU CAVES
There's a 140-foot-high golden statue of Murugan, the Hindu god of war, at the entrance to these striking caverns.

KAMPUNG KUANTAN
At night, these mangrove swamps sparkle with the lights of thousands of fireflies.

JOHOR BAHRU

MALACCA
It was here that European colonists first made contact with Malaysia. As a result, the city is full of British, Dutch, and Portuguese building

PETRONAS TWIN TOWERS
They're no longer the tallest buildings in the world, but these towers are still a striking addition to the Kuala Lumpur skyline.

BUTTERFLY PARK
Step inside a climate-controlled rain forest housing over 6,000 butterflies.

BUKIT BINTANG
Enormous shopping malls, busy hawker stalls, and late-night clubs make for nonstop action in the city's entertainment district.

MICHELLE YEOH
B.1962
Yeoh is famous for her Hong Kong action movies (she did all her own stunts!) and won an Oscar for *Everything Everywhere All at Once*.

SPECTACULAR FORESTS, FOOD, AND CULTURAL HERITAGE

Divided into two parts by the South China Sea, Malaysia is made up of the Peninsula side, which is the most populated part, and the Borneo side, which is wild and rugged.

For many years, the country lay on an important trade route for European colonial powers wanting to cash in on the profitable spice market. Because of this, Malaysia has a fascinating mix of cultures and religions, particularly on the Peninsula. The most dominant influences over the centuries have been Chinese, Indian, British, Dutch, and Portuguese, and these influences can be seen in the architecture, religious buildings, and the food. Seaside cities like Malacca are the best places to get a feel for the colonial past.

Malaysia's capital city, Kuala Lumpur, is a thriving metropolis, famous for its hawker food markets, enormous shopping malls, and the sky-piercing Petronas Twin Towers.

malaysia

KINABATANGAN RIVER
This river welcomes scores of wildlife to its banks, including the Asian elephant and the Borneo pygmy elephant.

MOUNT KINABALU
Some travelers get up at 2 a.m. to climb to the top of Borneo's tallest mountain (13,400 feet) in time for sunrise.

KOTA KINABALU

SEPILOK REHABILITATION CENTER
This center rescues baby orangutans orphaned by logging in Sabah's forests. These great apes are now endangered.

SARAWAK CULTURAL VILLAGE
See inside a traditional longhouse and watch dancing and music performances from five of the biggest tribes in Borneo.

NIAH CAVES
Inside these vast caves there's evidence of human habitation from 40,000 years ago.

BAKO NATIONAL PARK
This park is home to around 300 proboscis monkeys.

SIPADAN
The island of Sipadan is considered to be one of the best scuba diving places on Earth.

...JARA TURTLE ...ROJECT, PULAU ...OMAN
...ea turtles have ...een around for 130 ...illion years, but the ...st two centuries ...ave seen their ...umbers plummet; ...is project aims to ...alt this decline.

KUCHING CAT MUSEUM
Exhibits in the world's first cat museum range from a mummified Egyptian cat to delicate porcelain statues.

INDONESIA

GUNUNG GADING NATIONAL PARK
The rafflesia, the biggest flower in the world, blooms in this park. Don't get too close though—it's also one of the smelliest flowers in the world!

WAN AZIZAH WAN ISMAIL
B.1952
In 2018, this politician became the first Malaysian woman to become deputy prime minister.

CHEONG CHOON NG
B.1969
Cheong Choon Ng invented the loom band—remember that craze? His invention quickly made him a millionaire.

KEY FACTS	UNITY IS STRENGTH	
CAPITAL Kuala Lumpur	**MONEY** Malaysian ringgit	**NATION CODE** MY
LARGEST CITIES Kuala Lumpur George Town Ipoh Johor Bahru Petaling Jaya	**NAMED FOR** From the Malay word *Melayu*—meaning "land of mountains"	**OFFICIAL LANGUAGE** Malay
POPULATION 34,200,000	**FLOWER** *Hibiscus rosa sinensis*	**BIRD** Rhinoceros hornbill

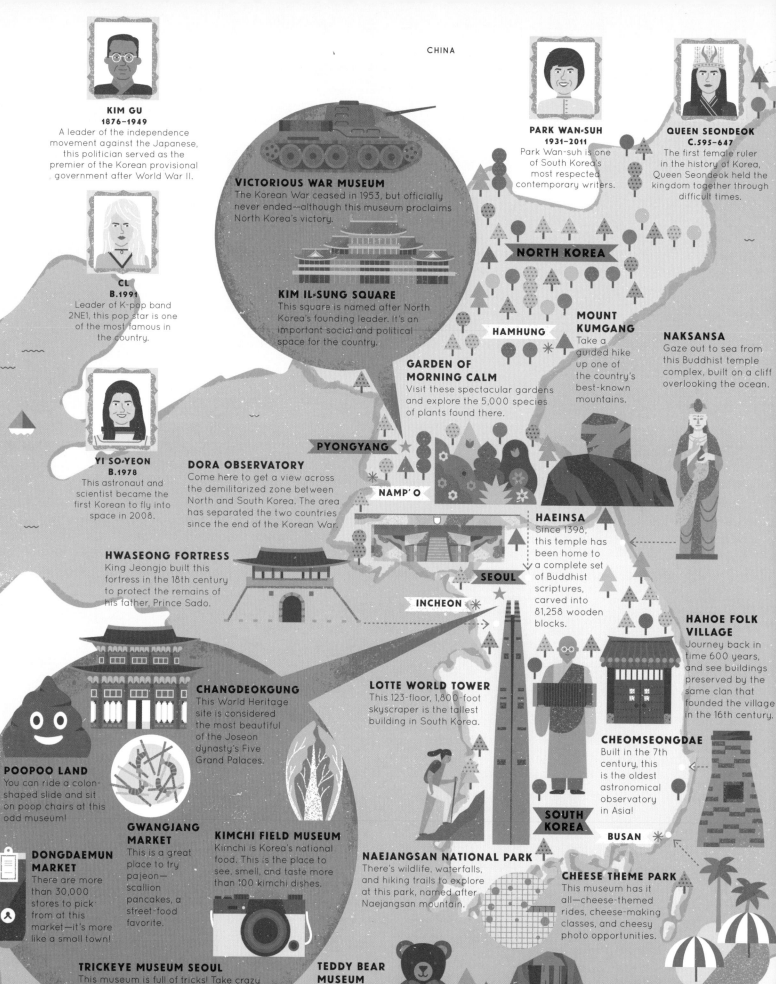

KIM GU
1876–1949
A leader of the independence movement against the Japanese, this politician served as the premier of the Korean provisional government after World War II.

CL
B.1991
Leader of K-pop band 2NE1, this pop star is one of the most famous in the country.

YI SO-YEON
B.1978
This astronaut and scientist became the first Korean to fly into space in 2008.

VICTORIOUS WAR MUSEUM
The Korean War ceased in 1953, but officially never ended—although this museum proclaims North Korea's victory.

KIM IL-SUNG SQUARE
This square is named after North Korea's founding leader. It's an important social and political space for the country.

NORTH KOREA

HAMHUNG

PARK WAN-SUH
1931–2011
Park Wan-suh is one of South Korea's most respected contemporary writers.

QUEEN SEONDEOK
C.595–647
The first female ruler in the history of Korea, Queen Seondeok held the kingdom together through difficult times.

MOUNT KUMGANG
Take a guided hike up one of the country's best-known mountains.

NAKSANSA
Gaze out to sea from this Buddhist temple complex, built on a cliff overlooking the ocean.

GARDEN OF MORNING CALM
Visit these spectacular gardens and explore the 5,000 species of plants found there.

PYONGYANG

DORA OBSERVATORY
Come here to get a view across the demilitarized zone between North and South Korea. The area has separated the two countries since the end of the Korean War.

NAMP'O

HAEINSA
Since 1398, this temple has been home to a complete set of Buddhist scriptures, carved into 81,258 wooden blocks.

HWASEONG FORTRESS
King Jeongjo built this fortress in the 18th century to protect the remains of his father, Prince Sado.

SEOUL

INCHEON

HAHOE FOLK VILLAGE
Journey back in time 600 years, and see buildings preserved by the same clan that founded the village in the 16th century.

CHANGDEOKGUNG
This World Heritage site is considered the most beautiful of the Joseon dynasty's Five Grand Palaces.

LOTTE WORLD TOWER
This 123-floor, 1,800-foot skyscraper is the tallest building in South Korea.

CHEOMSEONGDAE
Built in the 7th century, this is the oldest astronomical observatory in Asia!

SOUTH KOREA

POOPOO LAND
You can ride a colon-shaped slide and sit on poop chairs at this odd museum!

DONGDAEMUN MARKET
There are more than 30,000 stores to pick from at this market—it's more like a small town!

GWANGJANG MARKET
This is a great place to try pajeon—scallion pancakes, a street-food favorite.

KIMCHI FIELD MUSEUM
Kimchi is Korea's national food. This is the place to see, smell, and taste more than 100 kimchi dishes.

NAEJANGSAN NATIONAL PARK
There's wildlife, waterfalls, and hiking trails to explore at this park, named after Naejangsan mountain.

BUSAN

CHEESE THEME PARK
This museum has it all—cheese-themed rides, cheese-making classes, and cheesy photo opportunities.

TRICKEYE MUSEUM SEOUL
This museum is full of tricks! Take crazy photos of yourself that defy logic.

TEDDY BEAR MUSEUM
Play with the exhibits at this museum!

CHEONJEYEON WATERFALLS
Take a trip to Jeju Island and see this beautiful three-tiered waterfall.

THE LAND OF MORNING CALM

Korea is in fact two countries—North Korea and South Korea—the result of a division made after World War II. Having regained its land from the Japanese, and after many thousands of years of shared history, Korea and its people were separated. This division turned into the Korean War, which has left the two countries with a very tense relationship.

Since the fighting ended, South Korea has become one of the most successful economic nations on Earth, with a huge impact on modern life in the shape of cars and electronics. It's also introduced the world to K-pop—Korean pop music that's famous for its impressive dancing and catchy tunes. The cities are big and busy, and on every street, you'll find food that will blow your mind with its spicy flavors.

The people of North Korea have endured a very different life. It is a very closed country and is not easy to visit. North Korea is known for its totalitarian rule, and since the end of World War II, it has been controlled by one family. North Korea and South Korea are separated by a strip of land called the demilitarized zone.

MOMENTS TO REMEMBER

2333 BC: The god-king Dangun is said to have established the Gojoseon kingdom.

300 BC: The Jin state is established on the Southern Korean peninsula.

86 BC: The Dongbuyeo kingdom is established by a prince named Hae Buru.

AD 918: The Goryeo dynasty is founded by Wang Geon and rules Korea until 1392.

1392: General Yi Seong-gye establishes the Joseon dynasty, which survives until the 20th century.

1910: Japan takes over Korea and establishes it as a colony.

1945: After Japan's defeat in World War II, Korea is divided into two countries, North Korea and South Korea. North Korea is under Soviet occupation and South Korea under American occupation.

1948: Kim Il-Sung becomes premier of the Democratic People's Republic of Korea (North Korea).

1950: War begins between North Korea (with Russian and Chinese support) and South Korea (with support from the USA and its allies).

1953: Fighting stops between the two countries, though the war never officially ends.

1988: South Korea hosts the Olympic Games in Seoul.

1994: Kim Jong II becomes leader of North Korea after the death of his father Kim Il-Sung.

2000s: A phenomenon known as the "Korean Wave" sees Korean music, art, cinema, and fashion spread around the world.

2011: Kim Jong II dies, and his son Kim Jong-Un becomes the Supreme Leader of North Korea.

KEY FACTS

NORTH KOREA: POWERFUL AND PROSPEROUS NATION
SOUTH KOREA: TO BROADLY BENEFIT HUMANITY/DEVOTION TO HUMAN WELFARE

CAPITALS North Korea: Pyongyang South Korea: Seoul	**MONEY** North Korean won South Korean won	**NATION CODES** North Korea: KP South Korea: KR
LARGEST CITIES North Korea: Pyongyang Hamhung Namp'o South Korea: Seoul Busan Incheon	**OFFICIAL LANGUAGE** Korean **FLOWERS** North Korea: *Magnolia sieboldii* South Korea: Korean rose	**BIRDS** North Korea: Goshawk South Korea: Oriental magpie
POPULATION North Korea: 26,200,000 South Korea: 52,000,000		

JAPAN

KOREA

HAEUNDAE BEACH

Haeundae is one of South Korea's most popular beaches. After a swim, you can join the Sand Festival and build a giant castle!

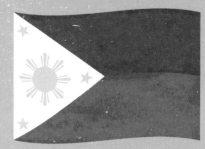

PHILIPPINES

CRISTETA COMERFORD B.1962
Comerford is the first woman and the first person of Asian descent to hold the post of official White House executive chef in the USA.

HANGING COFFINS, SAGADA
Local tradition states that the higher a coffin is hung on the mountainside, the more loved and respected the deceased person was.

VIGAN
Here, beautifully preserved Spanish buildings from the 18th century bring colonial history alive.

IFUGAO RICE TERRACES
If all Ifugao's rice terraces were stretched out in a straight line, they would wrap halfway around Earth.

TIMBAC MUMMIES
Hidden away in caves, these mummies were entombed in their wooden caskets over 500 years ago.

CALOOCAN
QUEZON CITY
MANILA

BINONDO
The world's oldest Chinatown (outside of China) is in Manila.

TAAL VOLCANO
Small but dangerous, this volcano is still very much an active threat.

INTRAMUROS
The Spanish began building the walled city of Intramuros in 1521 as their political and military base in Asia.

FORT SANTIAGO
This 16th-century Spanish fort was an important defensive fort for the spice trade to Europe and the Americas.

SHIPWRECKS, CORON
Just off the island of Coron, divers can explore the sunken wrecks of Japanese warships from World War II.

THE BIG LAGOON, EL NIDO
The turquoise waters of this stunning lagoon are surrounded by limestone cliffs, making it feel like a secret hideaway.

BARRACUDA LAKE
As you dive into the depths of this lake, the water warms up, before cooling again near the bottom! The change is due to a mix of salt and fresh water.

BORACAY
The tropical beaches of this resort island are so popular they closed for six months in 2018 to let nature rehabilitate.

VOLCANOES, SPANISH COLONISTS, AND PARADISE BEACHES

There are 7,641 islands in the archipelago known as the Philippines. Luzon is the most populated island, and is where you'll find the capital city, Manila. With this many islands, it's easy to see why the country is known for its amazing scuba-diving and snorkeling sites.

It's thought that the Philippines has been inhabited for close to 40,000 years, but it wasn't until its strategic position on trade routes between China, India, Indonesia, and Japan grew that it began to attract significant foreign interest. It was colonized by Spain in 1521 when the explorer Ferdinand Magellan arrived on the island of Cebu, and plenty of evidence of Spanish colonialism survives throughout the islands. One of the most striking sites is the walled city in Manila with its 16th-century defensive fort.

The Philippines is one of the countries that sits dangerously close to what's known as the Pacific Ring of Fire, a horseshoe-shaped area in the Pacific Ocean where lots of earthquakes and volcanoes occur. Smoking volcanoes are just one of the country's natural wonders. You can also see spectacular rice terraces and beaches surrounded by limestone karsts that create secret lagoons to explore.

PUERTO PRINCESA SUBTERRANEAN RIVER
Winding through 5 miles of limestone caves from the forest to the sea, this river can be explored by kayak.

TUBBATAHA REEF
This coral reef is considered one of the best diving spots in the Philippines. You might even see a sea turtle.

JOSÉ RIZAL
1861–1896
The country's nationalist hero, Rizal argued for a peaceful end to Spanish colonial rule. He was also a doctor, author, and poet!

REINABELLE REYES
B.1984
Reyes is an astrophysicist and data scientist who wrote a blog featuring young Filipino scientists.

ZAMBOANGA

FOR GOD, PEOPLE, NATURE, AND COUNTRY

CAPITAL
Manila

MONEY
Philippine peso

NATION CODE
PH

LARGEST CITIES
Quezon City
Manila
Caloocan
Davao City
Cebu
Zamboanga

NAMED FOR
In honor of King Philip II
of Spain

OFFICIAL LANGUAGES
Filipino and English

POPULATION
116,400,000

FLOWER
Jasminum sambac

BIRD
Philippine eagle

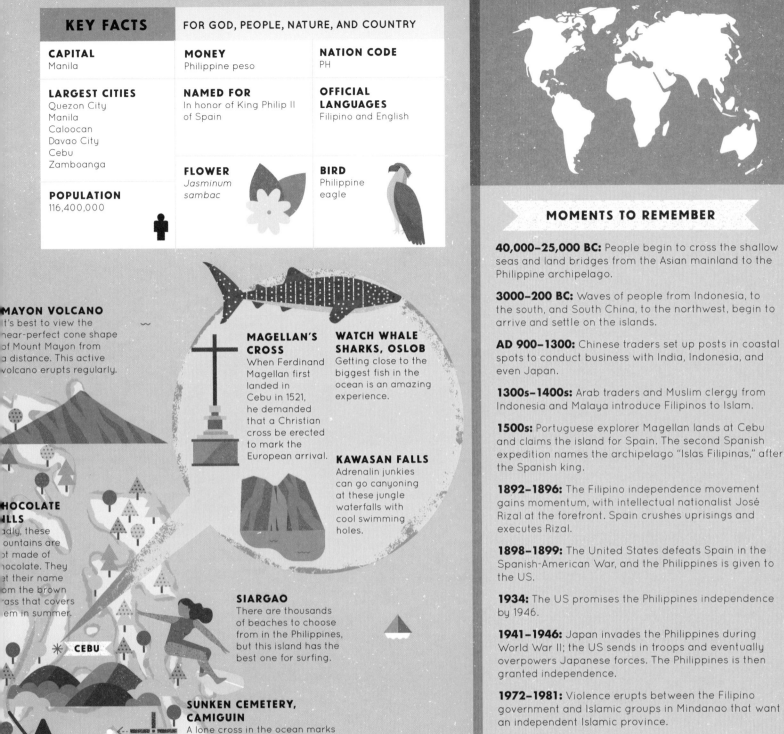

MOMENTS TO REMEMBER

40,000–25,000 BC: People begin to cross the shallow seas and land bridges from the Asian mainland to the Philippine archipelago.

3000–200 BC: Waves of people from Indonesia, to the south, and South China, to the northwest, begin to arrive and settle on the islands.

AD 900–1300: Chinese traders set up posts in coastal spots to conduct business with India, Indonesia, and even Japan.

1300s–1400s: Arab traders and Muslim clergy from Indonesia and Malaya introduce Filipinos to Islam.

1500s: Portuguese explorer Magellan lands at Cebu and claims the island for Spain. The second Spanish expedition names the archipelago "Islas Filipinas," after the Spanish king.

1892–1896: The Filipino independence movement gains momentum, with intellectual nationalist José Rizal at the forefront. Spain crushes uprisings and executes Rizal.

1898–1899: The United States defeats Spain in the Spanish-American War, and the Philippines is given to the US.

1934: The US promises the Philippines independence by 1946.

1941–1946: Japan invades the Philippines during World War II; the US sends in troops and eventually overpowers Japanese forces. The Philippines is then granted independence.

1972–1981: Violence erupts between the Filipino government and Islamic groups in Mindanao that want an independent Islamic province.

2013: The country suffers two natural disasters—an earthquake and then a typhoon. Around 6,500 people are killed.

MAYON VOLCANO
It's best to view the near-perfect cone shape of Mount Mayon from a distance. This active volcano erupts regularly.

MAGELLAN'S CROSS
When Ferdinand Magellan first landed in Cebu in 1521, he demanded that a Christian cross be erected to mark the European arrival.

WATCH WHALE SHARKS, OSLOB
Getting close to the biggest fish in the ocean is an amazing experience.

KAWASAN FALLS
Adrenalin junkies can go canyoning at these jungle waterfalls with cool swimming holes.

CHOCOLATE HILLS
Sadly, these mountains are not made of chocolate. They get their name from the brown grass that covers them in summer.

SIARGAO
There are thousands of beaches to choose from in the Philippines, but this island has the best one for surfing.

CEBU

SUNKEN CEMETERY, CAMIGUIN
A lone cross in the ocean marks the spot where a cemetery, and much of the surrounding city, sunk into the sea after a volcanic explosion in the 1870s.

SIQUIJOR
Filipinos believe there are magic powers at play on this island. It's popular with witch doctors and shamans.

DAVAO CITY

HINATUAN ENCHANTED RIVER
Like magic, the blue water of the Hinatuan River pops up from underground just before it flows out to sea.

ASIK-ASIK FALLS
Water seems to spout straight out of the mountain here before cascading over foliage to the rocks below.

MANNY PACQUIAO
B.1978
A 12-time world champion boxer, Pacquiao is considered by many to be one of the greatest of all time.

ROBERTO DEL ROSARIO
1919–2003
Rosario invented a machine called the Singalong in 1975, which makes him responsible for karaoke.

Cambodia

BANTEAY CHHMAR
Recent conservation efforts are helping to restore this Khmer temple complex, left crumbling for 800 years.

SEREI SAOPHOAN

TONLÉ SAP LAKE
There are over 170 floating villages on this huge freshwater lake.

PREAH VIHEAR TEMPLE
This 11th-century clifftop temple was claimed by Thailand and Cambodia. An international court decided it belonged to Cambodia.

TA PROHM TEMPLE
This 12th-century temple is overgrown with strangler figs. It's impossible to see where the temple ends and the forest starts.

ANGKOR THOM
Not a temple but an entire ancient city, surrounded by 26-foot-high walls with five grand gates.

BAYON TEMPLE
Enormous stone faces gaze at visitors to this Buddhist, then Hindu, temple.

SIEM REAP

BATTAMBANG

BAT CAVES, BATTAMBANG PROVINCE
Thousands of bats spend their days tucked up in these caves, emerging in droves at sunset.

BAMBOO TRAIN LINE, BATTAMBANG
Ride along a rickety track on the "bamboo train"—carts made from old truck parts and a bamboo platform.

SAMBOR PREI KUK
This crumbling temple site is slowly being swallowed up by jungle vines.

KEY FACTS — NATION, RELIGION, KING

CAPITAL	MONEY	NATION CODE
Phnom Penh	Riel	KH

LARGEST CITIES	NAMED FOR	OFFICIAL LANGUAGE
Phnom Penh, Ta Khmau, Battambang, Serei Saophoan, Siem Reap	Kambujadeśa, a Northern Indian tribe that helped form the Khmer Empire	Khmer

POPULATION	FLOWER	BIRD
16,900,000	Rumduol	Giant ibis

KIRIROM NATIONAL PARK
Cambodia's first national park is popular for its pine forests and waterfalls.

CARDAMOM MOUNTAINS
This tropical rain forest is home to Siamese crocodiles, elephants, tigers, and more.

PHNOM TAMAO WILDLIFE RESCUE CENTER
Here you can meet animals rescued from illegal traders and poachers.

PHNOM PENH

TA KHMAU

NORODOM BUPPHA DEVI
1943–2019
Devi was a princess, government minister, prima ballerina, and director of the Royal Ballet of Cambodia.

KOH RONG SAMLOEM
Swaying palm trees, turquoise waters, white sands—welcome to Cambodia's island paradise.

BOKOR HILL STATION
This abandoned ruin was once a summer retreat for French soldiers.

PHNOM CHHNGOK CAVE TEMPLE
This ancient cave temple is the only one of its kind in Cambodia it houses a temple dedicated to the Hindu god Shiva.

SIHANOUKVILLE
The country's most popular seaside resort offers all kinds of water sports, from paddle boarding to kayaking.

CRAB MARKET, KEP
Watch fishermen haul in giant crabs, squid, and piles of fish at this seaside town.

LAOS

KONGNGY HAV
B.1987
Social entrepreneur Kongngy created an eco-friendly and sustainable building brick so that houses could become more affordable in Cambodia.

KING JAYAVARMAN VII
C.1122–1218
King Jayavarman VII was responsible for building the Bayon temple as well as hospitals and rest houses.

VEUN SAI-SIEM PANG CONSERVATION AREA
This pristine forest is home to gibbons, rare giant ibises, and clouded leopards.

LAKE YEAK LAOM
This volcanic crater, surrounded by lush rain forest, forms an almost perfect circle.

TUOL SLENG GENOCIDE MUSEUM
The Khmer Rouge's brutal genocide is remembered in this museum that was once used as a prison and torture chambers.

THE ROYAL PALACE AND SILVER PAGODA
The palace has been the home of Cambodia's king since 1866; the Silver Pagoda contains national treasures.

ELEPHANT VALLEY PROJECT, MONDULKIRI
A small herd of elephants roam around freely at this 1,500-hectare sanctuary.

CAMBODIAN LIVING ARTS THEATER SHOW
Traditional theater and dance were virtually destroyed by the Khmer Rouge, but this organization helped to bring them back to life.

VIETNAM

FROM MIGHTY ANCIENT KINGDOM TO MODERN-DAY SURVIVOR

Cambodia has white-sand beaches with crystal-clear waters, picturesque waterfalls, volcanic crater lakes, floating villages, temple ruins disguised by jungle vines, and pristine tropical rain forests that hide wondrous wildlife such as ocelots, sun bears, elephants, and gibbons.

It's hard to believe that a country that was once home to the mighty Khmer Empire, responsible for constructing the largest religious monument in the world—the Temples of Angkor—is the same place that experienced a devastating genocide at the hands of the Khmer Rouge. Cambodia's history and hardships are impossible to ignore, but it's a country that has emerged as a proud nation of people who look to the future with optimism.

Cambodians are determined that they won't be defined by their dark past but instead by their rich ancient heritage, their pride in Khmer culture, and their passion for the future.

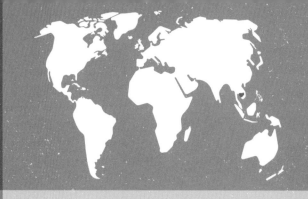

MOMENTS TO REMEMBER

AD 802–1431: The powerful and expansive Khmer Empire rules over most of today's Cambodia, Thailand, Laos, and Southern Vietnam.

1100s: The temple complex Angkor Wat is built—construction takes over 30 years.

1594: Thai forces capture the Cambodian capital of Lovek.

1658–1690: Vietnam invades Cambodia.

1820–1851: The Khmer people of Cambodia revolt against Vietnamese rule and eventually succeed in overthrowing the occupying forces.

1863: Cambodia becomes a protectorate of France.

1941–1946: Cambodia is occupied by Japan during World War II; after the war, France steps back in.

1953: Cambodia wins independence from France and becomes the Kingdom of Cambodia.

1969: The United States begins bombing North Vietnamese forces who have set up bases in Cambodia.

1975: The brutal dictator Pol Pot and his followers, known as the Khmer Rouge, seize power and begin executing hundreds of thousands of educated middle-class Cambodians.

1979–1989: Vietnamese forces invade and rename the country the People's Republic of Kampuchea; guerrilla warfare breaks out before Vietnam withdraws.

1998: Pol Pot dies, and the Khmer Rouge regime finally ends.

2003: Leaders of the Khmer Rouge are put on trial for their part in the violent acts carried out on the Cambodian people.

2012: Former King of Cambodia Norodom Sihanouk dies at age 89.

VANNARY SAN
B.1979
Vannary is the founder of a handicraft business established to revive the traditional Cambodian silk industry and support rural communities.

EAR UY
B.1983
Co-founder and CEO of Cambodia's first online gaming development studio, he helped create the popular "Asva the Monkey" game app.

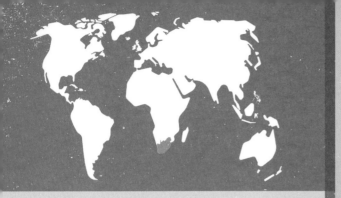

South Africa is the place where all your wild animal dreams come true. You can get up close to lions, elephants, hippos, rhinos, giraffes, zebras, leopards, buffalo, and many other spectacular creatures. If one thing can distract you from the wildife, it might be the country's vast and dramatic landscapes, which include majestic mountains, deserts, deep canyons, and stunning beaches.

Humans have lived in South Africa for thousands of years and left behind fossilized remains, tools, and rock art, much of which can still be seen today. Indigenous African tribes lived a hunter-gatherer and farming existence before Dutch and English colonists arrived. The history of this beautiful country has by no means always been peaceful and wars have been fought over land, and the gold and precious stones the land contains. Life today is more harmonious, and South Africa's largest cities are a fascinating blend of its past, with modern Western fashions sitting alongside local art, music, and traditions.

MOMENTS TO REMEMBER

200 BC–AD 400: Migrants from parts of Northern Africa move south and join with local San and Khoikhoi people.

1480–90: Portuguese navigators and explorers sail around the tip of South Africa and become the first Europeans to set foot in the country.

1652: The Dutch East India Company establishes the Dutch Cape Colony, which will eventually become Cape Town.

1795–1814: British and Dutch forces fight over control of the Cape Colony, with the British Empire overpowering the Dutch in 1814.

1835–1843: The Boers (descendants of the Dutch colonizers and French and German settlers) break from British rule and establish republics in the north and east.

1867–1902: The discovery of diamonds and gold in the Boer Transvaal Republic ignites a series of wars that the Boers lose to the British.

1910: The British form the Union of South Africa from the Cape Colony, Natal Colony, Transvaal Colony, and Orange River Colony.

1913: The Natives Land Act is introduced and results in land segregation along racial lines.

1931: South Africa becomes independent from the UK.

1948: The government introduces the apartheid policy, which separates people and land on the basis of race.

1963: Nelson Mandela, leader of the African National Congress, is jailed for fighting against apartheid. He is imprisoned until 1990.

1994: Apartheid ends and Black people vote in a national election for the first time. Nelson Mandela is voted in as president.

2006: South Africa becomes the first African country to allow same-sex marriage.

2010: South Africa hosts the soccer World Cup.

TABLE MOUNTAIN
Catch a cable car to the top of this flat-topped mountain for breathtaking views.

ATLANTIC OCEAN

ROBBEN ISLAND
Imagine being imprisoned because you wanted equality for all South Africans. That's what happened to Nelson Mandela on Robben Island.

BOULDERS BEACH
This sheltered beach, lined by boulders, attracts thousands of African penguins.

KIRSTENBOSCH NATIONAL BOTANICAL GARDEN
Medicinal plants, indigenous species, and endangered flora are some of the themed gardens found here.

SOUTH AFRICA

NELSON MANDELA
1918–2013
Mandela was devoted to ending racial segregation in South Africa. The country's first Black president, he was awarded the Nobel Peace Prize in 1993.

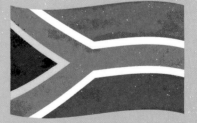

ELON MUSK
B.1971
Tech entrepreneur Musk helped to develop affordable electric cars and has plans to build a colony on Mars.

THATO KGATLHANYE
B.1993
Kgatlhanye invented a solar backpack, made from recycled plastic bags, which stores power so kids can use it for lighting at night.

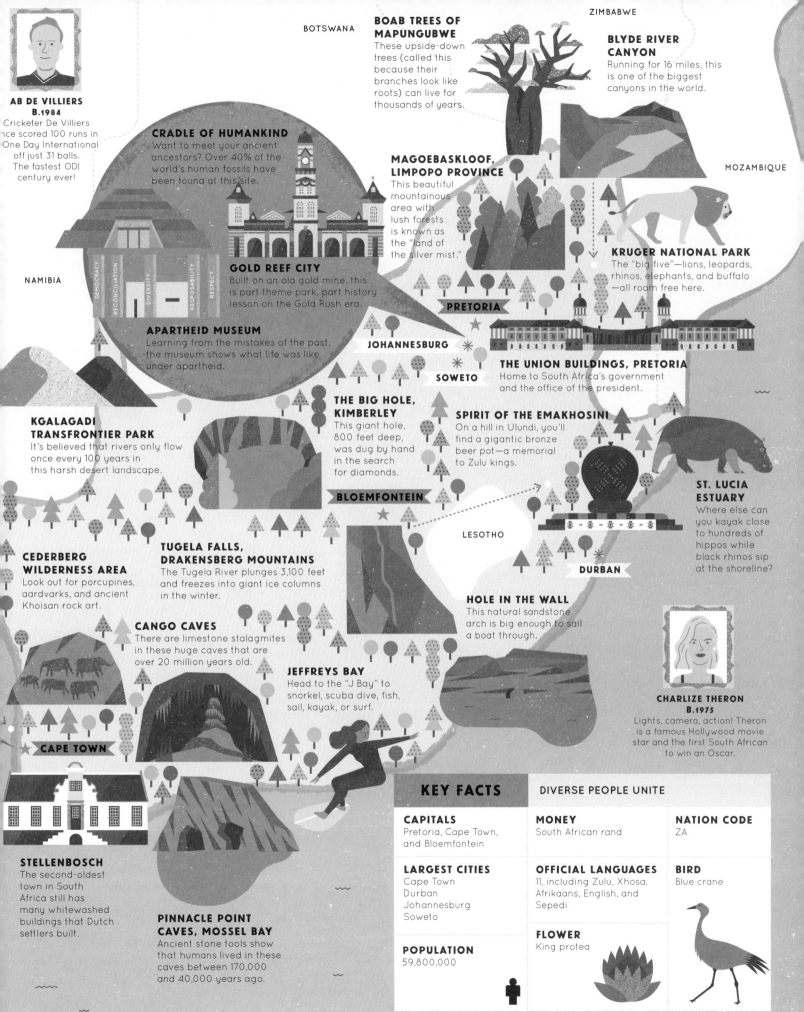

AB DE VILLIERS
B.1984
Cricketer De Villiers [on]ce scored 100 runs in [One] Day International off just 31 balls. The fastest ODI century ever!

ZIMBABWE

BOTSWANA

BOAB TREES OF MAPUNGUBWE
These upside-down trees (called this because their branches look like roots) can live for thousands of years.

BLYDE RIVER CANYON
Running for 16 miles, this is one of the biggest canyons in the world.

MOZAMBIQUE

CRADLE OF HUMANKIND
Want to meet your ancient ancestors? Over 40% of the world's human fossils have been found at this site.

MAGOEBASKLOOF, LIMPOPO PROVINCE
This beautiful mountainous area with lush forests is known as the "land of the silver mist."

KRUGER NATIONAL PARK
The "big five"—lions, leopards, rhinos, elephants, and buffalo —all roam free here.

NAMIBIA

DEMOCRACY RECONCILIATION DIVERSITY RESPOSABILITY RESPECT

GOLD REEF CITY
Built on an old gold mine, this is part theme park, part history lesson on the Gold Rush era.

PRETORIA

APARTHEID MUSEUM
Learning from the mistakes of the past, the museum shows what life was like under apartheid.

JOHANNESBURG

THE UNION BUILDINGS, PRETORIA
Home to South Africa's government and the office of the president.

SOWETO

KGALAGADI TRANSFRONTIER PARK
It's believed that rivers only flow once every 100 years in this harsh desert landscape.

THE BIG HOLE, KIMBERLEY
This giant hole, 800 feet deep, was dug by hand in the search for diamonds.

SPIRIT OF THE EMAKHOSINI
On a hill in Ulundi, you'll find a gigantic bronze beer pot—a memorial to Zulu kings.

BLOEMFONTEIN

ST. LUCIA ESTUARY
Where else can you kayak close to hundreds of hippos while black rhinos sip at the shoreline?

CEDERBERG WILDERNESS AREA
Look out for porcupines, aardvarks, and ancient Khoisan rock art.

TUGELA FALLS, DRAKENSBERG MOUNTAINS
The Tugela River plunges 3,100 feet and freezes into giant ice columns in the winter.

LESOTHO

DURBAN

HOLE IN THE WALL
This natural sandstone arch is big enough to sail a boat through.

CANGO CAVES
There are limestone stalagmites in these huge caves that are over 20 million years old.

JEFFREYS BAY
Head to the "J Bay" to snorkel, scuba dive, fish, sail, kayak, or surf.

CHARLIZE THERON
B.1975
Lights, camera, action! Theron is a famous Hollywood movie star and the first South African to win an Oscar.

CAPE TOWN

STELLENBOSCH
The second-oldest town in South Africa still has many whitewashed buildings that Dutch settlers built.

PINNACLE POINT CAVES, MOSSEL BAY
Ancient stone tools show that humans lived in these caves between 170,000 and 40,000 years ago.

KEY FACTS
DIVERSE PEOPLE UNITE

CAPITALS	MONEY	NATION CODE
Pretoria, Cape Town, and Bloemfontein	South African rand	ZA
LARGEST CITIES Cape Town Durban Johannesburg Soweto	**OFFICIAL LANGUAGES** 11, including Zulu, Xhosa, Afrikaans, English, and Sepedi	**BIRD** Blue crane
POPULATION 59,800,000	**FLOWER** King protea	

TUTANKHAMUN
C.1341–1325 BC
Known as the "Boy King" or King Tut, Tutankhamun became a pharaoh at just nine years of age and ruled for ten years before he died.

CATACOMBS OF KOM EL-SHOQAFA
This necropolis (City of the Dead) was dug deep underground to house over 300 corpses.

POMPEY'S PILLAR
This 100-foot-high column rises out of the ruins of the Temple of Serapeum.

CITADEL OF QAITBAY
This 600-year-old fortress was built to protect the city of Alexandria from invading forces.

THE CAIRO CITADEL
Built in the 12th century, this citadel was home to Egypt's rulers for over 700 years.

EGYPTIAN MUSEUM
Egyptians buried their royalty with gold, jewelry, and other precious items. Many of these are found here, including Tutankhamun's burial mask.

GREAT PYRAMIDS OF GIZA
The ancient Egyptians entombed their most important people inside these mammoth stone structures.

SAQQARA
The Step Pyramid is the oldest major stone structure in Egypt.

KHAN EL-KHALILI
Shop for souvenirs and admire the beautiful Islamic architecture at this 15th-century market.

ALEXANDRIA

MANSOURA

NILE RIVER DELTA
This is where the Nile River empties into the Mediterranean Sea.

GREAT SPHINX OF GIZA
The sphinx statue is more than 240 feet long and has the body of a lion and the head of a human.

CAIRO

GIZA

SUEZ CANAL
Every day, around 50 ships pass through the Suez Canal, which connects the Red Sea to the Mediterranean.

ST. CATHERINE'S MONASTERY
Near here, Moses is believed to have made his proclamation about the Ten Commandments.

MOUNT SINAI
The Bible says that God spoke to Moses from the top of Mount Sinai.

WADI AL-HITAN (WHALE VALLEY)
The fossilized remains of a long-extinct species of whale litter the landscape here.

SIWA OASIS
Siwa has mud-brick homes, palm trees, and clearwater springs.

WHITE DESERT
It might look like it's covered in snow, but it's actually chalk dust!

HURGHADA
Relax in Egypt's fanciest beach resort town!

THE TEMPLES OF ABYDOS
This site was a place of worship for Osiris, the Egyptian god of the dead.

SS THISTLEGORM DIVE SITE
This British Army freighter sank in the Red Sea in World War II. Today you can scuba dive through the ghostly wreck.

ANWAR SADAT
1918–1981
The former president of Egypt worked toward peace with Israel. He also wanted to help Egyptian people live free of poverty.

VALLEY OF THE KINGS
Egyptians stopped building pyramids and started burying their pharaohs here, in tombs cut into the rock face.

KARNAK TEMPLE COMPLEX
This complex was built over 2,000 years, with each pharaoh adding their own buildings.

RAMESSES II
C.1304–1214 BC
A brilliant military leader, Ramesses II is considered one of the greatest pharaohs who ever lived.

LAKE NASSER
This reservoir is shared by Egypt, Sudan . . . and Africa's largest reptile, the Nile crocodile.

ABU SIMBEL TEMPLES
These ancient temples were carved into the mountainside 3,000 years ago by Ramesses II.

ASWAN DAM
When you stop the flow of one of the world's largest rivers, you get the world's largest dam.

SUDAN

WELCOME TO THE LAND OF THE PHARAOHS

No place can capture your imagination the way Egypt can, with its mind-blowing giant pyramids and pharaohs. The majestic River Nile winds its way through desert sands and past cities with ancient citadels. This country's civilization starts thousands of years ago, and so many of its treasures can still be seen today, from the tombs in the Valley of the Kings to the artifacts in the Egyptian museum in Cairo.

When you've finished exploring the ancient world, there are all the wonders that nature provides, such as the White Desert and the majestic Mount Sinai. Watch white-sailed feluccas (a type of boat) on Lake Nasser and go exploring underwater shipwrecks in the Red Sea.

In the country's biggest cities, there are busy markets and modern shopping malls, beautiful mosques, and fascinating museums. In fact, the country's capital, Cairo, is so big and so full of history that Egyptians know it as Umm al-Dunya or the "mother of the world."

MOMENTS TO REMEMBER

3500–3000 BC: The Egyptians invent hieroglyphics—a system of writing that uses pictures and symbols.

2500 BC: The Great Pyramids of Giza and the Sphinx are built.

1500 BC: The pharaohs are no longer buried in pyramids; instead they are placed in tombs in the Valley of the Kings.

1390–1213 BC: The Temple of Luxor is built.

331 BC: The Macedonian king, Alexander the Great, conquers Egypt and establishes the city of Alexandria.

30 BC: The last pharaoh of Egypt, Cleopatra VII, dies and the country is ruled by the Roman Empire.

AD 639–646: Egypt comes under Arab rule and is converted to Islam.

969: Cairo becomes the capital of Egypt.

1517: Egypt is conquered by the Ottoman Empire.

1869: The Suez Canal, connecting the Mediterranean Sea with the Red Sea, is completed.

1953: The Republic of Egypt is established, and Egypt becomes a powerful Arab nation in the Middle East.

1978: President Anwar Sadat signs a peace treaty with Israel, known as the Camp David Accords, ending decades of hostilities.

2018: A beautiful 4,400-year-old tomb is discovered at the Saqqara pyramid complex—the most complete find in decades.

KEY FACTS

LIFE, HEALTH, WELL-BEING

CAPITAL Cairo	**MONEY** Egyptian pound	**NATION CODE** EG
LARGEST CITIES Cairo Alexandria Giza Port Said Suez	**NAMED FOR** The Greek word Aigyptos	**OFFICIAL LANGUAGE** Arabic
POPULATION 109,500,000	**FLOWER** Lotus	**BIRD** Steppe eagle

SAUDI ARABIA

EGYPT

CLEOPATRA VII
69–30 BC
The last Egyptian pharaoh to rule before the Roman conquest, Cleopatra was famed not just for her beauty but for her fiercely intelligent leadership.

LOTFIA EL NADI
1907–2002
El Nadi was the first Egyptian woman and first woman from the Arab world to become a licensed pilot.

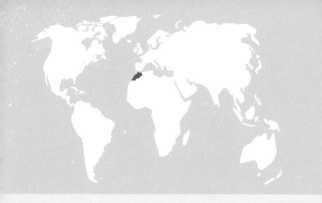

One day you might find yourself twisting and turning through narrow streets in an ancient kasbah, the next you're riding a camel along the shores of a golden-sand beach—this is Morocco! From the heights of the Atlas Mountains to the desert sands and shady oases of the Sahara, Morocco is a land of extremes. The country's history plays out in the cities and towns with stunning Islamic mosques, the mud-brick buildings of the Berbers, Moorish arches from Spain, and Roman ruins.

If the bustle of the big cities and buzzing marketplaces becomes too much, escape to dramatic national parks to see endangered monkeys or rock climb North Africa's tallest mountain, explore caves or snooze in the shade of a palm tree in an expansive oasis. Whichever way you turn in this African nation, you'll find history and natural wonders. The influences from Europe and the Arab world combined with stunning landscapes make Morocco a place like no other.

MOMENTS TO REMEMBER

1200 BC: Traders from Phoenicia (modern-day Lebanon) arrive.

500 BC: The Carthaginians from Tunisia control North Africa, including Morocco.

AD 40: The Roman Empire conquers Morocco.

278: Romans establish a regional capital at Tangier, in Northern Morocco.

600s: Arabs invade and bring with them the Arabic language and Islam.

1000s: The Berbers establish a series of powerful dynasties.

1500s–1600s: Arab dynasties conquer the Berbers; the Alaouite Dynasty comes to power in 1631 and still rules today.

1777: Morocco is the first country to recognize the United States as an independent nation.

1912: Morocco becomes a protectorate of France though Spain continues to have control over its coastal zones.

1956: The French protectorate ends, and Morocco becomes an independent nation known as the Kingdom of Morocco.

2011–2012: The Moroccan people protest against the unchecked powers of the king; he is forced to reform the constitution.

KOUTOUBIA MOSQUE
This 12th-century mosque was named after the booksellers who even today set up stalls at the base of the minaret.

BAHIA PALACE
This palace is now a museum where you can wander through the intricately designed rooms and gardens.

JEMAA EL-FNAA MARKET
This buzzing square and marketplace is full of food stalls and entertainers.

TAGHARTE BEACH, ESSAOUIRA
Swim, surf, or sunbathe on the golden sand . . . or go for a ride on a camel.

JBEL TOUBKAL
The highest peak in North Africa is here in the Atlas Mountains.

LEGZIRA BEACH
This remote and windswept beach has an enormous arch carved by the sea.

CHAIMA LAHSINI
B.1993
A human-rights campaigner, journalist, and feminist, Chaima works for gender equality and women's rights.

MOROCCO

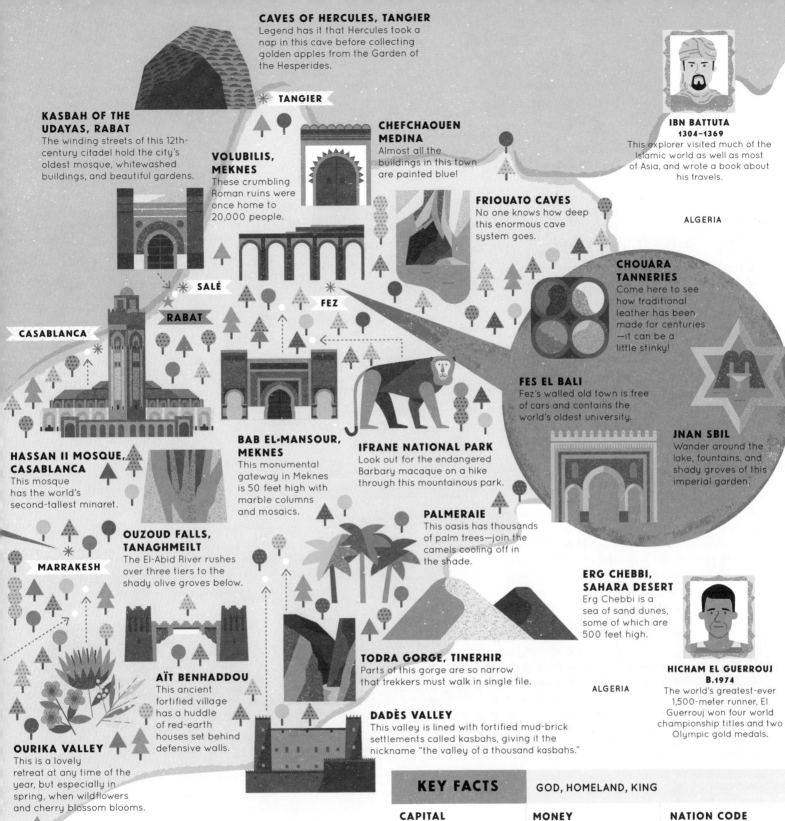

CAVES OF HERCULES, TANGIER
Legend has it that Hercules took a nap in this cave before collecting golden apples from the Garden of the Hesperides.

TANGIER

KASBAH OF THE UDAYAS, RABAT
The winding streets of this 12th-century citadel hold the city's oldest mosque, whitewashed buildings, and beautiful gardens.

VOLUBILIS, MEKNES
These crumbling Roman ruins were once home to 20,000 people.

CHEFCHAOUEN MEDINA
Almost all the buildings in this town are painted blue!

FRIOUATO CAVES
No one knows how deep this enormous cave system goes.

IBN BATTUTA
1304–1369
This explorer visited much of the Islamic world as well as most of Asia, and wrote a book about his travels.

ALGERIA

CHOUARA TANNERIES
Come here to see how traditional leather has been made for centuries —it can be a little stinky!

SALÉ

RABAT

FEZ

CASABLANCA

FES EL BALI
Fez's walled old town is free of cars and contains the world's oldest university.

JNAN SBIL
Wander around the lake, fountains, and shady groves of this imperial garden.

HASSAN II MOSQUE, CASABLANCA
This mosque has the world's second-tallest minaret.

BAB EL-MANSOUR, MEKNES
This monumental gateway in Meknes is 50 feet high with marble columns and mosaics.

IFRANE NATIONAL PARK
Look out for the endangered Barbary macaque on a hike through this mountainous park.

PALMERAIE
This oasis has thousands of palm trees—join the camels cooling off in the shade.

OUZOUD FALLS, TANAGHMEILT
The El-Abid River rushes over three tiers to the shady olive groves below.

MARRAKESH

ERG CHEBBI, SAHARA DESERT
Erg Chebbi is a sea of sand dunes, some of which are 500 feet high.

AÏT BENHADDOU
This ancient fortified village has a huddle of red-earth houses set behind defensive walls.

TODRA GORGE, TINERHIR
Parts of this gorge are so narrow that trekkers must walk in single file.

HICHAM EL GUERROUJ
B.1974
The world's greatest-ever 1,500-meter runner, El Guerrouj won four world championship titles and two Olympic gold medals.

ALGERIA

OURIKA VALLEY
This is a lovely retreat at any time of the year, but especially in spring, when wildflowers and cherry blossom blooms.

DADÈS VALLEY
This valley is lined with fortified mud-brick settlements called kasbahs, giving it the nickname "the valley of a thousand kasbahs."

MERIEME CHADID
B.1969
A groundbreaking explorer, astrophysicist, and astronomer, Dr. Chadid leads major scientific expeditions to the polar regions.

FRENCH MONTANA
B.1984
Born Karim Kharbouch, this rapper and DJ moved to New York when he was 13 and became an international recording artist.

KEY FACTS — GOD, HOMELAND, KING

CAPITAL
Rabat

MONEY
Moroccan dirham

NATION CODE
MA

LARGEST CITIES
Casablanca
Rabat
Fez
Salé
Marrakesh
Agadir

NAMED FOR
The Spanish word for Marrakesh, *Maruecos*. The name Marrakesh means "Land of God"

OFFICIAL LANGUAGES
Arabic and Berber

POPULATION
37,100,000

FLOWER
Rose

BIRD
Moussier's redstart

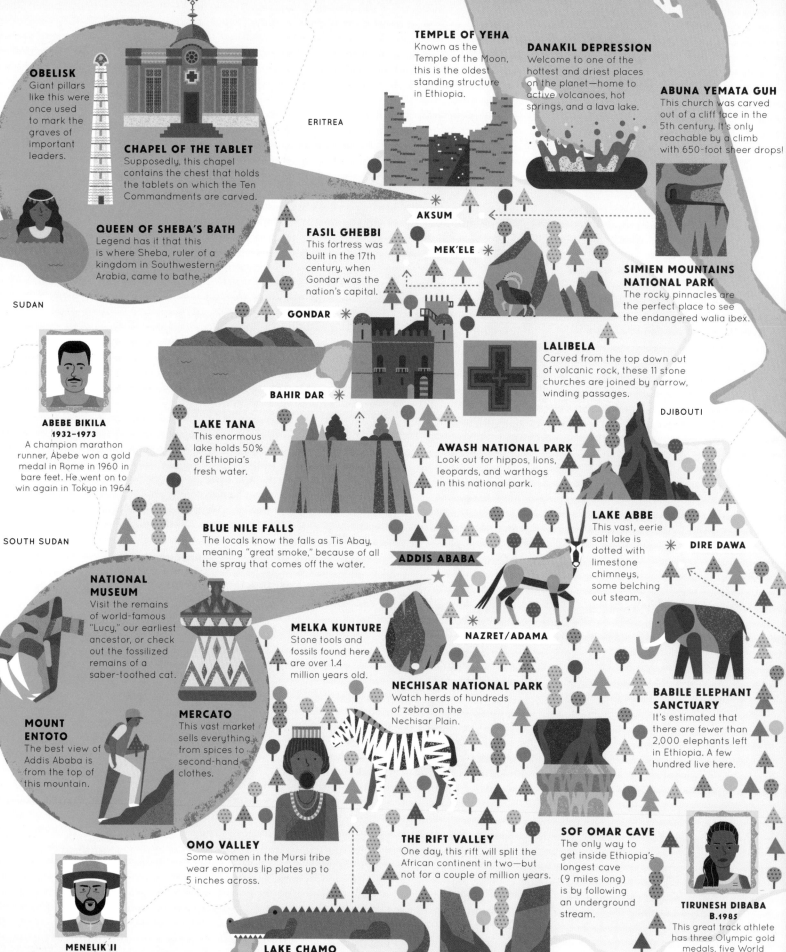

OBELISK
Giant pillars like this were once used to mark the graves of important leaders.

CHAPEL OF THE TABLET
Supposedly, this chapel contains the chest that holds the tablets on which the Ten Commandments are carved.

QUEEN OF SHEBA'S BATH
Legend has it that this is where Sheba, ruler of a kingdom in Southwestern Arabia, came to bathe.

TEMPLE OF YEHA
Known as the Temple of the Moon, this is the oldest standing structure in Ethiopia.

DANAKIL DEPRESSION
Welcome to one of the hottest and driest places on the planet—home to active volcanoes, hot springs, and a lava lake.

ABUNA YEMATA GUH
This church was carved out of a cliff face in the 5th century. It's only reachable by a climb with 650-foot sheer drops!

ERITREA

SUDAN

ABEBE BIKILA
1932–1973
A champion marathon runner, Abebe won a gold medal in Rome in 1960 in bare feet. He went on to win again in Tokyo in 1964.

AKSUM

FASIL GHEBBI
This fortress was built in the 17th century, when Gondar was the nation's capital.

MEK'ELE

SIMIEN MOUNTAINS NATIONAL PARK
The rocky pinnacles are the perfect place to see the endangered walia ibex.

GONDAR

LALIBELA
Carved from the top down out of volcanic rock, these 11 stone churches are joined by narrow, winding passages.

DJIBOUTI

BAHIR DAR

SOUTH SUDAN

LAKE TANA
This enormous lake holds 50% of Ethiopia's fresh water.

AWASH NATIONAL PARK
Look out for hippos, lions, leopards, and warthogs in this national park.

LAKE ABBE
This vast, eerie salt lake is dotted with limestone chimneys, some belching out steam.

BLUE NILE FALLS
The locals know the falls as Tis Abay, meaning "great smoke," because of all the spray that comes off the water.

DIRE DAWA

ADDIS ABABA

NATIONAL MUSEUM
Visit the remains of world-famous "Lucy," our earliest ancestor, or check out the fossilized remains of a saber-toothed cat.

MELKA KUNTURE
Stone tools and fossils found here are over 1.4 million years old.

NAZRET/ADAMA

MOUNT ENTOTO
The best view of Addis Ababa is from the top of this mountain.

MERCATO
This vast market sells everything from spices to second-hand clothes.

NECHISAR NATIONAL PARK
Watch herds of hundreds of zebra on the Nechisar Plain.

BABILE ELEPHANT SANCTUARY
It's estimated that there are fewer than 2,000 elephants left in Ethiopia. A few hundred live here.

OMO VALLEY
Some women in the Mursi tribe wear enormous lip plates up to 5 inches across.

THE RIFT VALLEY
One day, this rift will split the African continent in two—but not for a couple of million years.

SOF OMAR CAVE
The only way to get inside Ethiopia's longest cave (9 miles long) is by following an underground stream.

TIRUNESH DIBABA
B.1985
This great track athlete has three Olympic gold medals, five World Championships, and five World Cross Country titles.

MENELIK II
1844–1913
Emperor Menelik is credited with doubling the size of the Ethiopian Empire and repelling the Italian invasion.

LAKE CHAMO
The banks of this lake are often crowded with Nile crocodiles basking in the midday sun.

KENYA

WELCOME TO THE LAND OF OUR ANCIENT ANCESTORS

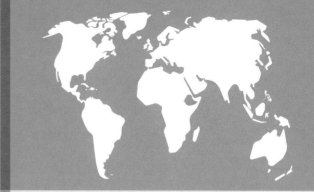

Ethiopia is one of the oldest countries on Earth, and its people are fiercely proud of the fact that they have never been colonized. Ethiopians are diverse, made up of over 80 different ethnic groups, each with their own language. This is a land of breathtaking natural sites, from the enormous Rift Valley to the source of the Blue Nile river, and the hottest, driest place on the planet, the Danakil Depression.

Through time, Ethiopia has endured the hardships of war and cruelty of famine. But it also has a rich history that has left behind stunning relics, from churches carved in stone to ancient obelisks and the most important of all—a prehistoric archeological site that tells us the story of how humans developed. In the nation's capital and largest city, Addis Ababa, you'll find an enormous open-air market, museums packed with precious artifacts, and a towering mountain covered in eucalyptus trees. At every turn, there is something uniquely striking to see and experience.

MOMENTS TO REMEMBER

3.2 million years ago: Early humans, known as hominids, begin to walk upright on the land.

1.75 million years ago: Humans known as *Homo erectus* begin to use stone tools at Melka Kunture.

10th century BC: An empire known as D'mt comes to power and establishes a capital city at Yeha.

1st century AD: The Aksumite Empire is founded and becomes known as one of the four major civilizations of the world (Rome, China, and Persia are the other three).

300s: Ethiopia becomes one of the first nations in the world to adopt Christianity.

615: The first Muslim settlement in Africa is established at Negash.

1632: Gondar is proclaimed capital of Ethiopia.

1769–1855: Gondar begins to lose influence and Ethiopia begins to be ruled by regions. This period is known as the "Era of the Princes."

1896: Italy attempts to invade Ethiopia, but is defeated by Ethiopian forces under Emperor Menelik II.

1936–1941: Italy invades again; they occupy the country for five years before the British help push them out.

1983–1985: One of the worst famines in world history results in the death of over 1.2 million Ethiopians.

1993–2000: Eritrea splits from Ethiopia and becomes an independent nation. Clashes on the border turn into war, before a peace accord is signed in 2000.

2005: Italy returns the final piece of the 4th-century Axum obelisk to Ethiopia 60 years after looting it.

2020: The brutal Tigray War breaks out between the government and forces in the Tigray region. A truce is called in November 2022.

KEY FACTS

ETHIOPIA STRETCHES HER HANDS UNTO GOD

CAPITAL Addis Ababa	**MONEY** Birr	**NATION CODE** ET
LARGEST CITIES Addis Ababa Dire Dawa Mek'ele Nazret/Adama Bahir Dar Gondar	**NAMED FOR** From the Greek words *aitho* meaning "I burn" and *ops* meaning "face"	**FLOWER** Calla lily **ANIMAL** Lion
POPULATION 115,800,000	**OFFICIAL LANGUAGE** Amharic	

HARAR
The oldest Islamic city in Africa has around 100 mosques within its walls.

SAHLE-WORK ZEWDE B.1950
Ethiopia's first female president is a trailblazer for women's rights, and a symbol of progress.

DINKNESH, AKA LUCY 3.2 MILLION YEARS OLD
"Lucy" is one of our earliest human ancestors. She had ape-like features and characteristics, and could walk on two feet.

ETHIOPIA

WELCOME TO AFRICA'S POWERHOUSE COUNTRY

This is Africa's most populated country and—after oil was discovered in 1956—one of its richest. It's estimated that the country's largest city, Lagos, has over 20 million inhabitants! The first people to make Nigeria their home are believed to be the Nok civilization, which existed well before Romans began building roads.

The countryside in Nigeria is made up of tropical rain forests, grasslands, mountain ranges, and coastal mangroves and swamps. Despite a difficult and often violent history of colonial occupation, slave trading, and civil war, there have been recent efforts to protect Nigeria's natural wonders by creating large national parks. These are some of the best places to see wildlife, such as pangolins, elephants, rhinoceroses, baboons, African buffalo, and lions.

Modern Nigeria is a mix of cities with skyscrapers, traditional thatched-hut villages, beautiful beaches, and sacred underground caves. It's a place where cultures, arts, architecture, and religions meet, creating a fascinating and constantly changing country.

MOMENTS TO REMEMBER

900 BC: A Neolithic civilization known as the Nok settle at the Jos Plateau in central Nigeria.

AD 800s–1400: The Hausa kingdoms and Borno dynasty are formed in the north, and the Oyo and Benin kingdoms are established in the south.

1472: Portuguese explorers arrive and begin trading brass and copper for pepper, cloth, and enslaved people.

1500s–1800s: British merchants capture, transport, and sell enslaved Africans from Nigeria, resulting in thousands of people being sent to the Americas.

1850–1914: The British strengthen their hold over the country they call the Colony and Protectorate of Nigeria.

1956: Oil is discovered in Nigeria at the Oloibiri oilfield.

1960: Nigeria achieves independence.

1967: Civil war breaks out when three eastern states attempt to become the Republic of Biafra.

1979–1990s: The country is caught up in a series of political coups and messy leadership changes.

1996: Nigeria's soccer team win gold at the Olympics.

2000: Tension between Muslims and Christians becomes violent and a series of tribal wars begin.

2014: Nigeria's economy becomes the largest in Africa.

2015: Muhammadu Buhari becomes president and promises to fight corruption. It is the first peaceful transfer of power between rival parties in the nation.

2022: A number of museums in the US and Europe decide to return looted Benin Bronzes to Nigeria.

CHIMAMANDA NGOZI ADICHIE
B.1977
Novelist Adichie writes about being a young, Black Nigerian woman and has won many international awards for her work.

NATIONAL THEATER
This striking building was designed to look like a military hat.

THIRD MAINLAND BRIDGE
Nigeria's longest bridge connects Lagos Island to the mainland.

LEKKI CONSERVATION CENTER
Suspended walkways let visitors stroll through the treetops at eye level with monkeys and birds, and at a safe distance from the crocodiles below.

**WIZKID AKA
AYODEJI IBRAHIM BALOGUN**
B.1990
Wizkid began recording his own songs at age 11 and in 2016 became a global superstar when his collaboration with Drake went to number-one in 15 countries.

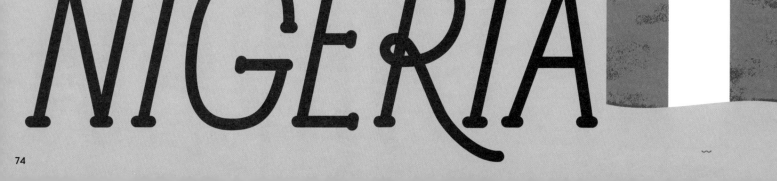

NIGERIA

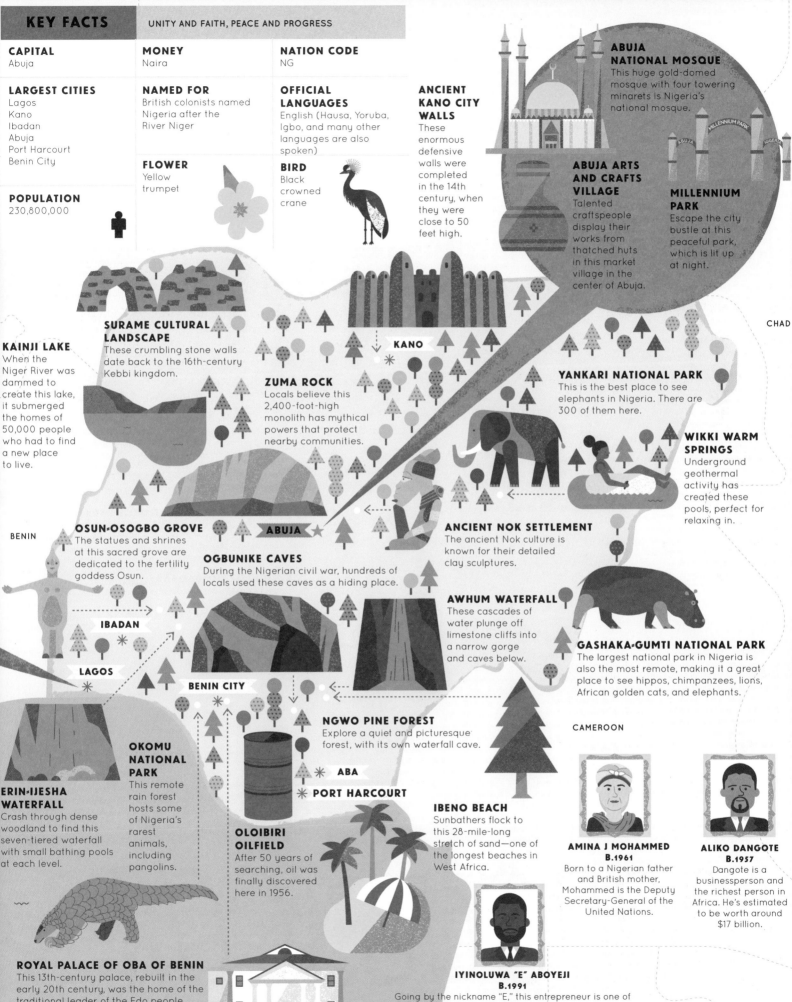

CAPITAL
Abuja

MONEY
Naira

NATION CODE
NG

LARGEST CITIES
Lagos
Kano
Ibadan
Abuja
Port Harcourt
Benin City

NAMED FOR
British colonists named Nigeria after the River Niger

OFFICIAL LANGUAGES
English (Hausa, Yoruba, Igbo, and many other languages are also spoken)

FLOWER
Yellow trumpet

BIRD
Black crowned crane

POPULATION
230,800,000

ANCIENT KANO CITY WALLS
These enormous defensive walls were completed in the 14th century, when they were close to 50 feet high.

ABUJA NATIONAL MOSQUE
This huge gold-domed mosque with four towering minarets is Nigeria's national mosque.

ABUJA ARTS AND CRAFTS VILLAGE
Talented craftspeople display their works from thatched huts in this market village in the center of Abuja.

MILLENNIUM PARK
Escape the city bustle at this peaceful park, which is lit up at night.

CHAD

SURAME CULTURAL LANDSCAPE
These crumbling stone walls date back to the 16th-century Kebbi kingdom.

KANO

KAINJI LAKE
When the Niger River was dammed to create this lake, it submerged the homes of 50,000 people who had to find a new place to live.

ZUMA ROCK
Locals believe this 2,400-foot-high monolith has mythical powers that protect nearby communities.

YANKARI NATIONAL PARK
This is the best place to see elephants in Nigeria. There are 300 of them here.

WIKKI WARM SPRINGS
Underground geothermal activity has created these pools, perfect for relaxing in.

BENIN

OSUN-OSOGBO GROVE
The statues and shrines at this sacred grove are dedicated to the fertility goddess Osun.

ABUJA

OGBUNIKE CAVES
During the Nigerian civil war, hundreds of locals used these caves as a hiding place.

ANCIENT NOK SETTLEMENT
The ancient Nok culture is known for their detailed clay sculptures.

IBADAN

AWHUM WATERFALL
These cascades of water plunge off limestone cliffs into a narrow gorge and caves below.

LAGOS

GASHAKA-GUMTI NATIONAL PARK
The largest national park in Nigeria is also the most remote, making it a great place to see hippos, chimpanzees, lions, African golden cats, and elephants.

BENIN CITY

NGWO PINE FOREST
Explore a quiet and picturesque forest, with its own waterfall cave.

CAMEROON

OKOMU NATIONAL PARK
This remote rain forest hosts some of Nigeria's rarest animals, including pangolins.

ABA

PORT HARCOURT

ERIN-IJESHA WATERFALL
Crash through dense woodland to find this seven-tiered waterfall with small bathing pools at each level.

OLOIBIRI OILFIELD
After 50 years of searching, oil was finally discovered here in 1956.

IBENO BEACH
Sunbathers flock to this 28-mile-long stretch of sand—one of the longest beaches in West Africa.

AMINA J MOHAMMED
B.1961
Born to a Nigerian father and British mother, Mohammed is the Deputy Secretary-General of the United Nations.

ALIKO DANGOTE
B.1957
Dangote is a businessperson and the richest person in Africa. He's estimated to be worth around $17 billion.

ROYAL PALACE OF OBA OF BENIN
This 13th-century palace, rebuilt in the early 20th century, was the home of the traditional leader of the Edo people.

IYINOLUWA "E" ABOYEJI
B.1991
Going by the nickname "E," this entrepreneur is one of Africa's most successful technology innovators.

THE EARTH'S BIODIVERSE WONDERLAND

When Madagascar split from the African mainland more than 160 million years ago, it began the process of evolving a vast array of unique flora and fauna. You might have heard of Madagascan wildlife—hundreds of species on the island are found nowhere else in the world. Its most famous furry resident is the wide-eyed lemur, and two of the rarest and most endangered of the species, the aye-aye and the golden bamboo lemur, are both found here. The island also has more than 11,000 unique species of plants.

Madagascar's isolation has had a significant impact on its human population as well as its flora and fauna. Despite being part of Africa, the people of Madagascar refer to themselves as Malagasies and have closer genetic ties to the people of Southeast Asia than Africa. It's thought that the first peoples arrived in long canoes from Indonesia. For centuries, the people of Madagascar managed to repel European invaders before finally falling to the French. The country became independent in 1960, but you will still see traces of the French in the language and the food.

The majority of the island lies within the tropics, but it is so big that the climate ranges from cold in the central highlands to hot and sunny in the west to wet and steamy in the rain forests of the east. On any given day, it's possible to experience unique wildlife, weather, and welcomes.

MOMENTS TO REMEMBER

160 million years ago: A large area of land splits off from what is now Africa, containing what becomes India and Madagascar.

80 million years ago: Madagascar separates from India and becomes the island it is today.

AD 700–1200: Austronesian peoples begin arriving to the island from Indonesia, on outrigger canoes.

800–900: Arab merchants begin trading with locals along the north coast of Madagascar.

1500: The Portuguese sea captain Diogo Dias is blown off course and becomes the first European to set foot on the island. He names it St. Lawrence.

1500s: English, French, Dutch, and Portuguese all attempt to establish trade routes in Madagascar, but they are fought off by the local Malagasy people.

Late 1500s: The Sakalava people become the first to form an empire here.

1600s: The east coast of the island becomes a lawless place and is largely controlled by pirates.

1810–1828: Radama I, king of the Merina people, unifies the country and overpowers the Sakalava Empire—with help from the British.

1890: The British agree to Madagascar becoming a French protectorate in exchange for influence in Zanzibar, Tanzania.

1960: After years of brutal fighting with the French, Madagascar becomes independent.

1975: Didier Ratsiraka takes control and forms a dictatorship that lasts for 18 years.

1993: Albert Zafy wins democratic elections to become the president of Madagascar.

2021: Scientists discover what could be the world's smallest reptile: a tiny chameleon the size of a sunflower seed!

QUEEN RANAVALONA I
1778–1861
Madagascar's "Mad Queen" cut ties with European powers, banned Christianity, and used forced labor to do public works.

TSINGY DE BEMARAHA NATIONAL PARK
The Malagasy word "tsingy" translates to "where one cannot walk barefoot." When you see this mass of limestone spikes, you'll see why!

AVENUE OF THE BAOBABS
These two rows of "upside-down" trees have trunks that measure 150 feet in circumference. Some are 800 years old!

ISALO NATIONAL PARK
The landscape here shifts from sandstone formations to fern-tree-lined canyons and waterfalls.

ILAKAKA SAPPHIRE MINES
The first sapphire was discovered here in 1998, kicking off a gem rush. The town grew from 40 to 60,000 people, and became the world's largest supplier of sapphires.

MADAGASCAR

NOSY BE
The name means "Big Island", but it's also known as "The Perfumed Island" because of all the ylang-ylang plantations.

ANKARANA CAVES
The combination of limestone and heavy rainfall has created cave systems here, with sinkholes and underground rivers.

MOUNT MAROMOKOTRO
The highest mountain in Madagascar is sometimes covered in snow at the peak.

ALBERT RAKOTO RATSIMAMANGA
1907–2001
Ratsimamanga was a scientist who researched the medicinal properties of Madagascar's unique flora.

PIRATE CEMETERY
When the pirates of this tropical island died, they were laid to rest here—a buccaneer burial ground.

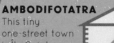

AMBODIFOTATRA
This tiny one-street town is Île Sainte-Marie's capital and the home of Madagascar's oldest church.

SHIPWRECKS AT PIRATE BAY
Several pirate shipwrecks lie off the coast of Île Sainte-Marie; many are thought to still contain treasure.

MAHAJANGA

ZAHAMENA NATIONAL PARK
67 of the bird species in this park are unique to Madagascar, including the serpent eagle.

NOSY MANGABE
This tropical island is home to the endangered long-fingered lemur, known as the aye-aye.

MASOALA NATIONAL PARK
From coral reefs to rain forests, it's believed that 50% of Madagascar's biodiversity can be found here.

ANALAVORY GEYSERS
These geysers erupt because of the activity from the aragonite mines nearby.

NOSY ALAÑAÑA LIGHT
At 200 feet, this lighthouse is the tallest in Africa. Its purpose is to stop boats running aground on this tiny Isle of Prunes.

ANDOHALO PLACE
This was the first marketplace in the city and the place where royal ceremonies were held.

TOAMASINA

ANTANANARIVO

ROVA ALASORA
Andriamanelo, a Merina king, built a fortified complex here in 1540. Only the foundations remain today.

AMBOHIMANGA
The Royal Hill of Ambohimanga was the home of Merina royalty; the site contains many of their burial tombs.

QUEEN'S PALACE
This rova (fortified castle) was originally designed for Ranavalona I.

ANTSIRABE

ANTONGONA
The Vazimba people were the first to build homes on these clifftops in the 16th century.

RANOMAFANA NATIONAL PARK
The steamy rain forests here are home to some of the world's rarest lemur species, including the golden bamboo lemur.

ALI KAMÉ
B.1984
An Olympic decathlon athlete, Kamé was a gold medalist at the African Championships and a bronze medalist at the All-Africa Games.

FIANARANTSOA

RANOMAFANA THERMAL BATHS
The hot springs in Ranomafana National Park are used to feed a public swimming pool.

MADAGASCAR SLIM
B.1956
A folk and blues guitarist, Slim won Canada's World Music Album of the Year in 2000.

TSARANORO MASSIF
The 2,600-foot sheer rock wall is a magnet for rock climbers from all over the world.

MAHAFALY TOMBS
The Mahafaly built large tombs topped with zebu horns and sculpted wooden columns to honor their dead. See them on the roadside in the country's south.

GISÈLE RABESAHALA
1929–2011
The first woman to become a minister in Madagascar's government, she devoted her life to fighting for human rights.

KEY FACTS
LIBERTY, FATHERLAND, PROGRESS

CAPITAL Antananarivo	**MONEY** Malagasy ariary	**NATION CODE** MG
LARGEST CITIES Antananarivo Toamasina Antsirabe Fianarantsoa Mahajanga	**NAMED FOR** The European interpretation of the Malagasy word *Madagasikara*	**OFFICIAL LANGUAGES** Malagasy and French
POPULATION 28,800,000	**FLOWER** Poinciana	**BIRD** Fish eagle

KENYA

UGANDA

MOMENTS TO REMEMBER

6 million BC: One of the earliest ancestors of humans, the hominid *Orrorin tugenensis*, lived in the Tugen Hills in Kenya.

1.8 million BC: Upright man (*Homo erectus*) begins using tools in the Lake Turkana region.

2000 BC: Nomadic tribes begin to arrive from Ethiopia.

2500–1500 BC: Bantu groups from Sub-Saharan Africa arrive in Kenya and begin working with metals.

AD 900: Islamic groups settle in Mombasa; this is the beginning of the Swahili civilization.

1498: The Portuguese arrive and establish a naval base at Mombasa; their arrival lessens the Arab dominance.

1840s: German missionaries and explorers Johann Krapf and Johannes Rebmann become the first Europeans to see Mount Kilimanjaro and Mount Kenya.

1890–1895: Kenya and Uganda come under the control of the British and become known as British East Africa.

1963: Kenya becomes an independent nation with Jomo Kenyatta as its first prime minister.

2013: Jomo Kenyatta's son, Uhuru Kenyatta, narrowly wins the presidential election.

2015: Archeologists discover stone tools at Lomekwi. Believed to be 3.3 million years old, they are the oldest tools ever discovered.

2022: Kenyan runner Eliud Kipchoge sets a new marathon world record: 2 hours, 1 minute, and 9 seconds. He is considered the greatest marathon runner of all time.

MOUNT KENYA
The highest mountain in Kenya and the second-highest in Africa, after Mount Kilimanjaro, is an extinct volcano.

OL PEJETA CONSERVANCY
At this sanctuary, lucky safari-goers might see the "big five"—elephant, lion, leopard, rhinoceros, and buffalo.

EWASO NYIRO RIVER
In the dry north, this river brings life to many animals, including Nile crocodiles.

LAKE NAKURU NATIONAL PARK
Black and white rhinos, endangered Rothschild's giraffes, and flamingos all call this park home.

THE GREAT RIFT VALLEY
Here in Kenya you can see Earth's crust moving. Two tectonic plates are moving apart and creating a giant crack.

KISUMU ✳

NAKURU ✳

NAIROBI

KARURU FALLS
Kenya's highest waterfalls have a 900-foot drop and are surrounded by lush forests.

LAKE NAIVASHA
At this birdwatcher's paradise, expect to see cranes, marabou storks, pelicans—and hippos!

MAASAI CULTURAL HERITAGE CENTER
This center aims to preserve Maasai culture and heritage while providing job opportunities for women artisans.

MAASAI MARA NATIONAL RESERVE
Each year, thousands of wildebeest cross the plains of this park in search of greener pastures. It's known as the Great Migration.

AMBOSELI NATIONAL PARK
Come here to get a dose of iconic Kenya—watch a herd of elephants crossing the dry plains with Mount Kilimanjaro in the background.

KEY FACTS
LET US ALL PULL TOGETHER

CAPITAL Nairobi	**MONEY** Kenyan shilling	**NATION CODE** KE
LARGEST CITIES Nairobi Mombasa Kisumu Nakuru Eldoret	**NAMED FOR** The second-highest mountain in Africa, Mount Kenya	**OFFICIAL LANGUAGES** Swahili and English
POPULATION 57,100,000	**FLOWER** Orchid 	**BIRD** Lilac-breasted roller

TANZANIA

SAVANNAS AND SEAPORTS—WELCOME TO KENYA

With its Indian Ocean coastline, Kenya has attracted its fair share of international visitors over the years—the Portuguese, Chinese, English, and Arab peoples all saw that this seaport was a treasure trove for trade, so all staked a claim to the land. Millions of years before the coast became a draw for outsiders, however, Kenya was home to the planet's earliest human beings. We know this because ancient stone tools have been discovered in the Turkana region.

Aside from all the human activity, Kenya is home to some of the world's most spectacular wildlife. Its national parks and conservation areas boast white and black rhinoceroses, elephants, lions, tigers, buffalo, leopards, giraffes, hippos, Nile crocodiles, and a critically endangered antelope. Wildebeest make their annual migration across Kenyan plains, and there's even a place you can stay where giraffes will join you for breakfast.

It should come as no surprise that a country with wildlife so spectacular would have a landscape to match. Sandstone canyons, plunging waterfalls, extinct volcanoes, wide-open savannas, and a valley where Earth's crust can be seen moving apart can all be found here. Kenya is a snapshot of the Africa that everyone dreams about.

JOMO KENYATTA
C.1897–1978
Kenyatta believed in Kenyan independence. He became the country's first prime minister in 1963.

WANGARI MAATHAI
1940–2011
Maathai was the first African woman to be awarded a Nobel Peace Prize for her work in reducing poverty and conserving the environment.

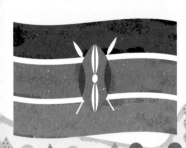

SAMBURU NATIONAL RESERVE
Samburu was home to a famous lioness known as Kamunyak, who adopted and protected more than orphaned oryx calves.

GIRAFFE MANOR
At this hotel, giraffes poke their heads through the windows hoping for a snack!

BOMAS OF KENYA
In one of Africa's largest auditoriums, more than 50 different bomas (homesteads) perform traditional music and dance.

NAIROBI SAFARI WALK
Stroll along a boardwalk with a view over cheetahs, lions, and other animals.

HELL'S GATE GORGE
This gorge is named after a narrow gap in the towering limestone cliffs.

LAMU ISLAND
The architecture on Lamu tells the story of its past. You'll see Arab, Indian, and Chinese influences.

MARAFA DEPRESSION
This sandstone canyon has been worn away over centuries to become a gorge with layers of pink, orange, and white.

MOMBASA

DIANI BEACH
This strip of sand has been voted Africa's best beach!

YATTA PLATEAU
This is no ordinary plateau—it is the world's longest lava flow!

LUGARD FALLS
These falls on the Galana River are more like a series of white-water rapids.

HIROLA ANTELOPE
The hirola is the world's rarest antelope. It's also known as the four-eyed antelope because of dark markings under its eyes.

MALINDI
For 300 years, Malindi was a port town trading in ivory and enslaved people, until slavery was abolished in 1873. Now it's popular with beach-loving tourists.

MOMBASA MARINE PARK
Warm tropical waters and coral reefs draw divers and snorkelers.

FORT JESUS
The 400-year-old fort was built by the Portuguese in Mombasa to protect their trading interests.

DAPHNE SHELDRICK
1934–2018
Sheldrick spent her life saving and rehabilitating wild animals.

DAVID RUDISHA
B.1988
The only person to have run 800 meters in under 1 minute 41 seconds, Rudisha is the 2012 and 2016 Olympic champion.

RICHARD TURERE
B.2000
To help save his family's livestock from being eaten by lions, Turere invented a light system that mimics the pattern of a person walking with a flashlight to scare off the lions.

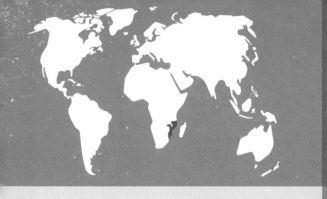

CAPITAL	MONEY	NATION CODE
Maputo	Metical	MZ
LARGEST CITIES	**NAMED FOR**	**OFFICIAL LANGUAGE**
Matola	An Arab trader named	Portuguese
Maputo	Mussa Bin Bique, or	
Nampula	Mossa Al Bique, who	
Beira	visited the coast and	
Chimoio	went on to live there	
POPULATION	**FLOWER**	**ANIMAL**
32,500,000	Maroon bell bean	African elephant

MOMENTS TO REMEMBER

AD 200: Bantu-speaking tribes from west and central Africa begin moving into the area now known as Mozambique.

1000s: The largely agricultural Shona Empire expands from Zimbabwe into present-day Mozambique.

1498: A Portuguese expedition, led by Vasco de Gama, arrives off the Mozambican coast.

1400s–1600s: The Portuguese establish forts and trading posts and take land for European settlers.

1700s–1800s: Mozambique becomes one of the biggest slave trade centers in the world.

1842: Portugal bans the slave trade, but it secretly continues.

1878: Portugal leases large sections of land to international companies that use local labor.

1930–1960s: The Portuguese decide to break up the trading companies and impose their direct rule over Mozambique. Thousands of Portuguese settlers flood into the country.

1975: After years of fighting for an end to Portuguese rule, the Mozambique Liberation Front (Frelimo) wins independence for the country and becomes the ruling party.

1977–1992: Civil war breaks out between the Frelimo government and Renamo rebels, who also want power.

2001: Close to 70,000 people are left homeless when the Zambezi Valley floods.

2013: Government forces and the rebel group Renamo begin fighting again. The violence means that thousands flee their homes.

2021: Mozambique's national soccer team achieves a historic victory, qualifying for the African Cup of Nations for the first time.

JOAQUIM CHISSANO
B.1939
President of Mozambique from 1986 to 2005, Chissano is recognized for bringing democracy to the country.

MARIA MUTOLA
B.1972
Mostly an 800-meter runner, Mutola is Mozambique's first Olympic gold medalist and won three World Championships.

CAHORA BASSA LAKE
A giant dam built on the Zambezi River in 1974 formed this huge lake.

THE LION HOUSE
This lodge in the Gorongosa Park was originally built for visitors, but was abandoned when it kept flooding . . . that's when the lions moved in!

CHINAMAPERE ROCK PAINTINGS
Thousands of years old, these rock paintings show animal and human figures.

CHIMOIO

GRANDE HOTEL

GRANDE HOTEL OF BEIRA
Built in 1954, this luxury hotel with an Olympic-sized pool closed in 1974 and has since become overrun with squatters.

NATURAL HISTORY MUSEUM
The main attraction here is the taxidermied native animals drinking at a neon-green waterhole.

TUNDURU BOTANICAL GARDENS
Escape the tropical heat of Maputo at this green oasis.

MAPUTO CENTRAL MARKET
There are so many stalls inside this Portuguese colonial market that sellers spill out into the street.

INHACA ISLAND
A mere 7,000 years ago, this island was part of the mainland. Today it's 30 miles offshore from Maputo.

MATOLA

MAPUTO

TANZANIA

NIASSA RESERVE
The largest protected area in Mozambique is home to 350 endangered African wild dogs.

MABU FOREST
Locals have known about this old-growth rain forest for centuries, but scientists didn't discover it until 2005!

MOUNT NAMULI
At 8,000 feet, this is the second-tallest mountain in Mozambique.

QUIRIMBAS NATIONAL PARK
The 12 main islands of this small archipelago are known for their white-sand beaches and beautiful coral reefs.

NAMPULA

GORONGOSA NATIONAL PARK
The civil war in Mozambique devastated the numbers of big mammals, like lions, but numbers have begun rising again.

STONE TOWN, MOZAMBIQUE ISLAND
This tiny island was once the capital of Portuguese East Africa. Stone Town, with its impressive defensive fort, was the colonial headquarters.

MAKUTI, MOZAMBIQUE ISLAND
Nothing like Stone Town, Mozambique's other city is made up of traditional thatched homes.

GOA ISLAND
To prevent ships from running aground on this tiny island, a large square lighthouse was built in 1876.

MALANGATANA NGWENYA
1936–2011
A painter and a poet, Ngwenya used the struggles of ordinary people and the Mozambican quest for independence as his inspiration.

SANTA CAROLINA
This tiny island in the Bazaruto Archipelago has all the tropical wonders of the other islands and is also home to an abandoned resort.

BENGUERRA ISLAND
The waters surrounding this island are still used by trading dhows (traditional boats).

THE AQUARIUM
This snorkeling reef off Bazaruto Island gets its name because of the numbers of tropical fish found there.

CLARISSE MACHANGUANA
B.1976
Basketball player Machanguana has played in America's WNBA and in Spain's national league.

BEIRA

MACUTI LIGHTHOUSE AND SHIPWRECK, BEIRA
Walk through a rusted shipwreck just below an abandoned lighthouse. Though it looks dramatic, the ship was deliberately run aground to form a breakwater.

MANYIKENI
This 12th–17th-century archeological site contained glass beads and seashells, suggesting the settlement traded with coastal towns.

POMENE RESERVE
You might see a rare dugong at this small marine reserve, which protects a pristine mangrove estuary.

TOFO BEACH
The ocean here is home to giant manta rays, dolphins, whale sharks, and even migrating humpback whales.

LUÍSA DIOGO
B.1958
Diogo was the first female prime minister of Mozambique. She has a reputation for being an intelligent economist.

DOLPHINS AT PONTA DO OURO
People come here for the chance to interact with lots of dolphins.

BEAUTIFUL BEACHES, HISTORICAL ISLAND FORTS, AND WILDLIFE RESERVES

With its stunning tropical coastline, the east African nation of Mozambique has attracted attention from traders and travelers for centuries, but it was the Portuguese who established a powerful trade colony here in the 16th century. The tiny Mozambique Island became the capital of their African empire, and it's still possible to see the crumbling remnants of this colonial past in the defensive fort in Stone Town. When Mozambique finally achieved independence from Portuguese rule in the 1970s, the country then suffered years of civil war and violent fighting while political parties struggled to establish a workable government.

Mozambique remains a poor country. However, the end to civil war has meant that industries like tourism and conservation have begun to grow. Animal populations have started to flourish again, and in places such as Gorongosa National Park and Niassa Reserve, it's possible to see large herds of elephants, endangered wild African dogs, hippos, lions, and wild buffalo.

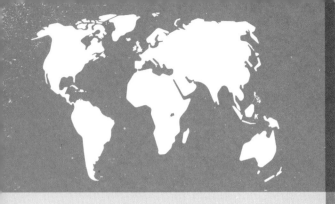

UGANDA

MOMENTS TO REMEMBER

10,000 to 3000 BC: The first people, known as the Twa, moved into the region.

5th to 11th century AD: Tribespeople known as Hutus arrive and start farming the land.

14th century: Tutsi tribespeople begin migrating to the region and use their superior fighting skills to become the dominant tribe.

19th century: Tutsi king Kigeri IV Rwabugiri establishes the boundaries of the kingdom of Rwanda.

1899: The German Empire colonizes the country, and it becomes known as German East Africa.

1916: Belgian forces invade and occupy Rwanda.

1946: The United Nations declares Rwanda a trust territory to be governed by Belgium; Tutsi kings rule indirectly.

1962: Rwanda proclaims itself a republic and becomes an independent country under Hutu president Grégoire Kayibanda.

1990: Rebel Tutsi forces from Uganda invade Rwanda and demand a change in rule.

1994: Hutu extremists go on a brutal rampage, killing hundreds of thousands of Tutsis. This is known as genocide.

2001: A new flag and national anthem is announced to help bring Hutus and Tutsis together as Rwandans.

2018: Rwanda becomes the second African nation to have an equal balance of women and men as government ministers.

MOUNT BISOKE
This active volcano last erupted in 1957. For now it's safe to hike to the top to see the beautiful crater lake.

MUSANZE CAVES
This cave complex includes the largest caves in Rwanda. It's over 1.25 miles long and houses thousands of bats.

MOUNT KARISIMBI
The peak of this lofty mountain, the highest in the Virunga Mountain Range, is covered in snow.

PFUNDA TEA ESTATE
During the busiest harvesting season this tea plantation processes 100 tons of tea per day!

NYAMYUMBA HOT SPRINGS
These pools of bubbling hot water are said to have special healing powers.

RUHENGERI

GISENYI

GISHWATI-MUKURA NATIONAL PARK
A protection program has saved the park from deforestation and created a safe home for golden monkeys and other animals.

KARISOKE RESEARCH CENTER
Founded by zoologist Dian Fossey, this center studies and protects endangered mountain gorillas.

LAKE KIVU
Rwanda's largest lake may look beautiful but it doesn't smell great. This is because of the high levels of methane gas in its waters.

GITARAMA

NDABA WATERFALL
Legend has it that this torrent of water was once honey, which attracted people from the forests.

KIBUYE (KARONGI)
Rwanda might be landlocked but it still has beaches! This sleepy beach resort lies on the shores of Lake Kivu.

GISUMA
In 2009, 56 women got together and decided to improve their lives by creating a coffee-bean growing collective. Their beans are now sold worldwide.

NYUNGWE FOREST NATIONAL PARK CANOPY WALK
Walk through the treetops and you might come eye to eye with a chimpanzee.

RWESERO ART MUSEUM, NYANZA
A modern art museum is housed inside a palace built for King Mutara III Rudahigwa.

HUYE

HUYE (BUTARE TOWN)
This university town is home to more students than any other in Africa

RWANDA

IBY'IWACU CULTURAL VILLAGE

Locals here will introduce visitors to Rwandan customs and traditions, including dances, songs, and food.

MOUNT SABYINYO

Locals call this mountain "Old Man's Teeth" because of the jagged peaks at its summit.

VOLCANOES NATIONAL PARK

This is one of the only places on Earth where you can see critically endangered mountain gorillas in their natural habitat.

BYUMBA

LAKE BURERA AND LAKE RUHONDO

These twin lakes are free of hippos and crocodiles —perfect spots for humans to swim in instead!

KIGALI

PRESIDENTIAL PALACE AND ART MUSEUM

The home of the president before the genocide is now a museum showing how he lived.

GENOCIDE MEMORIAL

Over 800,000 people were killed during the Rwandan genocide, which is too awful to imagine. This memorial aims to honor the victims.

KIMIRONKO MARKET

The busiest market in Rwanda's capital city sells everything from fruit to fabric to tourist trinkets.

TANZANIA

AKAGERA NATIONAL PARK

Look out for zebras, giraffes, rhinos, and more on the savanna plains of this national park.

LAKE IHEMA

The biggest lake in the park is a popular fishing destination. Visitors are usually more excited about seeing the hippos and crocodiles!

BIRDWATCHING

See a red-faced barbet, brown-throated weaver, or even an African finfoot.

The nation of Rwanda has overcome a recent history of horrific violence to emerge as a beacon of progress and peace on the African continent. There are solemn reminders of the atrocities that occurred, such as the Genocide Memorial in the capital city Kigali, but for the most part it's a place where the people are looking forward with optimism and pride.

It's no wonder Rwandans are proud of their country—it's one of the only places left on Earth where you can see the world's largest primate, the mountain gorilla, in its natural habitat. You can also visit huge freshwater lakes, giant caves carved from lava flows, volcanic snow-topped peaks, and epic savannas inhabited by black rhinos, zebras, giraffes, and elephants. Cultural traditions are kept alive in the towns and villages, and in museums and marketplaces, where visitors are welcome and encouraged to learn all about daily life, including the importance of music and dance, and crafts such as weaving, basket making, and pottery.

Concerted efforts to ensure democracy and peace, alongside economic endeavors such as coffee-bean production and adventure tourism, are Rwanda's way of showing the world that it's a country focused on the future, not defined by its past.

AGNES BINAGWAHO
B.1955
Pediatrician Binagwaho has won international awards for her work improving the health of children in Rwanda.

JEAN DE DIEU NKUNDABERA
Wheelchair athlete Nkundabera is Rwanda's first Paralympic medalist. He claimed bronze in 2004 in the 800-meter T46 sprint.

ANTOINETTE UWIMANA
Uwimana is the country director of Women to Women International, and has helped improve the lives of Rwandan women.

HENRI NYAKARUNDI
B.1977
Not everyone in Rwanda has access to electricity, so Nyakarundi invented a solar-powered cart that can charge up to 80 cell phones at a time.

JIMMY GATETE
B.1982
Soccer star Gatete scored for the national team during the 2004 African Cup of Nations, ensuring they made their first finals.

KEY FACTS — UNITY, WORK, PATRIOTISM

CAPITAL	MONEY	NATION CODE
Kigali	Rwandan franc	RW

LARGEST CITIES	NAMED FOR	OFFICIAL LANGUAGES
Kigali	The Rwanda-Rundi word *Rwanda*, meaning "large in size"	Kinyarwanda, French, English, and Kiswahili
Huye (Butare)		
Gitarama		
Ruhengeri		
Gisenyi		
Byumba		

POPULATION	FLOWER	BIRD
13,400,000	Red rose	Shoebill

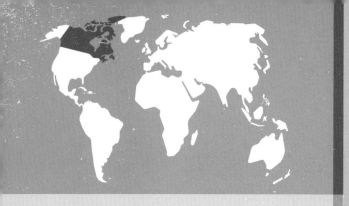

This vast and wild country is the second-largest on Earth (after Russia). It's full of snow-capped mountain ranges, enormous lakes, and miles of forests with wandering moose, munching musk ox, powerful bears, lumbering bison, sleek bobcats, gnawing beavers, and other wildlife. Unsurprisingly, there's lots to do outdoors, from kayaking and canoeing to skiing, hiking, and rock climbing.

In the 16th and 17th centuries, French and British explorers battled each other to colonize the land and the country still has strong ties to its French and English history. Canada is now regarded as one of the most multicultural countries in the world.

One of the best things to do in Canada is watch a game of hockey—the fast and rough winter national sport. But outside of the ice rink Canadians are famously friendly and peaceful.

MOMENTS TO REMEMBER

30,000–15,000 BC: Paleo-Indian peoples cross from Siberia into parts of the Yukon, Canada, and Alaska, USA.

AD 796: The Chippewa, Ottawa, and Potawatomi form an alliance known as the Three Fires Confederacy.

C.1450: The Haudenosaunee Confederacy is formed, bringing together five distinct nations from the Great Lakes District. No one knows for sure how old the Confederacy is.

1497: Italian explorer John Cabot lands in Newfoundland and claims the territory for England.

1534: French explorer Jacques Cartier claims the Gulf of Saint Lawrence for France.

1608: Quebec City is founded and over time becomes the capital of what is known as New France.

1763: After suffering defeat during the Seven Years' War, France gives control of its Canadian territories to Britain.

1857: Queen Victoria declares Ottawa to be the new capital of Canada.

1867: The Dominion of Canada is formed.

1914: Canada joins British troops to fight in World War I.

1931: British parliamentary power over Canada ends.

1939: Canada declares war on Germany and joins World War II.

1965: The red maple leaf on a white background becomes Canada's national flag.

1982: Queen Elizabeth II signs off on Canada's first independent constitution.

2014: A Canadian lab creates a vaccine to combat Africa's deadly Ebola virus.

2015: The Truth and Reconciliation Commission of Canada releases its report on the damage the government's policies have done to Indigenous peoples.

2019: The Toronto Raptors become the first non-US team to win the National Basketball Association title.

ROBERTA BONDAR
B.1945
Canada's first female astronaut and the first neurologist in space, Bondar worked as the head of space medicine at NASA.

CALGARY STAMPEDE
The Calgary Stampede shows off Western Canadian culture alongside rodeo events such as bull-riding and barrel racing.

BANFF NATIONAL PARK
This national park is known for glaciers, ice fields, forests, and the turquoise waters of Lake Moraine.

WANUSKEWIN HERITAGE PARK
Learn the story of the Northern Plains peoples at this cultural and historical center of First Nations.

CAPILANO SUSPENSION BRIDGE
Hold tight as you walk across this narrow bridge, 230 feet above the Capilano River.

STANLEY PARK
Vancouver's biggest park has almost half a million trees. The Hollow Tree is a stump that could fit an elephant inside!

GROUSE MOUNTAIN
In winter, Grouse Mountain is packed with skiers, snowboarders, and skaters; in summer, hikers walk the trails.

CALGARY

VANCOUVER

PACIFIC OCEAN

LAURA SECORD
1775–1868
Secord walked 100 miles to warn British, Canadian, and Indigenous troops of an imminent American attack during the War of 1812.

WAYNE GRETZKY
B.1961
Considered the greatest hockey player of all time, Gretzky holds the record for being the fastest player to reach 500 goals in the NHL.

SPOTTED LAKE
Each summer, most of the water in this lake evaporates, leaving behind hundreds of round puddles. The spots change color depending on the minerals in the soil.

DINOSAUR PROVINCIAL PARK
Almost 60 different dinosaur species were discovered here.

UNITED STATES OF AMERICA

CANADA

TERRY FOX
1958–1981
After losing a leg to cancer, Fox started a run across Canada to raise money for cancer research. After 143 days, his cancer returned, forcing him to stop.

LOUIS RIEL
1844–1885
As a politician and defender of the rights and culture of the Métis people, Riel led violent rebellions against the Canadian government to safeguard Métis land.

KEY FACTS	FROM SEA TO SEA	
CAPITAL Ottawa	**MONEY** Canadian dollar	**NATION CODE** CA
LARGEST CITIES Toronto Montreal Vancouver Calgary	**OFFICIAL LANGUAGES** English, French, and Mi'kmaw	
POPULATION 38,500,000	**NATIONAL TREE** Maple tree	**BIRD** Gray jay

TORONTO
Toronto is famed for being one of the most multicultural and peaceful cities in the world.

NIAGARA FALLS
You can see Niagara Falls from Canada and the USA. Horseshoe Falls is North America's most powerful waterfall.

CN TOWER, TORONTO
This communications and observation tower is the tallest free-standing structure in the Western Hemisphere.

LAKE HURON
Lake Huron has over 30,000 islands, including Manitoulin Island —the world's largest freshwater island.

POLAR BEARS IN CHURCHILL, MANITOBA
Hundreds of polar bears make their way toward the pack ice on Hudson Bay to begin the hunting season.

OLD QUEBEC
Quebec was first founded in 1608, and it is the only North American city north of Mexico that has preserved fortifications from this time.

MONT ROYAL
Walk to the top of Mont Royal for great views over the city. On a clear day, you can see all the way to the Adirondack Mountains in the USA.

OLD MONTREAL
French fur traders used the port in Montreal for close to 400 years. A more permanent French settlement was established in 1642.

LA BANQUISE RESTAURANT
Ready for gooey melted cheese and gravy on French fries? This restaurant serves over 30 varieties of poutine, the Quebec classic.

OTTAWA
Canada's capital is the seventh-coldest on Earth!

RIDEAU CANAL, OTTAWA
Connecting Ottawa with Lake Ontario and the Saint Lawrence River, this canal freezes in winter, making it the largest skating rink in the world.

L'ANSE AUX MEADOWS NATIONAL HISTORIC SITE
Dating from AD 1000, this is North America's only known Viking settlement. The site has reconstructed Norse turf houses.

ATLANTIC OCEAN

ST. JOHN'S, NEWFOUNDLAND
These colorful waterfront houses capture the unique, creative spirit of the town.

OTTAWA

MONTREAL

TORONTO

BAY OF FUNDY
More than 175 billion tons of water move in and out of the Bay of Fundy every day, creating the most extreme tides in the world.

UNITED STATES OF AMERICA

MIGUEL HIDALGO Y COSTILLA
1753–1811
Miguel was a priest who became a leader in the War of Mexican Independence.

TIJUANA

CIUDAD JUAREZ

CENTRO HISTORICO
In Mexico City's heart, you'll find ruins of an Aztec temple, Latin America's oldest cathedral, and a striking domed arts center.

PANCHO VILLA
1878–1923
Mexico's Robin Hood, Pancho was a revolutionary leader who fought for the rights of the poor.

SAN IGNACIO LAGOON
In winter, this lagoon is a top spot to see Eastern Pacific gray whales.

COPPER CANYON
If all six of these interconnecting canyons were joined together, they would be bigger than the USA's Grand Canyon.

XOCHIMILCO CANALS
In Xochimilco, colorful barges sail along quiet canals past floating gardens.

NATIONAL MUSEUM OF ANTHROPOLOGY
This is the largest museum in Mexico with more than 600,000 artifacts. Don't miss the 24-ton Sun Stone.

EL ARCO DE CABO SAN LUCAS
El Arco ("the arch") sits at the very tip of the Baja California Peninsula, where the Pacific Ocean becomes the Gulf of California.

PUERTO VALLARTA
A stroll along Puerto Vallarta's broadwalk is the best of both worlds—beach and city.

MORELIA
This city is known for its beautiful pink stone colonial architecture.

MAYAN RUINS OF CHICHEN ITZA
When the sun hits the central temple during the equinoxes, it crea[tes] a shadow that looks l[ike] a giant snake slitherin[g] down the outside.

HIDDEN BEACH
Swim through a long tunnel to emerge at a secret beach, lapped by crystal waters and lit by an enormous hole in the roof.

TEOTIHUACAN
The ruins of this ancient city show canals, palaces, and plazas.

GUADALAJARA

MEXICO CITY

PUEBLA

CULTURAL INSTITUTE CABAÑAS
Originally built as a hospital, this complex now houses contemporary Mexican art.

MONARCH BUTTERFLY BIOSPHERE RESERVE
Each year, millions of monarch butterflies travel from North America to spend winter here.

OAXACA
Famous as a foodie destination; a popular street snack here is a cup of fried grasshopper[s]

GUACHIMONTONES
This grass-covered stepped pyramid is the 2,000-year-old remnant of the Teuchitlán culture.

ACAPULCO CLIFF DIVERS
Watch in stunned silence as professional high divers leap from the cliffs of La Quebrada into the sea 130 feet below. Please leave this one to the experts!

LA BARRANCA DE HUENTITÁN
On the outskirts of the city is this stunning canyon —walk to the bottom to find thermal pools.

PACIFIC OCEAN

ELSA AVILA
B.1963
Avila is the first Latin American woman to reach the summit of Mount Everest.

FRIDA KAHLO
1907–1954
One of the world's most famous artists, Kahlo used her country's culture as inspiration for her work.

KEY FACTS
THE HOMELAND IS FIRST

CAPITAL Mexico City	**MONEY** Mexican peso	**NATION CODE** MX
LARGEST CITIES Mexico City Guadalajara Puebla Ciudad Juárez Tijuana	**NAMED FOR** The Aztec tribe, the Mexica	**OFFICIAL LANGUAGE** Spanish
POPULATION 129,900,000	**FLOWER** Dahlia 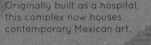	**BIRD** Crested caracara 

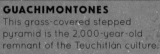

WELCOME TO A COUNTRY OF ANCIENT CULTURES, NATURAL WONDERS, AND STRIKING CITIES

What do you think of when you think about Mexico? Is it the white-sand beaches with shimmering turquoise water? Or the spicy, fragrant food from markets and street stalls? Perhaps it's the spectacular ancient ruins that tell the story of cultures from thousands of years ago? Or maybe you think about modern cities with skyscrapers and bustling plazas? Mexico is all these things and more. It's colorful, busy, loud, and proud.

Few places bring history and culture to life the way Mexico does. One day you can find yourself exploring an ancient Maya temple, the next you could be scuba diving through underground limestone tunnels. There are jungles and mountaintops, mega cities, and local villages. And if that's not enough, you should know . . . Mexico is where chocolate was invented!

MOMENTS TO REMEMBER

1400 BC: The sophisticated Olmec civilization forms.

1000–100 BC: The Maya civilization forms. They build pyramids to honor their gods.

AD 1000–1200: The Maya culture collapses, and the Aztecs arrive in Mexico.

1325–1440: The Aztecs establish the city of Tenochtitlan, and the Aztec Empire expands under Montezuma I.

1517–1521: Spanish explorers arrive. Hernán Cortés defeats the Aztecs and claims the land for Spain. Mexico City is built on the same spot as Tenochtitlan.

1600s: Mexico becomes part of the colony of New Spain and Spanish settlers begin to arrive.

1810–1821: The Mexican War of Independence is fought, ending in Spanish defeat. Mexico becomes a republic.

1846–1848: Mexico and the United States go to war over Texas. When the US occupies Mexico City, Mexico agrees to give up much of its land.

1917: The current Mexican constitution is adopted.

1929: The National Revolutionary Party (later the Institutional Revolutionary Party, or PRI) is formed. They hold power for the next 70 years.

1985: A huge 8.1 magnitude earthquake hits Mexico City, killing over 10,000 people.

2000: Vincente Fox becomes the first president who is not from the PRI party to be elected in over 70 years.

2020: Archeologists discover a 3,000-year-old Maya ceremonial complex, the oldest and largest ever found.

ISLA HOLBOX
This is one of the best places in the world to see flamingos or swim with whale sharks.

ISLA MUJERES
The Maya people saw this island as a place of worship devoted to the goddess of childbirth and medicine.

CENOTE DOS OJOS
Swim in crystal-clear water in this ancient cenote (natural sinkhole). Its name means "two eyes" because there are two interconnecting cenotes.

COZUMEL
The vast barrier reef around the island of Cozumel is perfect for snorkeling or scuba diving.

XEL-HÁ PARK
This is a natural water park, with caves, underground rivers, and water slides.

TULUM
There's no shortage of astounding ruins on the Yucatán Peninsula, but Tulum's Maya castle perched above the sea is hard to beat.

BONAMPAK MURALS
Inside the Temple of the Murals at this ancient Maya site, you'll see bold paintings depicting battles and sacrifices.

CARIBBEAN SEA

MONTEZUMA
C.1398–1469
The second Aztec emperor and fifth king of Tenochtitlan, he put all his effort into strengthening and expanding Aztec rule.

MEXICO

THE LAND OF THE FREE

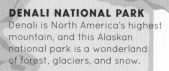

DENALI NATIONAL PARK
Denali is North America's highest mountain, and this Alaskan national park is a wonderland of forest, glaciers, and snow.

The USA really does have it all! It's the fourth-largest country in the world and has an abundance of natural resources that have made it one of the wealthiest places on Earth. It's full of large cities, beautiful national parks, and more movie stars than you can count!

The modern city as we know it, with skyscrapers and freeways, was born in the USA—and the names of many American cities are known throughout the world. This is largely due to another major export of the USA—TV and movies. Hollywood has been making movies for more than 100 years, and American TV shows are broadcast almost everywhere.

One of the USA's most famous exports must be fast food! Hamburgers, hot dogs, and fries—is it possible that you've never eaten fast food? It seems very unlikely!

WAIKIKI BEACH
Clear water, white sand, and a city built to the edge makes this beach on the island of O'ahu in Hawai'i a must-swim destination!

GOLDEN GATE BRIDGE
The bridge is an icon of San Francisco, even if it's not golden at all! The red steel structure was completed in 1937.

YOSEMITE VALLEY
Sheer stone cliffs 3,000 feet high ring Yosemite Valley. Check out the rock climbers on the walls!

YELLOWSTONE NATIONAL PARK
Marvel at geysers, mud volcanoes, bears, and bison at the USA's first national park.

MOUNT RUSHMORE
At around 60 feet tall, the four faces of US presidents George Washington, Thomas Jefferson, Theodore Roosevelt, and Abraham Lincoln are carved into the rock.

DEATH VALLEY
This is the hottest, driest, lowest place in the USA. Despite that, it has snow-capped mountains!

MESA VERDE NATIONAL PARK
This site is famous for the 800-year-old stone dwellings nested in the cliffs.

UNIVERSAL STUDIOS
This movie studio has been running since 1912. Some of the world's most popular films have been made here.

LOS ANGELES ✳

PHOENIX ✳

UFO MUSEUM & RESEARCH CENTER
Read stories about extra-terrestrial encounters at this museum in the town of Roswell, New Mexico.

DISNEYLAND
Walt Disney was an animator and entrepreneur who created the most famous theme park in the world.

THE NEON MUSEUM
Las Vegas is a neon wonderland, so of course there's a museum celebrating these bright gassy tubes.

HOUSTON ✳

GRAND CANYON
Two billion years of history can be seen in the canyon walls, in layers of stone eroded by the Colorado River.

KEY FACTS	IN GOD WE TRUST	
CAPITAL Washington, DC	**MONEY** US dollar	**NATION CODE** US
LARGEST CITIES New York Los Angeles Chicago Houston Phoenix	**NAMED FOR** Italian explorer Amerigo Vespucci	**OFFICIAL LANGUAGE** English
POPULATION 335,600,000	**FLOWER** Rose	**BIRD** Bald eagle 

AMELIA EARHART
1897–1937
The first woman to fly solo across the Atlantic. She and her plane later disappeared as she attempted to fly around the world.

SERENA WILLIAMS
B.1981
Williams holds 23 Grand Slam tennis titles and was ranked the world's number-one player for 319 weeks!

MEXICO

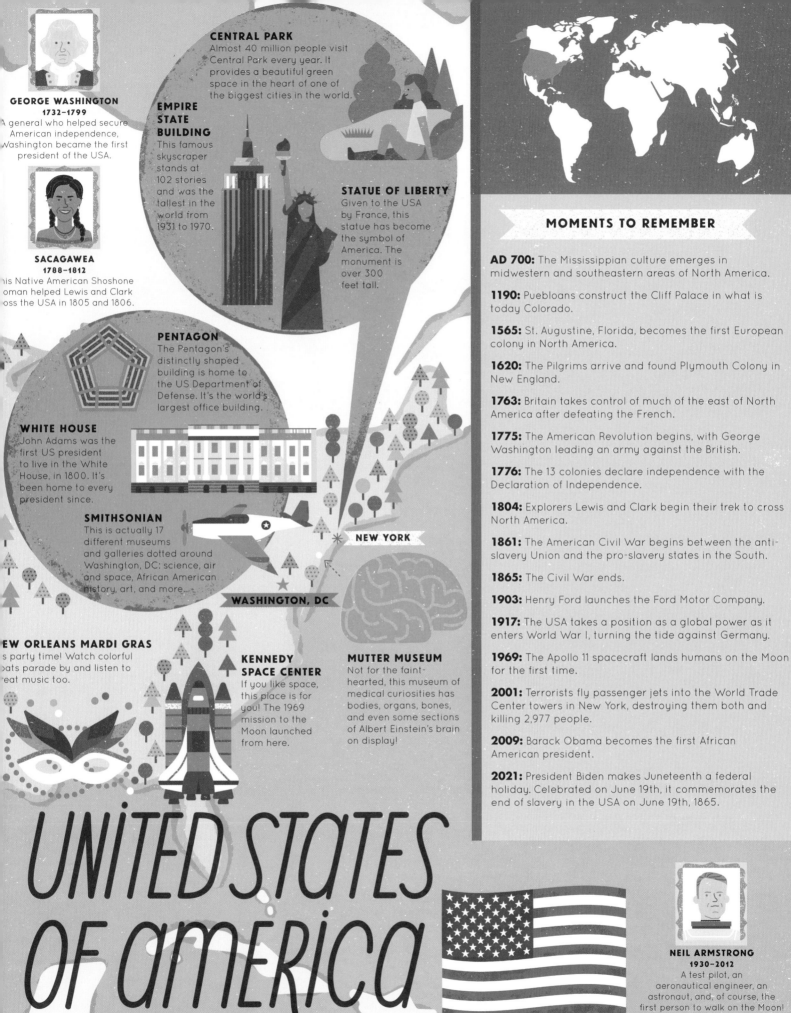

GEORGE WASHINGTON
1732–1799
A general who helped secure American independence, Washington became the first president of the USA.

SACAGAWEA
1788–1812
This Native American Shoshone woman helped Lewis and Clark cross the USA in 1805 and 1806.

CENTRAL PARK
Almost 40 million people visit Central Park every year. It provides a beautiful green space in the heart of one of the biggest cities in the world.

EMPIRE STATE BUILDING
This famous skyscraper stands at 102 stories and was the tallest in the world from 1931 to 1970.

STATUE OF LIBERTY
Given to the USA by France, this statue has become the symbol of America. The monument is over 300 feet tall.

PENTAGON
The Pentagon's distinctly shaped building is home to the US Department of Defense. It's the world's largest office building.

WHITE HOUSE
John Adams was the first US president to live in the White House, in 1800. It's been home to every president since.

SMITHSONIAN
This is actually 17 different museums and galleries dotted around Washington, DC: science, air and space, African American history, art, and more.

NEW YORK

WASHINGTON, DC

NEW ORLEANS MARDI GRAS
It's party time! Watch colorful floats parade by and listen to great music too.

KENNEDY SPACE CENTER
If you like space, this place is for you! The 1969 mission to the Moon launched from here.

MUTTER MUSEUM
Not for the faint-hearted, this museum of medical curiosities has bodies, organs, bones, and even some sections of Albert Einstein's brain on display!

UNITED STATES OF america

MOMENTS TO REMEMBER

AD 700: The Mississippian culture emerges in midwestern and southeastern areas of North America.

1190: Puebloans construct the Cliff Palace in what is today Colorado.

1565: St. Augustine, Florida, becomes the first European colony in North America.

1620: The Pilgrims arrive and found Plymouth Colony in New England.

1763: Britain takes control of much of the east of North America after defeating the French.

1775: The American Revolution begins, with George Washington leading an army against the British.

1776: The 13 colonies declare independence with the Declaration of Independence.

1804: Explorers Lewis and Clark begin their trek to cross North America.

1861: The American Civil War begins between the anti-slavery Union and the pro-slavery states in the South.

1865: The Civil War ends.

1903: Henry Ford launches the Ford Motor Company.

1917: The USA takes a position as a global power as it enters World War I, turning the tide against Germany.

1969: The Apollo 11 spacecraft lands humans on the Moon for the first time.

2001: Terrorists fly passenger jets into the World Trade Center towers in New York, destroying them both and killing 2,977 people.

2009: Barack Obama becomes the first African American president.

2021: President Biden makes Juneteenth a federal holiday. Celebrated on June 19th, it commemorates the end of slavery in the USA on June 19th, 1865.

NEIL ARMSTRONG
1930–2012
A test pilot, an aeronautical engineer, an astronaut, and, of course, the first person to walk on the Moon!

OLD HAVANA
Founded in 1519, the oldest part of Havana is still laid out as it was 500 years ago.

MALECON
This 5-mile-long seaside esplanade is one of Havana's most popular spots for a stroll.

CASTILLO DE LOS TRES REYES DEL MORRO
This fortress had holes built into the back walls so that prisoners could be fed to sharks!

FIDEL CASTRO
1929–2016
Revolutionary and political leader Castro was Cuba's premier and president for nearly 60 years. He made Cuba the first communist state in the Western Hemisphere.

SATURNO CAVE
Dive into the clear blue waters of this underground swimming hole, complete with stalactites and stalagmites.

VARADERO ECOLOGICAL PARK
The top sights in this park are two huge caves containing resident bat colonies and ancient Indigenous rock art.

VARADERO BEACH
Cuba's most famous and exclusive beach resorts are found along these soft white sands.

VIÑALES VALLEY NATIONAL PARK
Spectacular limestone mounds rise from the valley floor, where tobacco plants have been farmed for centuries.

GUANAHACABIBES NATIONAL PARK
This park is popular for scuba diving, but the thousands of scuttling land crabs steal the show.

HAVANA

MATANZAS
Around 500 years ago, pirates hung out in this small bay. These days it's poets, artists, and scholars.

PENINSULA DE ZAPATA
This peninsula has a giant swamp where you might see the world's smallest bird, the bee hummingbird.

SANTA CLARA
Che Guevara's mausoleum is here; there's also a museum with his personal belongings.

SCUBA DIVING AT MARÍA LA GORDA
Legend has it there is pirate treasure buried off the coast here. Even if you can't find it, the coral reefs are a decent alternative.

PLAYA PARAISO
In English this translates as "Paradise Beach." The crystal-clear waters, palm trees, and white sand are pretty close to perfect.

TRINIDAD
Spanish colonialists made lots of money from sugar farming and built grand homes in Trinidad—all painted in vibrant colors.

SANCTI SPÍRITUS
One of the original seven Spanish settlements in Cuba, this pretty city has the country's oldest bridge and oldest church.

FROM REVOLUTION TO NATURE'S RICHES

From Spanish colony to communist state, Cuba has a past filled with invasion and rebellion. Its heroes are those who have fought for its independence and a Cuban identity. Despite a tumultuous history, the natural beauty of this island—the largest in the Caribbean—is beginning to gain the country a new reputation for tourism and biodiversity. Cuba's colonial past is present in the grand buildings of its cities, built on the back of sugarcane and tobacco farming; its future can be seen in the increasing number of national parks and biosphere reserves, where you can see creatures like the miniature bee hummingbird and the tiny Monte Iberia frog, both the smallest of their kind in the world.

Cuba's pre-colonial inhabitants have left their mark on their homeland in the form of rock art and ancient burial sites. It's also possible to visit re-created villages that show how Indigenous tribes lived all those centuries ago. Today's Cubans are proud and fun-loving, with dancing, eating, and promenading all part of everyday life. Who wouldn't want to sing and dance about a place that brings together such a fascinating mix of remote wilderness, grand cities, simple rural villages, steep mountain ranges, and spectacular coastlines?

ALICIA ALONSO
1920–2019
Alonso was a prima ballerina and choreographer who established the Cuban National Ballet Company in 1955.

JAVIER SOTOMAYOR
B.1967
The world record holder for high jump, Sotomayor is the only human being to have jumped 2.45 meters (8 ft).

ANA BETANCOURT
1832–1901
Betancourt fought for Cuban independence from Spain. She was from a wealthy family but lived in the forest with the revolutionaries.

CELIA CRUZ
1925–2003
One of the most popular Latin American singers in the 20th century, Cruz made 37 studio albums and won two Grammy awards.

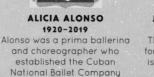

KEY FACTS — HOMELAND OR DEATH, WE SHALL OVERCOME!

CAPITAL
Havana

MONEY
Cuban peso

NATION CODE
CU

LARGEST CITIES
Havana
Santiago de Cuba
Camagüey
Holguin
Guantánamo

NAMED FOR
The Taíno word *cubao* meaning "where fertile land is abundant"

OFFICIAL LANGUAGE
Spanish

FLOWER
Mariposa

BIRD
Cuban trogon

POPULATION
11,200,000

CUBA

CAGUANES NATIONAL PARKS
This coastal park has swamps populated with birds and shy manatees, and over 70 caves.

CAYO COCO
Large colonies of flamingos stop off on their seasonal migration at this beautiful beach.

CAMAGÜEY

SIERRA MAESTRA MOUNTAINS
The highest mountain range in Cuba was used as a remote hideout by revolutionaries such as Fidel Castro.

HOLGUIN

ALEJANDRO DE HUMBOLDT NATIONAL PARK
This park is famous for being one of the most biologically diverse places in the world.

GUAMÁ
There are few places left in Cuba that give an insight into how the ancient Taíno people lived. This re-created village is one.

SANTIAGO DE CUBA

GUANTÁNAMO

CASTILLO DE SAN PEDRO DEL MORRO
After the city of Santiago was raided by pirates in the 16th century, the people decided to build this mighty fortress as protection.

MADRE VIEJA
Peer closely under the ferns in this mountain ridge and you might be lucky enough to see one of the world's tiniest frogs, the Monte Iberia Eleuth.

BARACOA
Cuba's oldest and most isolated town hugs a beautiful bay and is backed by a flat-topped mountain called El Yunque (The Anvil).

PARQUE BACONAO
The residents at this park include rare bats, spiders, and dozens of life-sized models of dinosaurs!

MOMENTS TO REMEMBER

1000 BC: The Guanahatabey people from South America arrive in Cuba.

AD 1200: The Taíno people arrive, settle, and begin farming maize, tobacco, yucca plants, and cotton.

1492: Explorer Christopher Columbus becomes the first European to arrive in Cuba. He claims the country for Spain.

1511: Diego Velazquez establishes the first Spanish settlement, known as Baracoa. The Europeans also introduce diseases, which kill thousands of Taíno people.

1607: Havana is named the capital of Cuba.

1898: Cuban independence fighters join the USA in a war against Spain; when the USA is victorious, Cuba becomes its protectorate.

1902: Cuba becomes independent, but leases Guantánamo Bay to the USA.

1952–1959: Fulgencio Batista becomes dictator of Cuba. Many unhappy Cubans support a revolution by rebel leader Fidel Castro. Castro overthrows Batista and declares Cuba a socialist country and ally of Russia.

1961–1962: Cuba is caught in the middle of the Cold War between the USA and the Soviet Union. The USA fails to overthrow Castro in the Bay of Pigs invasion.

2002: Following the collapse of the Soviet Union in 1991 Russia begins to lose influence, and in this year, the last Russian military base on Cuba is closed.

2008: Fidel Castro retires and hands over power to his brother, Raul.

2015: US President Barrack Obama and Raul Castro reestablish diplomatic ties between the two countries.

ISCHIGUALASTO
Ancient rock formations dot this barren park, also known as the Valley of the Moon.

TAFÍ DEL VALLE MENHIRES
Los Menhires Archeological Park is home to 50 carved standing stones that are almost 3,000 years old.

BOLIVIA

BRAZIL

CAMPO DEL CIELO METEORITE FIELD
This crater field was created by a large iron meteorite that broke up as it entered Earth's atmosphere.

IGUAZÚ FALLS
The Iguazú Falls, on the border with Brazil, is the largest system of waterfalls in the world.

SALINAS GRANDES
This huge salt flat is more than 13,000 feet above sea level and shines bright in the sun!

IBERA WETLANDS
This is the second-largest wetland in the world—look out for anacondas, jaguars, capybaras, caimans, and more!

BORGES MEMORIAL MAZE
Located in the grounds of Finca Los Alamos, this modern hedge maze was designed in honor of the famous author Jorge Luis Borges.

THERMAL BATHS OF VILLAVICENCIO
Jump into the mineral springs at Villavicencio, which apparently have healing properties.

CÓRDOBA

ROSARIO

MENDOZA

URUGUAY

ACONCAGUA
At roughly 23,000 feet tall, this is the tallest mountain in the Southern Hemisphere.

LAGUNA DEL DIAMANTE
This beautiful but toxic lake lies at the foot of a volcano and is home to flamingos.

BUENOS AIRES

GAUCHOS
Gauchos became famous as Argentina's very own cowboys, herding and protecting cattle.

FLORALIS GENÉRICA
This metal sculpture of a flower in Buenos Aires opens in the mornings and closes again in the evenings!

PACIFIC OCEAN

MALBA
Explore the art of Latin America at this modern museum, designed by three Argentinian architects.

BUTCH CASSIDY'S CABIN
Butch Cassidy was an American Wild West criminal who fled to Argentina, where he settled for a while in this cabin.

NAHUEL HUAPI LAKE
Hit this lake for kayaking and fishing. It's a glacial lake, so is a little chilly for swimming!

LA RECOLETA CEMETERY
Considered one of the most beautiful cemeteries in the world, you'll find the tombs of many famous Argentinians here.

CAVE OF HANDS
The stenciled handprints and paintings on the walls of this cave are about 10,000 years old.

CERRO FITZ ROY
This jagged mountain on the border with Chile often appears pink at sunrise.

VALDÉS PENINSULA
Check out this large coastal nature reserve, home to orcas, seals, sea lions, and whales.

ATLANTIC OCEAN

PERITO MORENO GLACIER
This frozen river of ice 19 miles long and 3 miles wide edges its way slowly into Lake Argentino.

BOSQUES PETRIFICADOS DE JARAMILLO NATIONAL PARK
An ancient conifer forest became covered in ash from nearby volcanic eruptions—turning remnants of the forest to stone.

TIERRA DEL FUEGO
This chain of islands at the tip of South America is made up of mountains, glaciers, and fjords—hop in a sea kayak to explore!

ANTARCTIC CRUISE
Jump on a ship from Ushuaia, the most popula starting poir for cruises t Antarctica.

MUSEO DEL FIN DEL MUNDO
Take a tour through the history of the land at the end of the world —shipping, whaling, and historic photos.

USHUAIA

KEY FACTS

CAPITAL
Buenos Aires

MONEY
Argentine peso

NATION CODE
AR

LARGEST CITIES
Buenos Aires
Córdoba
Rosario
Mendoza

NAMED FOR
"Argentum", the Latin
word for "silver"

**OFFICIAL
LANGUAGE**
Spanish

POPULATION
46,600,000

FLOWER
Erythrina

BIRD
Rufous hornero

CHE GUEVARA
1928–1967
Guevara was a
doctor, writer, and
revolutionary who
helped Fidel Castro
overthrow Cuba's
dictatorship.

LIONEL MESSI
B.1987
One of the world's
best soccer players,
Messi has scored
more goals than any
other Argentinian.

JORGE LUIS BORGES
1899–1986
Borges was an
author and poet who
influenced many
writers with his
innovative style.

DIEGO MARADONA
1960–2020
Perhaps the most
famous name in
soccer history,
Maradona led
Argentina to World
Cup victory in 1986.

WELCOME TO THE LAND OF SILVER

Dazzlingly beautiful Argentina is home to long, winding
coastlines, some of the world's tallest mountains, the incredible
Iguazú Falls, magnificent glaciers, and beautiful modern cities.
And a trip to the southern tip of this carrot-shaped country will
have you within a snowball's throw of the Antarctic!

People (or at least, our distant relatives) have lived in
this part of South America for three million years. Argentina
is a country full of natural wonders and a dizzying range of
wildlife. You'll love the llamas, jaguars, and capybaras.

The capital, Buenos Aires, is a colorful and cosmopolitan
city where you can always find something exciting to do.
Maybe discover some of the country's delicious street food, such
as choripán or empanadas, or learn the steps of the great dance
invented here—the tango!

MOMENTS TO REMEMBER

c. AD1400s–1530: The Incas arrive in the lands
that will become Argentina.

1516: Juan Diaz de Solis is the first European to
visit the Incan lands, searching for gold.

1536: The city of Buenos Aires is founded by
Pedro de Mendoza. The city is later abandoned
and re-founded in 1580.

1810: The first government of Argentina forms.

1816: Argentina declares its independence
from Spain.

1853: Argentina becomes a republic with the
launch of its constitution.

1944: The San Juan earthquake leaves a third of
the population homeless.

1946: Juan Perón becomes president.

1947: Argentinian women get the right to vote.

1978: Argentina hosts the FIFA World Cup,
and wins!

1982: The Falklands War with the UK takes place.

2013: Argentina-born Jorge Mario Bergoglio
becomes Catholic Pope Francis.

EVA PERÓN
1919–1952
Actor and activist Eva Perón
was married to President
Juan Perón and was known
as the spiritual leader of
the country.

ARGENTINA

BRAZIL

MOMENTS TO REMEMBER

AD 1500: Portuguese explorer Pedro Álvares Cabral arrives and claims the already-inhabited land for Portugal.

1542: Spanish conquistador Francisco de Orellana completes the first European navigation of the Amazon River.

1654: After a brief occupation by Dutch forces, Portugal fights back and claims ownership of Brazil.

1727: The first coffee bush is planted at Para in the north of the country. Brazil will go on to be the biggest coffee producer in the world.

18th to 19th centuries: Millions of Africans are brought by force to Brazil to be sold as slaves and made to work on the coffee plantations.

1822: Brazil breaks ties with Portugal and declares its independence.

1888: Slavery is abolished.

1889–1891: The monarchy is overthrown in a military coup and Brazil becomes a republic.

1917: Brazil joins World War I on the side of the Allies.

1958: Brazil wins the FIFA World Cup for the first time.

2010: Dilma Rousseff is the first woman to be elected president of Brazil.

2018: Brazil's National Museum burns down in a fire. Millions of priceless artifacts are destroyed.

PELÉ
1940–2022
Of all Brazil's soccer heroes, Pelé is thought by many to have been the best player in the history of the game.

GISELE BÜNDCHEN
B.1980
Winning her first modeling competition aged 13, Bündchen has become one of Brazil's most famous faces.

MARTA VIEIRA DA SILVA
B.1986
Soccer stars don't get much bigger than this! Marta was FIFA's player of the year five years in a row.

AMAZON RIVER DOLPHINS
These pink-colored dolphins have the biggest brains of all dolphin species!

AMAZON RAIN FOREST
If the Amazon rain forest was its own country, it would be one of the largest in the world, at 2 million square miles.

MEETING OF WATERS, MANAU
The pale-colored Rio Solimoes and the dark Rio Negro, converge here . . . and run side by side without mixing for 4 miles!

PANTANAL
The largest wetland on the planet has the biggest concentration of caimans anywhere—more than 10 million!

BONITO REGION
You can explore caves and snorkel in crystal-clear rivers in this ecotourist paradise. Look out for macaws, monkeys, and capybaras!

IGUAZÚ FALLS
This waterfall system on the border with Argentina is made up of 275 waterfalls!

PACIFIC OCEAN

BOLIVIA

PERU

PARAGUAY

WELCOME TO A SHOWCASE OF NATURE'S GREATEST HITS

From wildlife to wild street parties, Brazil has it all! This land of jaw-dropping natural beauty is home to the world's largest rain forest and the second-largest river, both known as the Amazon—it's no wonder that the country is home to over 150,000 species of plants and animals, including jaguars, pumas, sloths, armadillos, tapirs, toucans, and over 75 species of monkey. And it's not just rain forest that can be found here—there are waterfalls, wetlands, mountains, dunes, beaches, and blue lagoons too.

As well as being famous for its natural wonders, Brazil hosts an enormous street party called Carnival. At Carnival, you'll see people in colorful costumes dancing on elaborately decorated floats that parade through the city. When Brazilians aren't kicking their heels up at Carnival, you're likely to see crowds flocking to the spectacular beaches such as Rio de Janeiro's Copacabana or cheering wildly at a soccer game.

SÃO MIGUEL DAS MISSÕES
These ruins were once home to Jesuit missionaries and the local Indigenous population they were trying to convert.

URUGUAY

ARGENTINA

ATLANTIC OCEAN

CAPITAL	MONEY	NATION CODE
Brasília	Real	BR
LARGEST CITIES	**NAMED FOR**	**OFFICIAL LANGUAGE**
São Paulo Rio de Janeiro Brasília Salvador	The brazilwood tree	Portuguese
POPULATION	**FLOWER**	**BIRD**
218,700,000	Yellow ipê	Rufous-bellied thrush

FERNANDO DE NORONHA
This archipelago is a protected marine park, home to sea turtles, dolphins, stingrays, and reef sharks.

...NÇÓIS MARANHENSES ...ATIONAL PARK
...certain times of year, ...nwater creates huge ...e lagoons among ...e vast, sloping ...nd dunes here.

FORTALEZA

CATHEDRAL OF BRASÍLIA
With its circular floorplan and stained-glass ceiling, this curvy cathedral is like no other on Earth.

POÇO ENCANTADO AND POÇO AZUL
When sunlight hits the blue water in these caves, it becomes so clear that swimmers look like they're floating on air.

PORTO DE GALINHAS
This beach is famous for its turquoise waters, white sand, and reef pools packed with marine life.

SALVADOR

PELOURINHO, SALVADOR
The oldest part of Salvador is full of colorful colonial buildings. It was once a marketplace for the slave trade.

BRASÍLIA

INHOTIM MUSEUM, BRUMADINHO
At this modern, open-air museum, 500 artworks are displayed in beautiful botanic gardens.

OURO PRETO
Gold and gemstones mined in the nearby hills allowed this colonial city to build beautiful buildings.

RIO DE JANEIRO

SÃO PAULO

TARSILA DO AMARAL
1886–1973
Born on a coffee farm in a small town, Tarsila went on to become a famous modernist artist.

OSCAR NIEMEYER
1907–2012
Niemeyer was a modernist architect who designed concrete buildings that look like giant bendy sculptures.

NITERÓI CONTEMPORARY ART MUSEUM
Museum or space ship? This Oscar Niemeyer-designed building is perched on a cliff with panoramic views of Rio de Janeiro.

CHRIST THE REDEEMER
Arms outstretched, this iconic 125-foot-high soapstone statue of Christ towers over Rio de Janeiro.

SUGARLOAF MOUNTAIN
You can take a glass-sided cable car to the summit of this famous peak overlooking the city.

APARADOS DA SERRA NATIONAL PARK
This national park contains the steepest canyons in Brazil. From the top, it's a sheer 2,300-foot drop to the canyon floor!

MASP
Like a giant Lego brick on São Paulo's busiest street, this gallery contains more than 10,000 works of art.

LIBERDADE
Home to the biggest Japanese population outside Japan, Liberdade feels more like Tokyo than São Paulo.

MUSEU DO FUTEBOL
Discover Brazil's love of the "beautiful game" at this interactive museum.

COPACABANA BEACH
This 2.5-mile beach becomes the biggest party on the planet during Carnival.

JARDIM BOTÂNICO
There are 8,000 different plant types in Rio's botanic gardens, including over 600 species of exotic orchids!

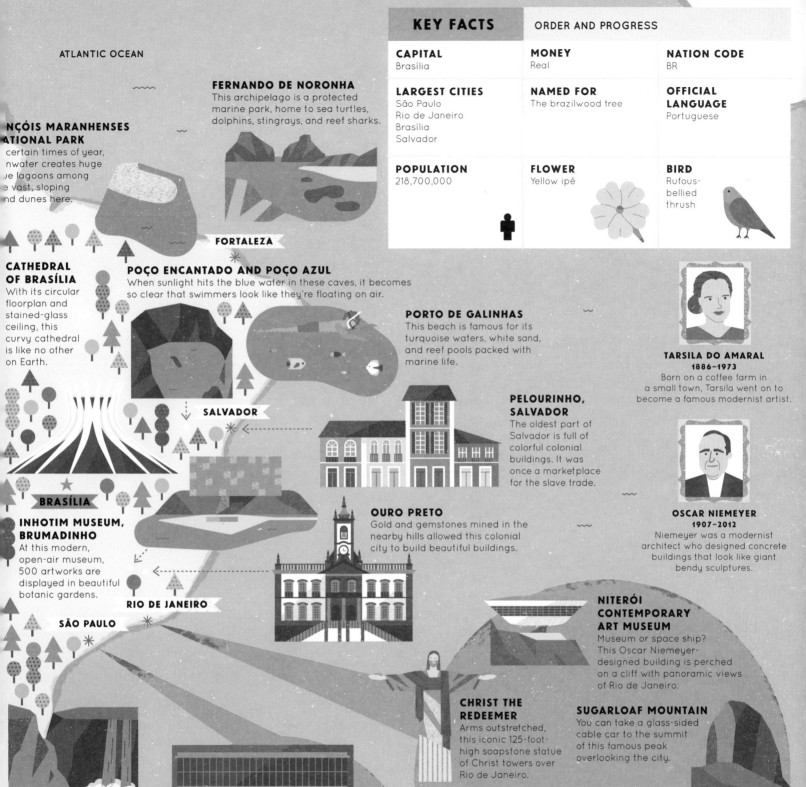

PERU

MOMENTS TO REMEMBER

8000 BC: Human beings are living in the Ancash region of Peru, apparently farming crops.

900–200 BC: Chavin culture develops; the people construct a temple complex at Chavin de Huantar.

200 BC–AD 600: The Nazca culture creates the mysterious Nazca Lines, patterns and drawings of animals best seen from the air.

100 BC–AD 700: Moche culture rises to power. Their rulers are entombed at Huaca Rajada in Sipán.

1200: The Incas begin to absorb small tribes in the Cusco area under the leadership of Manco Capac.

1460: The ninth Inca, Pachacutec, builds the magnificent Machu Picchu.

1533: Civil war breaks out between the Inca empires and the civilization is destroyed.

1534–1543: Spanish conquistadors invade Cusco; Lima becomes the first capital of this new colonial government.

1810–1824: Peruvians wage a war of independence against the Spanish, clinching victory in 1824.

1879: Chile declares war on Peru and Bolivia.

1948–2000: Peru's political leadership seesaws between military coups and free elections.

1998: A peace treaty is made with Ecuador, ending a long-running dispute between the two countries.

2007: A huge 7.9 magnitude earthquake hits Pisco province, destroying 85% of the city's buildings.

2010: Novelist Mario Vargas Llosa receives the Nobel Prize in Literature.

PACHACUTEC INCA YUPANQUI
C.1418–1471
This powerful Inca ruler expanded the Kingdom of Cusco and founded Machu Picchu.

LADY OF CAO
C. AD 420–450
Mummified 1,700 years ago, she wears a gold crown, leading archeologists to believe she was a powerful Moche priestess.

ECUADOR

KUELAP
The Chachapoya culture built this walled settlement in the 6th century to house 300,000 people.

GOCTA WATERFALL
Water plunges nearly 2,600 feet to the jungle floor below. Can you hear the call of howler monkeys over the noise?

MOCHE MUMMIES AT HUACA RAJADA, SIPÁN
Inside these pyramids, archeologists discovered the mummified remains of Moche leaders along with valuable artifacts.

✳ **PIURA**

CHICLAYO

HUACA DEL SOL AND HUACA DE LA LUNA
The Moche culture used the Sun Temple for administrative purposes and the Moon Temple for ceremonies.

✳ **TRUJILLO**

CHACHAPOYA MUMMIES, LAGUNA DE LAS MOMIAS
Hundreds of mummies were entombed in this steep rockface. Some are now in museums, but many still remain.

LAGUNA 69, CORDILLERA BLANCA
One of around 300 lakes in the Huascarán National Park, Lake 69 is a spectacular bright blue.

MARKAWASI
This towering mountain range looks like it's made up of hundreds of faces carved into the rock.

CHAVIN DE HUANTAR
Some believe that the pitch-dark passageways in this ancient temple complex were created to make it seem like any sounds were the voice of a god.

LIMA

MAGIC WATER CIRCUIT
Winding paths circle 13 enormous fountains in this park. At night, they light up like a kaleidoscope!

ISLA BALLESTAS
A birdwatcher's paradise: pelicans, penguins, and boobies all use Ballestas as a base.

HUACA PUCLLANA
The Indigenous Lima culture built clay pyramids like this one before the reign of the Incas.

CONVENTO DE SAN FRANCISCO
In the crypt of this monastery lie the bones of 70,000 people, laid out in strange patterns!

HUACACHINA
It might look like a movie set, but this desert oasis is the real deal, complete with lagoon, palm trees, and sand dunes.

NAZCA LINES
It's still a mystery as to why the Nazca people etched these enormous lines, patterns, and drawings of animals into the ground.

MARIO VARGAS LLOSA
B.1936
Peru's most famous writer, Vargas Llosa is also known for being a politician, journalist, and professor.

PACAYA-SAMIRIA NATIONAL RESERVE
Taking a dip in one of the world's most magnificent rivers becomes a truly magical experience if you manage to see a Peruvian manatee.

IQUITOS

DORIS GIBSON PARRA DEL RIEGO
1910–2008
During a time when women were expected to stay at home, Doris Gibson started up one of Peru's most successful magazines.

BRAZIL

MACHU PICCHU
This stunning Inca citadel, built high in the Andean Mountains, is one of the most famous archeological sites in the world.

RAMÓN CASTILLA
1797–1867
Castilla was a Peruvian president who abolished slavery; he also worked to build schools and improve transport.

OLLANTAYTAMBO
Five-hundred-year-old Inca ruins surround this Sacred Valley village.

PISAC MARKET
This bustling craft market is a great place to buy handmade crafts or sample local delicacies like roasted "cuy" (guinea pig!).

CUSCO

COLCA CANYON
This gigantic canyon is twice as deep as the Grand Canyon in the US; giant Andean condors can be seen coasting on updrafts.

BOLIVIA

AREQUIPA

SILLUSTANI
These cylindrical structures look like watchtowers, but they're prehistoric tombs once used by the Qulla people.

LAKE TITICACA
The Incas believed that this lake was the birthplace of the Sun, so there are many ancient ruins around its banks.

CHILE

WELCOME TO THE LAND OF ANCIENT CULTURES AND NATURAL WONDERS

The sights of Peru defy imagination—the country is home to a large part of the world's biggest rain forest, the second-highest mountain range, ancient cultures, mountaintop temples, gigantic canyons, desert oases, the highest navigable lake on Earth, and mysterious lines carved into the ground that are perhaps thousands of years old (and best seen from the air).

The rich and powerful Inca culture dominated Peru for hundreds of years and left countless ancient ruins. But there were many Indigenous cultures that existed before them, like the Moche culture, who buried their dead in pyramids with precious artifacts. In more recent times, Spanish conquistadors colonized the country, building churches and introducing the Spanish language. Peru's cities tell the story of these ancient cultures and colonization, and today you'll find cathedrals built on the ruins of temples.

In South America's third-largest country, be prepared to encounter spectacular landscapes, fascinating ancient cultures, prehistoric sites, unusual wildlife, and unique cuisine. Word of warning, the humble guinea pig is something of a national dish —you might want to check before you chomp.

KEY FACTS
FIRM AND HAPPY FOR THE UNION

CAPITAL Lima	**MONEY** Sol	**NATION CODE** PE
LARGEST CITIES Lima Arequipa Trujillo Chiclayo Piura Iquitos	**NAMED FOR** A local ruler, Birú, who was encountered by Spanish explorers in the early 16th century	**OFFICIAL LANGUAGES** Spanish, and co-official languages including Quechua and Aymara
POPULATION 32,400,000	**FLOWER** Cantuta	**BIRD** Andean cock-of-the-rock

KORIKANCHA (SUN TEMPLE) AND CHURCH OF SANTO DOMINGO
The temple of Korikancha was the Inca's tribute to the sun god. It was destroyed by Spanish conquistadors, who built the Church of Santo Domingo on the ruins.

PLAZA DE ARMAS
The city's central square is lined with restaurants and coffee shops. In the middle stands a huge statue of the Inca ruler Patchacutec.

INTI RAYMI FESTIVAL
This colorful Inca festival takes place in the temple ruins of Sacsayhuamán during the winter solstice, to celebrate the coming of the Sun.

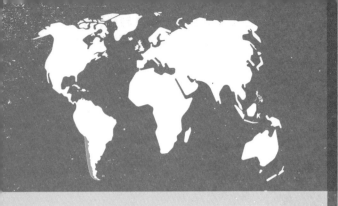

KEY FACTS BY RIGHT OR MIGHT

CAPITAL Santiago	**MONEY** Chilean peso	**NATION CODE** CL
LARGEST CITIES Santiago Valparaíso Concepción Puente Alto Antofagasta	**NAMED FOR** From the Indigenous Mapuche word *chilli*, meaning "where the land ends" or "the deepest point of the Earth"	**OFFICIAL LANGUAGES** Chilean Spanish, and Indigenous languages including Mapudungun
POPULATION 18,500,000	**FLOWER** Chilean bellflower	**BIRD** Andean condor

RAPA NUI (EASTER ISLAND)
Chile claimed this Polynesian island in 1888. On it they found over 900 enormous stone statues with oversized heads, known as moai.

MOMENTS TO REMEMBER

14,000 BC: Nomadic tribes are living in the area that is now Chile.

8000–1000 BC: The Chinchorro tribe becomes the dominant civilization. They begin farming and fishing.

AD 200: The Mapuche people start to emerge as the leading tribe in the area.

c.1475: Incas invade Northern Chile and push south until they're stopped by the Mapuche at the Battle of the Maule.

1520: Portuguese explorer Magellan is the first European to see Chile when he sails around the southern tip.

1540–1541: Pedro de Valdivia claims Chile for Peru (which is under Spanish rule); he becomes the governor of Chile and establishes Santiago.

1807–1818: Spain is conquered by France, so Chile takes its chance to declare independence. Spanish troops and Chilean independence fighters battle it out until the Spanish resistance is overpowered.

1850s: Mapuche tribes begin a series of rebellions against the government. They are eventually quashed.

1949: Women are given the right to vote (men were granted the same right 24 years earlier).

1973: General Augusto Pinochet leads a military coup to overthrow the government. He establishes a brutal dictatorship where his opponents are persecuted or killed.

2010: Thirty-three miners are trapped underground in Copiapó for 69 days before they are all rescued!

2014: After becoming the first woman to be Chile's president in 2006, Michelle Bachelet becomes the first woman to be reelected.

2019: A rise in subway fares in Santiago sparks months of mass demonstrations and riots around the country, in protest against inequality and living costs.

GET TO KNOW A LAND OF GLACIERS AND GEYSERS

Measuring 2,653 miles in length along the west coast of the South American continent, but only 276 miles across at its widest point, Chile is the narrowest country on Earth. Despite Chile's skinny shape it doesn't scrimp on amazing sights, cultural cities, fascinating history, or mind-blowing natural wonders. The southernmost tip of the country is the jumping-off point for Antarctica, while in the north is the Atacama Desert, a moon-like landscape that is the driest place on the planet. From desert sands, active volcanoes, and geothermal fields packed with geysers, to snowfields, creeping glaciers, and coastal caves carved from marble, Chile packs a world of beauty within its borders.

Chile's Indigenous peoples, the Mapuche, have inhabited Southern Chile for over 2,000 years and have fought hard to retain their culture, languages, and land; today they make up nearly 10% of the Chilean population. Chile was conquered by Spain in the 16th century and remained under Spanish rule until declaring independence in 1818. Despite conquests and civil wars, Chileans are fiercely proud of their country and it is one of the most beautiful countries in South America.

CHILE

PABLO NERUDA
1904–1973
Neruda's father wanted him to study math, but he had other plans. He began writing poetry and went on to win the Nobel Prize in Literature in 1971.

RODOLFO AMANDO PHILIPPI
1808–1904
Philippi was a paleontologist and zoologist who described three new species of South American lizards.

LAKE CHUNGARÁ, LAUCA NATIONAL PARK
Llamas and alpacas graze at the edge of this lake, overlooked by the snow-capped peak of the Parinacota volcano.

THE HUMBERSTONE AND SANTA LAURA SALTPETER WORKS
The discovery of synthetic nitrate for gunpowder turned these sodium nitrate mines into ghost towns.

VALLE DE LA LUNA (MOON VALLEY)
Parts of the Atacama Desert have never seen rain, which has created landscapes that look like the Moon.

TATIO GEYSERS
Over 80 geysers shoot up steam and hot water in this geothermal field. Watch where you step!

ANTOFAGASTA

ARGENTINA

HAND OF THE DESERT
Artist Mario Irarrázabal created this enormous sculpture of a stone hand, which rises from the sand in the Atacama Desert.

OJOS DEL SALADO
This is the highest point in Chile and the highest active volcano in the world, at 23,000 feet.

CHILE'S LARGEST SWIMMING POOL
A giant 20-acre pool in Algarrobo costs over $2 million a year to keep running!

ELQUI VALLEY
High elevation and cloud-free nights make this one of the best places on the planet to stargaze.

ROBINSON CRUSOE ISLAND
The true story of a young man marooned on this island for four years with only a musket, a knife, a Bible, and some tools, inspired the famous book.

VALPARAÍSO

SANTIAGO

CERRO SAN CRISTÓBAL
For the best views over Chile's capital city, hike or take a cable car to the mountain peak of Cerro San Cristóbal.

PARQUE QUINTA NORMAL
Have a picnic, hire a paddle boat, or check out a creepy 170-year-old crumbling greenhouse in this park.

PUENTE ALTO

LA ARAUCANÍA
This is the best place to get to know the ancient culture of the Mapuche people, including their intricate jewelry-making techniques.

VILLARRICA VOLCANO, PUCON
Venture into some of the only accessible volcanic caves on Earth at this active volcano.

MUSEUM OF MEMORY AND HUMAN RIGHTS
This museum commemorates those who disappeared during the dark years of Pinochet's dictatorship.

CONCEPCIÓN

TERMAS GEOMETRICAS, PANGUIPULLI
These natural hot springs are hidden deep in a lush forest; each of the 17 pools are connected by red wooden walkways.

PUMALIN PARK
An American billionaire bought the land that is now Pumalin Park in 1991 to preserve its landscape of glaciers, volcanoes, rain forests, lakes, and rivers.

GABRIELA MISTRAL
1889–1957
Mistral was the first Latin American to win a Nobel Prize in Literature. She won in 1945.

CHILEAN LAKE DISTRICT
Hike through beautiful scenery or ski on the slopes of active volcanoes!

CHILOE ISLAND
The largest of Chile's offshore islands is home to the world's smallest deer, the pudú.

QUEULAT NATIONAL PARK
The park's Hanging Glacier perches precariously over the edge of a cliff.

CAVERNAS DE MARMOL, LAKE CARRERA
Waves lapping at this marble peninsula have created spectacular caves that are lit up by the bright blue water on a sunny day.

ATLANTIC OCEAN

MARIO HAMUY
B.1960
Hamuy is an astronomer who studies supernovae, stars that explode at the end of their life.

CHINCHORRO MUMMIES
7020–5050 BC
Egyptian mummies get all the attention, but the Chinchorro mummies, in the north of Chile, are the oldest mummies on the planet by at least 2,000 years.

GREY GLACIER, TORRES DEL PAINE NATIONAL PARK
Part of the Southern Patagonian Ice Field, this 4-mile-wide glacier occasionally carves off huge icebergs into Grey Lake.

LOS PINGÜINOS NATURAL MONUMENT
Magdalena Island in the Strait of Magellan has no human inhabitants but thousands of, you guessed it, penguins.

TIERRA DEL FUEGO
The southernmost tip of the South American continent is claimed by both Chile and Argentina and is the jumping-off point for Antarctica.

EVO MORALES
B.1959
President of Bolivia 2006–19, he was the first to come from the country's Indigenous population.

CARMEN ROSA
B.1970
The founder of Bolivia's first Indigenous and female-run wrestling foundation, Rosa fights in her traditional dress and is known in her hometown of La Paz as "The Champion."

PERU

MADIDI NATIONAL PARK
This park in the Amazon River basin is home to jaguars, ocelots, spectacled bears, giant otters, and pink dolphins.

VALLE DE LAS ANIMAS
These towering spires of mud rock are so unusual that locals once believed they were the petrified souls of people reaching for the sky.

CABLE CAR
Some cities have buses, but La Paz goes one better with its cable car public transport system.

VALLE DE LA LUNA
The mountains of "Moon Valley" have been eroded into intricate peaks.

APACHETA CHUCHURA PASS
This is the highest point on the popular El Choro hiking trail, an ancient Inca path.

BOLIVIAN DEATH ROAD
No prizes for guessing how this road got its name—one side has a sheer 2,000-foot drop.

THE WITCHES' MARKET
The streets of this strange market are lined with potions and charms used to cast spells.

ISLA DEL SOL
The Incans believed this was the birthplace of the Sun. It's easy to see why when you watch the sunrise over the world's highest lake.

COPACABANA
Red-roofed Copacabana sits pretty on the banks of Lake Titicaca, the largest lake in South America.

NOEL KEMPFF MERCADO NATIONAL PARK
This pristine park is named after the biologist who first campaigned to protect the area.

EL ALTO ✳ LA PAZ

NOEL KEMPFF MERCADO
1924–1986
A pioneering biologist and environmentalist, Mercado was tragically murdered by drug traffickers.

SAJAMA NATIONAL PARK
Highlights at this remote park include volcanoes, thermal springs, and the highest forests in the world.

TIWANAKU
This archeological site was the capital city of an ancient empire.

GUEMBE BIOCENTER
You can visit the world's biggest butterfly sanctuary here.

COCHABAMBA

SANTA CRUZ DE LA SIERRA ✳

ORURO

PAMPAS DEL YACUM
Anacondas, caimans, and capybaras are just a few of the creatures found in this national park.

POTOSÍ
Potosí became the biggest city in the Americas after silver was discovered nearby in 1545.

SUCRE

LIDIA GUEILER TEJADA
1921–2011
Bolivia's first female president, she was the second woman to hold this position in the Americas.

SALAR DE UYUNI
The world's biggest and most spectacular salt flat is so blindingly white you'll need sunglasses!

SUCRE
Beautiful Sucre is known as the White City because of its whitewashed buildings.

LAGUNA HEDIONDA
Its name in English means "stinky lake," but that doesn't seem to bother all the flamingos that stop off here on their migration.

TRAIN CEMETERY
Ever wondered what happens to trains when they stop working? It seems as though they all come here!

ARTHUR POSNANSKY
1873–1946
This archeologist, entrepreneur, and explorer was born in Austria but became a Bolivian citizen. He introduced the first car to Bolivia!

ÁRBOL DE PIEDRA
The bizarre "Stone Tree" was formed by sand being whipped by wind against the rock.

CERRO RICO
The "Rich Mountain" is also known as the "mountain that eats men" because of the deadly conditions miners were forced to work under to extract silver.

SOL DE MAÑANA
Watch the earth bubble and steam in this colorful geyser field dotted with aqua-hued pools.

SALVADOR DALÍ DESERT
The eerie landscapes of this desert have been compared to the surreal paintings of Salvador Dalí.

ARGENTINA

Once part of the powerful Incan civilization until defeated by Spanish conquistadors in the 16th century, Indigenous Bolivians lived under the rule of the Spanish until the country became independent in 1825. Bolivia has struggled through political instability, with revolutions, uprisings, and riots. But through it all, Bolivia's rich Indigenous history has survived, and you can find examples of ancient civilizations all over the country, from burial towers to city ruins and centuries-old pilgrimage routes.

Bolivians speak over 35 different languages and are loyal and proud of their heritage. Bolivia's human history and human-made sights are stunning, but it's the beautiful landscapes that make Bolivia a must-see destination.

Of the overabundance of Bolivia's natural wonders, there are some world-beaters—including the highest lake on Earth, Lake Titicaca, and the largest salt lake on the planet, Salar de Uyuni. There are active volcanoes, geyser fields, snow-capped peaks, mountains full of silver, jungles filled with jaguars, and deserts with curious rock formations. And we haven't even begun on the cities, with their whitewashed buildings, fascinating markets, and busy cable cars. Get to know South America's jewel of a country.

MOMENTS TO REMEMBER

1st century AD: The Aymara people find the Tiwanaku civilization and build an enormous city.

1400s: Incans expand their empire to include parts of what is now Bolivia.

1538: Spanish forces conquer the area now known as Bolivia; it was called Upper Peru.

1545: Silver is discovered at Cerro Rico in Potosí—it becomes one of the richest silver mines in history.

1824–1825: Simón Bolívar, the Venezuelan freedom fighter, liberates Bolivia from Peru, and becomes the country's first president.

1879–84: Bolivia loses territory to Chile and becomes landlocked in the process.

1932: Bolivia and Paraguay go to war over an area of land believed to be rich in oil. Both sides suffer huge loss of life, and Bolivia loses the war.

1952: The Bolivian Revolution occurs—power shifts from the white ruling class to Indigenous communities.

1960–1970s: Bolivia suffers through a series of military coups; the decades are characterized by corruption and human-rights abuses.

1990: Four million acres of rain forest are allocated to Indigenous peoples.

2006: Evo Morales becomes the first Indigenous Bolivian to be elected president.

2019: Morales resigns amid allegations that he rigged an election.

KEY FACTS
UNITY IS STRENGTH

CAPITALS
Sucre and La Paz

MONEY
Boliviano

NATION CODE
BO

LARGEST CITIES
Santa Cruz de la Sierra
El Alto
La Paz
Cochabamba
Oruro

NAMED FOR
Simón Bolívar—the Venezuelan leader in the war of Spanish American independence

OFFICIAL LANGUAGES
Spanish and 36 Indigenous languages

FLOWER
Kantuta

BIRD
Andean condor

POPULATION
12,200,000

PARAGUAY

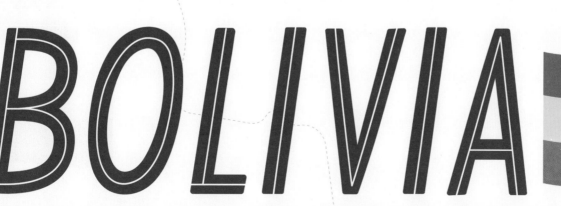

MOMENTS TO REMEMBER

9790 BC: Tibitó, north of Bogotá, is the site of the earliest human occupation in Colombia.

AD 1525–1538: The first permanent Spanish settlement is established at Santa Marta; conquistador Gonzalo Jiménez de Quesada discovers gold in the Andes.

1700s: Spain joins together Colombia, Venezuela, Ecuador, and Panama, and names the huge colony the Viceroyalty of New Granada.

1819: Colombia gains independence and Simón Bolívar becomes the first Colombian president.

1903: Panama splits from Colombia with the support of the USA, giving the USA control over the Panama Canal.

1948–1958: A civil war between those on the liberal and those on the conservative side of politics breaks out and over 250,000 people are killed.

1984: The country is plagued by violence between powerful drug cartels (associations) and the government.

2000: Colombia receives nearly US $1 billion in aid to help fight drug trafficking.

2007: The Nevado del Huila volcano, the highest in Colombia, erupts after being dormant for 500 years.

2012: The government begins peace talks with rebel leaders responsible for the drug trade.

2014: For the first time, the Colombian men's soccer team makes it to the quarter-finals of the FIFA World Cup.

2016: The government signs a historic peace deal with rebel forces, ending more than 50 years of drug-related violence.

2023: The women's soccer team become national heroes when they reach the quarter-finals of the FIFA Women's World Cup.

PARQUE ARVI
Medellín is Colombia's second-largest city, but you can escape the crowds at this nature reserve.

FLOWER FESTIVAL
Each year the city celebrates the annual flower festival with parades, pageants, and concerts.

PLAZA BOTERO
Fernando Botero is Colombia's most famous sculptor. This park is filled with his wonderful creations.

CABO SAN JUAN
You can only reach this tropical beach paradise by a two-hour hike.

BARRANQUILLA

CARTAGENA

EL PEÑÓN DE GUATAPÉ, ANTIOQUIA
The criss-cross staircase that takes you to the top of this massive rock has 649 steps!

MARÍA CANO
1887–1967
Colombia's first female political leader, Cano fought for civil and workers' rights. She was also a writer and poet.

SHAKIRA
B.1977
Singer-songwriter Shakira has sold over 140 million albums worldwide and has won more than 400 awards for her music.

CARLOS VALDERRAMA
B.1961
Valderrama played in 111 international games for the Colombian national soccer team, scoring 11 times.

LA CUEVA DEL ESPLENDOR
Walk inside this mountain cave and be awed by the waterfall cascading from a hole in the roof.

MEDELLÍN

THE COCORA VALLEY
The palm trees in ths valley are the tallest in the world, up to 200 feet tall!

TATACOA DESERT
Visit two distinct landscapes— the craggy red desert and the Moon-like gray desert.

CALI

SAN AGUSTÍN ARCHEOLOGICAL PARK
Statues of gods and mythical creatures are dotted around this park, making up the largest group of religious monuments in South America.

CAJONA CANYON, LAS DALIAS NATURAL RESERVE
This narrow canyon is lined on both sides with tropical rain forest.

COLOMBIA

PERU

TAROA DUNES, GUAJIRA
At the most northerly part of South America, steep sand dunes plunge into the Caribbean waters.

LOS FLAMENCOS SANCTUARY, GUAJIRA
Flocks of stately flamingos feed and roost at this wildlife sanctuary.

CIUDAD PERDIDA
High in the mountains are the 1,000-year-old ruins of an ancient Tairona settlement. The lost city was discovered by hunters in 1972.

THE POISON DART FROG, EL CHOCÓ
If you spot this colorful little frog in the rain forest, be sure to only look, not touch —its skin is so poisonous it can kill you.

CHICAMOCHA CANYON, SANTANDER
This is the second-largest canyon in the world!

LAS GACHAS, SANTANDER
The stream running along this riverbed has formed dozens of circular pools—pick one and take a dip!

★ **BOGOTÁ**

LAGUNA NEGRA, GUAVIARE
On a still day, this jungle lake creates a crystal-clear reflection of the sky.

NUEVO TOLIMA, GUAVIARE
The rock paintings here were created thousands of years ago by Indigenous tribes.

CAÑO CRISTALES
Between June and November, a species of plant blooms underwater in this river, making it bright red with spots of green and yellow.

COLORFUL CITIES AND NATURAL WONDERS

Sitting right at the top of South America, Colombia gets its name from the Italian explorer Christopher Columbus, who led the colonization of the Americas. Before Columbus, it was a Spanish colony called New Granada, and before that it was home to the ancient civilizations of the Quimbaya, the Chibcha, and the Kalina. Evidence of these civilizations can still be seen across the country in the form of religious monuments and city ruins.

The human history of Colombia is a fascinating one, but it's fair to say that the country tells its most exciting story through its stunning scenery. Colombia has coastlines along the Caribbean Sea and the Pacific Ocean, which makes for some beautiful beaches. Away from the coast, you'll find everything from tropical rain forests to snow-capped mountains. You'll encounter huge rocks (believed to be the oldest on the planet), ancient canyons, rainbow-colored rivers, and waterfalls that flow into underground caves.

With topography like this, it won't surprise you that there's some pretty wondrous wildlife here too, including the pint-sized poison dart frog. Colombia really does have it all!

MAVECURE HILLS, GUAINÍA
These three rock mountains are some of the oldest on the planet. Indigenous tribes believed they were houses for the gods.

BOLÍVAR SQUARE
This square at the heart of Bogotá has been used as a circus ground and even a bullfighting ring.

MONSERRATE
The mountain of Monserrate towers over the capital city and is topped with a whitewashed church.

GOLD MUSEUM
Discover the world's largest collection of gold artifacts, sacred to Colombia's Indigenous cultures.

BRAZIL

KEY FACTS	**LIBERTY AND ORDER**	
CAPITAL Bogotá	**MONEY** Colombian peso	**NATION CODE** CO
LARGEST CITIES Bogotá Medellín Cali Barranquilla Cartagena	**NAMED FOR** Christopher Columbus— the explorer who began the colonization of the Americas	**OFFICIAL LANGUAGES** Spanish and English
	FLOWER Christmas orchid 	**BIRD** Andean condor
POPULATION 49,300,000		

GABRIEL GARCÍA MÁRQUEZ
1927–2014
This Nobel Prize-winning novelist is Colombia's most famous writer. He created the writing style known as magical realism.

ADRIANA OCAMPO
B.1955
Planetary geologist Ocampo works at NASA in the USA and studies the impact (craters) created by asteroids.

AUSTRALIA & NEW ZEALAND

WELCOME TO THE GREAT LANDS DOWN UNDER

Australia is an enormous island nation, but did you know it's the smallest continent on Earth? It's home to the oldest continuous culture in the world—the Aboriginal and Torres Strait Islander peoples. You can see some of their stories in the country's ancient rock paintings. In New Zealand, the history of the Indigenous Māori is proudly brought to life at Wellington's Te Papa Tongarewa museum.

Australia and New Zealand have plenty going on—museums, striking buildings, and beautiful parks, but it's the unique wildlife and the extraordinary wilderness that wows the world. From beaches to mountain ranges, deserts to glaciers, rain forests to wetlands—you name it, they've got it!

KAKADU NATIONAL PARK
This park has huge termite mounds, ancient rock art, and 10,000 crocodiles!

DAINTREE NATIONAL PARK
It's hot in the rain forest, but don't be tempted to cool off in the Daintree River—it's full of crocs!

GREAT BARRIER REEF
This amazing reef is about the same size as Italy!

DINOSAUR TRACKS
130-million-year-old fossilized dinosaur footprints are the must-see sight of Western Australia.

NELLIE MELBA
1861–1931
In the early 20th century, there was no singer more famous than Nellie, an amazing soprano.

KANGAROO ISLAND
This island is serious about conservation. Look out for koalas, wombats, kangaroos, possums, sea lions, and penguins.

MELBOURNE
In Australia's second-largest city, you'll find its biggest sports stadium—the Melbourne Cricket Ground (MCG).

ULURU
This enormous rock in Australia's center is a sacred site for Aboriginal people.

EDITH COWAN
1861–1932
A tireless campaigner for women's and children's rights, Cowan was the first Australian woman to serve as a member of parliament.

ALBERT NAMATJIRA
1902–1959
This gifted artist was the first Indigenous person to receive Australian citizenship.

AUSTRALIA

BRISBANE

SYDNEY

CANBERRA

WELLINGTON
New Zealand's capital shows off the awesomely enormous Te Papa Tongarewa museum, which walks visitors through NZ's rich history.

MELBOURNE

KEY FACTS

AUSTRALIA: ADVANCE AUSTRALIA
NEW ZEALAND: ONWARD

CAPITALS	MONEY	NATION CODES
Australia: Canberra	Australian dollar	AU
New Zealand: Wellington	New Zealand dollar	NZ

LARGEST CITIES	NAMED FOR	POPULATION
Australia: Sydney, Melbourne New Zealand: Auckland, Christchurch	Australia: The Latin Terra Australis ("south land") New Zealand: The Dutch province of Zeeland—the Dutch called it Nova Zeelandia	Australia: 26,500,000 New Zealand: 5,100,000

OFFICIAL LANGUAGES	FLOWERS	BIRDS
Australia: English New Zealand: English and Māori	Australia: Golden wattle New Zealand: Silver fern	Australia: Emu New Zealand: Kiwi

GREAT OCEAN ROAD
Take a road trip and admire the views along this iconic coastal highway.

TASMANIAN DEVILS
These furry creatures are the world's largest carnivorous marsupials.

FRANZ JOSEF GLACIER
One of thousands of glaciers in NZ, the Franz Josef has beautiful ice caves and crevasses.

MILFORD SOUND
Early Europeans were wrong to call this a sound—it's actually a fjord!

SYDNEY OPERA HOUSE
Perched on the edge of Sydney Harbor, the Opera House looks like it could sail away!

BLUE MOUNTAINS
Droplets of eucalyptus oil in the air create the blue haze that gives these mountains their name.

BONDI BEACH
Few beaches are more famous than this stretch of sand on the city's east coast.

JACINDA ARDERN
B.1980
When Ardern became the New Zealand prime minister in 2017, she was the youngest-ever female head of state.

FIJI

MAUNGAKIEKIE (ONE TREE HILL)
This volcanic cone overlooking Auckland was once home to over 5,000 Māori from the Te Wai-O-Hua tribe.

SKY TOWER
For a bird's-eye view of NZ's biggest city, travel to the top of the 1,000-foot Sky Tower.

PIHA BEACH
Sink your toes into the sand on this wild beach, bookended by craggy cliffs.

SIR EDMUND HILLARY
1919–2008
In 1953, Hillary and Nepalese mountaineer Tenzing Norgay became the first climbers to reach the top of Mount Everest.

TE PUKATEA BAY, ABEL TASMAN NATIONAL PARK
There's a walking track from the sandy beach that leads up the headland to an ancient Māori fort.

AUCKLAND

TONGARIRO NATIONAL PARK
The volcanic mountains and other sites in this park are sacred to the Māori.

ROTORUA
No, that's not rotten eggs you can smell, it's the sulfide gas coming from the bubbling mud pools arond town.

NEW ZEALAND

WELLINGTON

WAITOMO CAVES
Take a boat trip and marvel at thousands of glow worms.

CHRISTCHURCH

QUEENSTOWN
If you like skiing or snowboarding, then it doesn't get much better than the runs around Queenstown.

KAIKŌURA
Swim with the dolphins near this South Island town or stay dry and watch the sperm whales.

MOMENTS TO REMEMBER

AUSTRALIA

65,000 years ago: The first people arrive in Australia and establish what is now the oldest-surviving culture in the world.

AD 1400–1500: Aboriginal people experience their first contact with the outside world and set up trade relations with people from Indonesia.

1768–88: Captain James Cook claims to have discovered Australia, and colonization on behalf of Great Britain begins.

1851: Gold is discovered in Victoria, which attracts thousands of migrants and creates thriving cities.

1901: Australia is proclaimed a commonwealth; parliament is formed, and the first prime minister is voted in.

2000: Sydney hosts the Olympic Games and Cathy Freeman becomes the first Aboriginal Australian to win an individual gold medal.

NEW ZEALAND

AD 1200–1300: Polynesian people discover and begin to settle in New Zealand; they became known as Māori.

1642: Dutch explorer Abel Tasman is the first European to see New Zealand. The coastline is charted by Dutch cartographers.

1700–1800: Captain James Cook becomes the first European to circumnavigate New Zealand—he is followed by other explorers, missionaries, and traders.

1840: Māori chiefs sign the Treaty of Waitangi with the British Crown, making New Zealand part of the British Empire.

1893: New Zealand is the first country in the world to give women the vote.

1947: New Zealand declares its independence from Great Britain.

2011: An earthquake hits Christchurch, killing 185 people.

2015: The All Blacks become the first team to win the Rugby World Cup twice in a row.

GLOSSARY

AERONAUTICS
The science and design of building and flying aircraft.

AGRICULTURE
Farming.

ALGEBRA
A branch of mathematics that uses letters to represent numbers.

ALGORITHM
A rule or process followed in calculations and problem-solving.

ALPINE
To do with high, mountainous regions.

AMPHITHEATER
A large, open-air theater, especially in the ancient world.

ANNEX
A small building attached to a larger building.

APARTHEID
A system of separating people, especially along racial lines.

AQUEDUCT
A large, artificial channel used to transport water from one place to another.

ARCHIPELAGO
A group of many islands.

ARCHITECTURE
The study and design of buildings.

ARISTOCRACY
The very upper classes in society.

ARTIFACT
A human-made object, usually with historical significance.

ASTROLOGY
The study of the supposed effect of stars and planets on everyday life.

ASTRONAUT
A person who works in space.

ASTRONOMY
The study of stars, planets, space, and the universe.

ATOMIC
To do with the immense energy release of nuclear fission or fusion bombs.

AUDITORIUM
A space for an audience to watch a performance.

AURORA BOREALIS
A natural light-show that occurs in the sky near the North Pole, also called the Northern Lights.

AVALANCHE
Huge amounts of snow and ice falling down a mountainside.

AVANT-GARDE
Art that goes against the mainstream.

BARBARIAN
Any people who, in ancient times, didn't belong to a main culture such as the Romans.

BARRACKS
A place where soldiers live.

BASILICA
A large, ornate style of church.

BIODIVERSITY
The variety of plant and animal life in a given region.

BIOLOGIST
A person who studies living things.

BIOME
A community of animals and plants living in one area.

BIOSPHERE
A building or human-made area containing an ecosystem.

BLOC
A group of allied countries or political parties.

BOTANY
The study of plants.

BUBONIC
Causing black swellings, called buboes, on the body.

BUREAUCRAT
A person who works in a government department.

CALCIFY
Harden into an element called calcium.

CALDERA
A crater formed in the collapsed mouth of a volcano.

CARTOGRAPHY
The study and making of maps.

CATACOMB
An underground cemetery containing many tombs.

CIRCUMNAVIGATE
Travel around something, especially by boat.

CITADEL
A fortress built on high ground.

CIVIL WAR
A war fought between people from the same country.

COLONY
An area in one country controlled by another.

COMMONWEALTH
An independent country or a group of such countries.

COMPOSER
A person who writes and makes music.

CONQUISTADOR
A Spanish word meaning "conqueror."

CONSTITUTION
A set of rules for how a country should be governed.

CONVERGE
When several things, especially rivers, meet and become one.

COSMONAUT
Another word for astronaut, used in Eastern Europe.

COUP
A violent uprising against a ruler or government.

CREVASSE
A deep crack in land or ice.

CRUSADES, THE
Christian wars against Muslim lands in the Middle Ages.

CULTIVATE
To grow a crop.

DEFORESTATION
Cutting down trees.

DELTA
A landform at the mouth of a river, caused by a buildup of sand and mud.

DEMOCRACY
A system in which people vote for their preferred leaders or policies.

DICTATORSHIP
A society ruled over by one person with total power.

DOMESTICATE
Tame and train an animal to live with humans.

DROUGHT
A long time without rain, causing a water shortage.

DYKE
A wall built to prevent flooding.

DYNASTY
A series of rulers who each inherited power from the one before, usually a parent.

ENDANGERED
At risk of going extinct.

ENTREPRENEUR
A person who sets up a business.

ENVIRONMENTALISM
Belief that the natural world should be protected and actions taken to do so.

EQUINOX
The date, twice a year, when day and night are of equal length.

ESPLANADE
An open, flat space for walking along a coast.

ESTUARY
A river-mouth that opens into the sea.

EXCAVATION
A dig-site for archeological remains.

FAMINE
A severe lack of food.

FEUDALISM
A system in which the upper classes own land that the lower classes work on.

FJORD
An inlet of the sea between tall cliffs.

FREIGHTER
A ship that transports goods.

FRESCO
A painting on a wall or ceiling.

FUNICULAR
A type of lift going up and down a steep hillside.

GENETICIST
A person who studies genes, which are what make each living thing unique.

GENOCIDE
The murder of a very large number of people.

GEODESIC
A building style that uses connected struts to form a dome.

GEOTHERMAL
To do with heat that comes from deep inside Earth.

GEYSER
A hot spring that, when it boils, sends bursts of water and steam into the air.

GLACIER
A river of ice that moves very slowly.

GORGE
A narrow valley between steep cliffs.

GROTTO
A small cave.

GROVE
A small group of trees.

GUERRILLA
A soldier who fights with a loosely organized group, rather than with an army.

GULF
A large area of ocean partially surrounded by land.

HYDRAULIC
To do with movement by a liquid.

INDIGENOUS
Originally from a given place.

KARST
A landscape of jagged rocks, caves, and sinkholes.

KIMONO
A traditional Japanese gown.

LAGOON
An area of saltwater separated from the sea.

MAGMA
Hot, half-fluid, half-solid substance that flows beneath Earth's surface.

MARITIME
To do with boats, shipping or the sea in general.

MARSUPIAL
Mammals whose young are carried in the mother's pouch.

MAUSOLEUM
A grand building that houses a tomb or tombs.

MEDIEVAL
From the Middle Ages, approximately AD 400–1400.

METROPOLIS
A huge city.

MINARET
A tower attached to a mosque, from which Muslims are called to prayer.

MODERNISM
Artistic movement that shunned traditional methods in the beginning of the 20th century.

MONARCHY
A society ruled by a king or queen.

MONASTERY
A place where monks live.

MONOLITH
A large stone that forms part of a monument or structure.

MONSOON
A season of heavy rainfall in parts of Asia.

MOSAIC
Artwork made of tiny pieces of glass or stone.

NATURALIST
A person who studies the natural world.

NEOLITHIC
From the late Stone Age.

NEUROLOGIST
A person who studies nerves and the nervous system.

NOMAD
A person who moves around without settling in one place.

OBELISK
A tall, narrow standing stone with a pointed top.

OBSERVATORY
A building where telescopes are used to study the sky.

OCCUPATION
A period during which one country's military is stationed in another country's territory.

ORANGERY
A greenhouse for growing oranges and other fruits.

OUTRIGGER
A style of boat with floats projecting from both sides.

PAGODA
A tower used as a Hindu or Buddhist temple.

PALEOLITHIC
From the early Stone Age.

PARLIAMENT
A group of people in a democracy who make laws and represent the general public.

PAVILION
A large tent or open-sided building in a park or garden.

PEDIATRICIAN
A doctor specializing in helping children.

PENINSULA
A landform jutting out from the mainland, into a sea or lake.

PETRIFY
Turn to stone.

PHARAOH
What ancient Egyptians called their kings.

PHILOSOPHY
The study of knowledge, reality, and existence.

PILGRIM
A person who journeys to a place sacred to their religion.

PLANETARIUM
A dark room for viewing projections of the stars and planets.

PLANTATION
An estate where crops are grown, especially luxuries such as sugar, coffee, and tobacco.

PLATEAU
An area of flat land at the top of a cliff or hill.

PREFECTURE
A district run by a governor or prefect.

PREHISTORIC
From a time before written, historical records.

PROMENADE
To promenade is to walk through a public place to be seen by others.

PROTECTORATE
A state or country controlled and protected by another.

PYRAMID
A building with a large base and pointed top, especially in ancient Egypt.

RAVINE
A very deep, narrow gorge.

REHABILITATION
Restoring a person or animal that is ill or injured to a healthy condition.

RELIC
An important object from an earlier time.

RENAISSANCE
The period from the 14th to the 17th century, during which European arts, sciences, and politics made important progress.

REPUBLIC
A society in which people elect other people to represent and govern them, without a king or queen.

REVOLUTIONARY
A person who supports or brings about a drastic change in government.

RICE PADDY
A flooded field where rice is grown.

SAMURAI
A member of a class of warriors in medieval Japan.

SAVANNA
A flat, grassy plain in hot regions.

SCRIPTURE
The sacred writings of a religion.

SEGREGATION
Keeping one group of people away from another.

SHAMAN
A person thought to have special powers and knowledge of spirits.

SLUICE
An artificial channel used to control the flow of water.

SOPRANO
A singer who sings the highest notes.

SOUND
A small area of sea connecting two larger areas of sea.

SPIT
A long beach extending out to sea.

STALACTITES
Cones of rock hanging from a cave ceiling, formed by dripping water over thousands of years.

STALAGMITES
Cones of rock on a cave floor, formed by water droplets building up over thousands of years.

STORM SURGE
A rise in sea level due to a storm.

STRAIT
A narrow body of water connecting two other bodies of water.

STUPA
A dome-shaped Buddhist shrine.

SUMO
A form of wrestling from Japan.

SUPERSONIC
Faster than the speed of sound.

TAXIDERMY
Preparing and displaying stuffed animals in a lifelike way.

TECTONIC PLATES
Large slabs of Earth's crust that move very slowly over time. Where they meet, volcanos erupt and earthquakes shake the ground.

TERRORISM
The use of violence and fear to achieve political aims.

TOPOGRAPHY
The physical features of a given area.

TURRET
A small tower attached to a fort or castle.

UNIFY
Bring and join together.

WAT
A Buddhist monastery or temple in Southeast Asia.

X-RAY
An invisible wave of energy that can pass through and form images of solid objects.

INDEX